Revolt
OF THE
Rebel Angels

THE FUTURE
OF THE
MULTIVERSE

TIMOTHY WYLLIE

Bear & Company
Rochester, Vermont • Toronto, Canada

Bear & Company
One Park Street
Rochester, Vermont 05767
www.BearandCompanyBooks.com

Text stock is SFI certified

Bear & Company is a division of Inner Traditions International

Library of Congress Cataloging-in-Publication Data
Wyllie, Timothy, 1940–
  Revolt of the rebel angels : the future of the multiverse / Timothy Wyllie.
    p. cm.
  Includes index.
  Summary: "A rebel angel's perspective on the Lucifer Rebellion 200,000 years
ago and her insight into its past and future effects on consciousness"—Provided by
publisher.
  ISBN 978-1-59143-174-9 (pbk.) — ISBN 978-1-59143-751-2 (e-book)
  1. Devil—Miscellanea. 2. Demonology—Miscellanea. 3. Consciousness—
Miscellanea. 4. Spiritual life—Miscellanea. 5. Earth—Forecasting—Miscellanea.
I. Title.
  BF1999.W97 2013
  133.4'2—dc23
                                                              2013006735

Printed and bound in the United States by Lake Book Manufacturing, Inc.
The text stock is SFI certified. The Sustainable Forestry Initiative® program
promotes sustainable forest management.

10 9 8 7 6 5 4 3 2 1

Text design by Virginia Scott Bowman and layout by Brian Boynton
This book was typeset in Garamond Premier Pro with Baskerville and Agenda as
display typefaces

To send correspondence to the author of this book, mail a first-class letter to the
author c/o Inner Traditions • Bear & Company, One Park Street, Rochester, VT
05767, and we will forward the communication, or contact the author through his
website: **www.timothywyllie.com.**

Contents

Acknowledgments

First and foremost, my deepest gratitude goes to Georgia for the privilege of this unusual collaboration. It was never a project I expected or consciously asked for, and yet in addressing the relevant issues in her books, she is throwing invaluable light on the angelic revolution that has puzzled me for over thirty years.

I was fortunate to have Anne Dillon, the editor of two of my previous books with Bear & Company (*The Return of the Rebel Angels* and *Confessions of a Rebel Angel*) and who knows my work well by now, to undertake the primary edit on this volume. As before, I'm grateful for Anne's intelligence, her kindness, and her scrupulous attention to detail. Over the course of preparing this book for publication I also worked with another editor, Chanc VanWinkle Orzell, who brought a fresh, new, and perceptive eye to Georgia's narrative. I particularly appreciated Chanc's unflagging enthusiasm and wise counsel through the later stages of bringing *Revolt of the Rebel Angels* to print.

Susan P. Marie, a reader who is also an adept with the pendulum, has become an important asset to the publication of Georgia's *Confessions*. She combs through the manuscripts, sentence by sentence, dowsing the degree of resonant truth to Georgia's statements. I then make the necessary adjustments after discussing them with Georgia. I'm most grateful for Susan's interest and the insights gained from her skill with the pendulum. It's also a credit to Georgia that Susan's dowsing has indicated only the most minimal of modifications.

Robert Davis of the Daynal Institute was the first person to recognize the value of Georgia's voice and has been a solid support throughout this collaboration. His rare spiritual intelligence, his kindness—Robert is the only person who has read all of Georgia's volumes completed to date—and his continuing enthusiasm for this project all mean a great deal to me.

My love and gratitude go again to June Atkin ("Juno") my New York City Art Partner—or "Artner" for the neologist—for the graphics we work on together with our Prismacolor pencils, mailing the emerging image back and forth from New York to New Mexico, each adding to it and then sending it back. I've chosen to include two of these images (plates 3 and 8) for their symbolic relevance to some of Georgia's insights. But more than that: Juno's intuitive wisdom—she reads Georgia's books in manuscript form—has greatly helped Georgia to clarify some of her more obscure statements.

All writers need a few people to have faith in our work and who will read our books just to make sure we are still making sense. Juno is the foremost of a handful of people who are kind enough to review my books prior to publication. Also included in this small group are Daniel Mator, Nikola Wittmer, Edward Mason, Roberta Quist, Gordon Phinn, Rob Drexel, Urszula Bolimowska, and Byron Belitsos of Origin Press. I'm most grateful for their intelligent comments and their open-mindedness in reviewing material as unconventional as Georgia's *Confessions*.

I'm thrilled Inner Traditions/Bear & Company has chosen to publish *Revolt of the Rebel Angels,* the second volume of Georgia's *Confessions.* I'm most grateful to Jon Graham, the acquisitions editor, for his continuing interest in my work; also I'm extremely thankful for the support of John Hays, the director of sales and marketing. While I've not had the chance to meet in person the publisher, Ehud Sperling; nor have I met Jeanie Levitan, the editor in chief, or Janet Jesso, the managing editor, I really appreciate that they find my work of sufficient value to invest the care and time to make such elegant and readable books. As a graphic designer myself, I'm an admirer of Peri Swan's evocative cover designs as well as the clarity of Virginia Scott Bowman's text design and layout. I'm also most grateful to Manzanita Carpenter and to others I haven't met who copy-edit, proofread, design, and market the books with such professionalism.

I've been most encouraged by Barbara Hand Clow's glowing endorsement of Georgia's previous book, and I trust this volume also meets her generous appreciation. I feel privileged by Ms. Hand Clow's recognition of the value of Georgia's narrative.

A big thank you, too, to all those readers whose letters tell me they can't wait for the next volume of Georgia's *Confessions* to emerge. I'm glad her words are striking a familiar chord in so many people.

Further acknowledgments must also go to the many personalities, both mortal and celestial, who appear in this narrative. I've changed a few names for privacy's sake, but the events and discussions described here occurred as Georgia perceived and understood them.

Finally, I acknowledge the consistent spiritual support and guidance of my two companion angels I've named Joy and Beauty, who've contributed so much to smoothing out the rough edges of my life, allowing me the peace and isolation from the humdrum world for this most intimate of writing projects. However, it is the Great Spirit, the Creator we all serve, whether we are celestial or mortal and whether we are aware of it or not, to whom my most heartfelt love and gratitude goes for the opportunity to collaborate in this "Great Work" of narrative alchemy. I would never have had the courage to delve into the reality of Lucifer and the rebel angels had I not experienced the love of the Creator so firmly in my heart. And, for that, I'm supremely grateful.

Note to the Reader
Regarding a Glossary of Terms
and the Angelic Cosmology

In this work the author has coined or provided specialized definitions of certain words, some of which are derived from *The Urantia Book,* a key source text. A complete list of these terms and their meanings has been provided in the glossary at the back of this book for your ready reference. The reader will find a brief overview of the Angelic Cosmology, also drawn from *The Urantia Book,* in the appendix.

Collaborating with a Discarnate Rebel Angel

When Georgia first made it known that she wanted to collaborate with me on this project, I agreed to do it more for personal reasons—I was fascinated by her dispassionate viewpoint—than with any thought of publication. It was a very liberating experience. However, on completing the first volume, *Confessions of a Rebel Angel,* and as her narrative unfolds, I have realized that she is talking to a wider audience than just me.

I have also come to accept what Georgia has been telling me these last few years: that there are now many tens of millions of fallen rebel angels who have incarnated into human bodies at this key point in human history. There are perhaps now as many as 120 million and more coming in every day.

The reasons for this influx of angels into human form are complex and arcane, and they underlie the basic theme of this story. As a consequence, it seems to me that Georgia's insights and revelations have a more general value, especially to other rebel angel reincarnates who are seeking to understand their place in the world. Since so few reincarnates are aware of their angelic heritage and the current era is generally dismissive of other realms of existence, these waves of reincarnates have remained an open secret—a secret, if you like, that keeps itself. And quite rightly so. The very point of incarnating as a human being is to fully experience a human lifetime.

The times, however, are no longer simply changing—they have

1

actually changed for many of us. Self-knowledge, even unwelcome self-knowledge, is the key to how each one of us, as individuals, will handle the coming global transformation. Knowing who we truly are, as well as having a basic understanding of the Multiverse and the role our planet is playing within it, will prove to be a vital lifeline in the times ahead.

Georgia has made her intentions clear. She has set out to survey her half-million-year posting on this planet to examine the decisions and steps taken in the past that have led to the current state of the world. And she has no illusions about how dark the global situation has become.

In Georgia's first book *Confessions of a Rebel Angel* and now in this one, she is gradually revealing how this has come about, as well as slowly coming to the realization for herself of the deeper, mysterious purpose behind what appears to be a failed experiment. As an angel, she has been observing the actions and behavior of early humanity, together with their celestial guides and overseers, from the time of the arrival of the Planetary Prince Caligastia and his staff—also identified by some to be the Nephilim or Annunaki—five hundred thousand years ago.

In Georgia's examination, she appears to be focusing on personalities and events that established the original patterns that have led to our downward spiral of social inequality, corporate indentured servitude, ecological suicide, spiritual ignorance, emotional instability, and all the mental shackles we use to limit ourselves.

When the Lucifer Rebellion broke out some 203,000 years ago, everything changed. Prince Caligastia's decision to follow his superior, Lucifer, into the revolution resulted in this and thirty-six other planets being quarantined and isolated from the larger Multiverse, from the realms of the celestials and the reality of extraterrestrials. In this Georgia is supported by the information available in *The Urantia Book* (UB).

However, her insights are starting to reveal another, far deeper, layer of purpose to what otherwise has been painted by the UB as an interplanetary tragedy, and the rebel angels as sadly deluded victims of a charismatic and power-maddened leadership.

The Revolt of the Rebel Angels, as well as my choice to so title this book, calls for some explanation. Readers who've been following my work over my previous books will likely have formed their own opinions about this recondite, but profoundly important, event. However, the reality of this angelic rebellion in an unimaginably distant past and the impact of this uprising still resonate in the ways of the world today. So this seems to be of immense importance if we're going to understand what is occurring on Earth.

In fact, the rebellion is of such profound significance that knowledge of it has been almost completely eradicated from human understanding. Except for some enigmatic references to a "War in Heaven," or its equivalent, in a number of ancient cosmologies, there would be nothing known whatsoever.

The Urantia Book, which I discovered in 1979 and which maintains that it is transmitted from the angels themselves, redresses that imbalance by describing the angelic rebellion, but from the point of view of MA (Multiverse Administration), the very administration against which the angels were rebelling. In part, this is what makes Georgia's observations so intriguing: she is reporting from the point of view of an angel who followed Lucifer into the revolution. She may have her disagreements with how *The Urantia Book* frames the Lucifer Rebellion as well as its impugning of the motives of the protagonists, yet she finds no disagreement with the general Multiverse context as presented by the book.

The Lucifer Rebellion clearly didn't occur in a vacuum. Although it has had a profound impact on the thirty-seven planets affected by it, it was a relatively low-level affair. To get a feel for this, you need to wrap your mind around some extremely large figures. The Multiverse may be utterly vast, but, according to *The Urantia Book,* it is finite. It has also been created and organized for the benefit of sentient life. The UB takes 2,097 closely reasoned pages to describe all this in agonizing detail, so my description here will, of necessity, be brief and hopefully won't overload the reader.

Much of what follows will require readers to look past the current mechanistic conceptual framework used by conventional science to explore the Universe and open themselves to the wider possibility of a vast and inhabited Multiverse and a deeply meaningful purpose to every human life. Contrary to a cold and purposeless existence, mortals on all third-density planets are deeply cared for by the angels who exist within the inner worlds of the imaginal realms.

I use the term *Multiverse* to include both the inner worlds of the celestials and the outer worlds of Time and Space. This is one of the primary divisions in the Multiverse. The worlds of Time and Space are composed of seven Superuniverses, each of which supports about 100,000 Local Universes. A Local Universe is made up of 10 million inhabited or to-be-inhabited worlds. Our Local Universe is numbered 611,121 and is positioned within the seventh Superuniverse. From that we can deduce that ours is one of the newer of the 700,000 Local Universes.

Equally clearly, it shouldn't be surprising to find that such a massive enterprise would need a masterful administration to keep it all running smoothly. Thus, each Local Universe is organized as a relatively autonomous social and political unit, which is itself subdivided in a series of nested hierarchies, down to the level of a Local System, which supports a mere one thousand inhabited or to-be-inhabited worlds.

Within the angelic hierarchy of our Local System, Lucifer, the then–System Sovereign, was in overall charge of the approximately 670 planets currently inhabited in this System, of which Earth is numbered 606.

When the revolution broke out some 203,000 years ago on Jerusem, the headquarters world of this Local System, the uprising spread to only thirty-seven of the third-density worlds, one of which was Earth. Just as each Local System has a celestial overseer, each planet has a couple of Planetary Princes, celestials of a fairly junior position who represent MA on their planets. On Earth, the main celestial administrator, the aforementioned Prince Caligastia, and his second-in-command, the conveniently named Prince Daligastia, were the administrative pair who aligned this planet with the angelic revolution.

Prince Caligastia has drawn much of Georgia's attention. The Prince is her titular chief, the one with whom she arrived on the planet half a million years ago, along with the first of the intraterrestrial missions, to work on this world.

In *Revolt of the Rebel Angels,* Georgia picks up her narrative soon after the angelic revolution had broken out and the conditions on Earth were beginning to deteriorate under the progressively dissolute leadership of Caligastia. There are signs emerging that Prince Caligastia is growing increasingly demented and unbalanced by the powers he awards himself and the behavior of his midwayers.

The second thread running through Georgia's books constitutes an examination of my own life, but from her own unique perspective. This volume initially finds me as a young man in my midtwenties, together with a community I'd had a hand in founding some three years earlier, and settled on an isolated plantation on the wild coast of the Yucatán Peninsula.

We had been led there by Beings of the imaginal realms by whom we'd been contacted through our group meditations. The community, which will later come to be known as the Process, was at that point composed of about thirty young men and women, mostly in our twenties. Once we might have been thought of as the cream of the English educational class system. We had rejected England in the spring of 1966 and set out for the Caribbean to find an island where we could start over, following our own ways. Failing to do that, we started to follow the guidance of the mysterious Beings who'd dropped into our meditations. Having been guided to Mexico City, and then further to Mérida in the Yucatán, we finally ended up in the tiny village of Sisal, penniless and with no idea where to go or quite why we were there at the end of the road.

Following a group meditation three days later, the Beings gave us images of what we'd find if we walked far along the beach. And the next day, when we all set off, I did indeed find the place we were guided to by the Beings, after walking over seventeen kilometers along the beach in the scorching tropical sun. We settled there on the site of a ruined salt factory we later discovered was called Xtul (pronounced Sh-tool) in the Maya language and started rebuilding the structures. We were happy in the knowledge that we'd found our spiritual home, the place to which we'd been guided by the gods.

So would start a new phase in the development of the Process community in which the psychotherapy we'd originally practiced, and which had drawn us all together, was gradually morphing from the psychological into the spiritual.

Xtul, which we now thought of as our spiritual home and a "Place of Miracles," would have some unexpected surprises for us and would bind the community into the tightest of group minds when it appeared to save our lives from the ravages of the terrible hurricane Inez that bore down directly on the Yucatán Peninsula in early October 1966.

Mary Ann and Robert, the community's two leaders, were starting to assert their power in the group and much of the literature that emerged from Robert's passionate and controversial thinking would be produced at Xtul. Yet it would be Mary Ann who proved to have the intuitive intelligence and the necessary clout to wield ultimate control over the group, becoming in our eyes the enigma of the incarnate Goddess and the spiritual center of our lives.

There were to be some harsh lessons and some glorious revelations, but the experiences we all had in Xtul, and which are described here through Georgia's eyes, so closely united us that when it came time to return to civilization we would become one of the most intriguing and controversial of the religious groups that sprang up in the 1960s and '70s.

Georgia's choice to align herself with the revolutionary faction has somewhat clipped her wings, as well as changing her status from an angel who accompanied the Prince's mission to one of "Watcher." I've also seen a gradual change taking place in her opinions and feelings about the rebellion among the angels, as she has observed the impact it has had on the state of the planet.

Those who have read the first volume, *Confessions of a Rebel Angel,* will know how I originally encountered Georgia. This book will further chronicle the nature of our developing relationship. Suffice it to say here that she is using her perception of my seventy-three swings around the sun as both an anchor for her much broader historical narrative and a way of keeping me involved and interested enough to spend ten hours a day, every day, at the keyboard.

She also needs me for my vocabulary, as well as my digits. Our working relationship has been changing over the course of this project. For the first third of *Confessions of a Rebel Angel,* she essentially channeled through me. That was when she was establishing that she could do it—and that I wouldn't freak out. She could and I didn't.

However, taking dictation from a discarnate Watcher interested me far less than having a more deeply collaborative association with Georgia. We now write together, but under rather curious conditions. She has me listen to talk radio on my headphones (in order to distract my monkey-mind, she says). Then I simply wait for her words to drift up from my subconscious—or down from my superconscious. We then both work to structure her narrative into a readily accessible form. I don't know what is coming next, and I can only trust that Georgia does. Strangely, when we have finished for the day, I find that I have little or no memory of what has just been written.

It is a curious process. Yet its value lies in the extent to which Georgia's observations offer authentic insights for those Watchers who have already entered human incarnation and are as yet unaware of their true backgrounds.

Finally, she wishes to remind all incarnate rebel angels of the profound privilege of living a mortal life in this exceptional world at this point in her history. Georgia hopes her words will help awaken reincarnates to their long angelic heritages.

I will step back now and let Georgia, the true author of this work, take up her narrative as our little community was struggling to survive in Xtul, deep in the wilds of the Yucatan coastal jungle.

Since it is being said that you are my twin and true friend, examine yourself and understand who you are, how you exist, and how you will come to be.

BOOK OF THOMAS: NAG HAMMADI (HC 11,7)

Our imagination is stretched to the utmost, not, as in fiction, to imagine things which are not really there, but just to comprehend those things which "are" there.

RICHARD FEYNMAN

To come into separate being was to have fallen away from what the orthodox called the original Abyss but the Gnostics called the Foremother and Forefather. The angel Adam was a fallen angel as soon as he could be distinguished from God. As a latter-day Gnostic I cheerfully affirm that we are all fallen angels.

HAROLD BLOOM, *FALLEN ANGELS*

Among us, there are those who are not among us.

FROM THE 2009 JIM JARMUSCH FILM
THE LIMITS OF CONTROL

1

Angelic Conspiracies

Watchers, Angels and Serpents, Islands of Mu, and Archetypes and Other Gods

Xtul—the Place of Miracles—is how the community came to think about the old ruins on their estate on the Yucatán coastline in eastern Mexico.

Twenty-six young men and women, mostly from Britain, arrived in the early summer of 1966 on the coast of the Yucatán Peninsula, some more confident than others that they were being guided by invisible and mysterious Beings, to find a place to settle down and create a utopian community. As a group of intelligent young people, they had become disenchanted with Western society and wished nothing more than to turn their backs on all the corruption, blame, and irresponsibility, and make a fresh start for themselves.

Yet there was an unusual and, for me, a most interesting, aspect to this community, which Mein Host had joined two years earlier. (I should add that the Germanic ring to the name I've given my ward remains a puzzle as much for him as it probably is for the reader. I've promised to reveal the reason in due time but for now he has to live with not knowing.) Anyway, this community was led by a woman of such brilliance and raw emotional power that by the time they got to Xtul most of them had started to accept that Mary Ann was the incarnate Goddess.

Mein Host, the young man I consider as my ward and whom I have encountered frequently in a number of his previous incarnations, wholeheartedly believed that in Mary Ann he had indeed met the Goddess in human form. A powerful personal revelation some months earlier had transformed him from an atheist to a person who could barely believe his good fortune. I could see he felt sure that, upon meeting Mary Ann, he had come home. He truly believed he had found what he had spent lifetimes searching for. He knew he had found Her, and lost Her, and found Her again, only to lose Her and find Her countless times, through many lifetimes. She was the One who truly knew him; the only one who had ever understood him and loved him for who he was.

He had even found Xtul for his Goddess.

Mein Host had been the one to walk the farthest along the beach. He had the intuition to turn back into the jungle at precisely the right point to find the perfect spot to accommodate the group. The place was completely invisible from the beach, as the estate lay well back behind a low cliff. Yet when he scrambled up and across the dunes, he found the very place to which the Beings had been so patiently guiding them over the previous few months.

And Xtul itself? A thin strip of the coast, some two or three miles long, situated between the tiny Maya villages of Sisal and Chuburna Puerto. Although it wasn't something the community found out until later, Xtul actually lay on an island, since the long coastal strip had a river a couple of miles behind it that inconspicuously separated the island from the mainland. Although it wasn't quite the lush desert island the group had visualized when they set out on their search back in London, the fact that Xtul was on an island retrospectively affirmed the rightness of their being there.

They'd been told by a local that the name for the place, *Xtul,* meant "terminus" in Maya, which seemed singularly appropriate to them at the time. Much later, an academic translation turned out to be more along the lines of the Place of the White She-Rabbit.

Xtul had once been an operating salt-extraction factory, but the buildings had fallen into disuse and ruin long ago. A hurricane earlier in the twentieth century most likely put an end to the enterprise. All that remained of the factory when Mein Host poked his head over the cliff edge that day in the summer of 1966 was one extremely large building. There were ragged gaps in the thick walls and the stucco in some places had crumbled back to the massive stonework beneath it. The building was now roofless and yet with its high, white walls—one of the signs the Beings had predicted—and its enormous, pointed, triangular eaves at either end, both rising to at least eighty feet above the ground, there seemed no doubt in Mein Host's mind that he had found the right place.

A smaller structure, also a roofless, windowless ruin, was set among the coconut palms and stood across from the large building that would soon be known as the monastery. The smaller one would be called the temple, and was intended as a residence for Mary Ann and her husband, Robert. The third building was a rickety wood structure with half a roof, broken glass for windows, and a cracked tile floor. This would become the building in which most of the community bedded down in their sleeping bags and blankets.

Regardless of all the obvious challenges facing a group of city-bred, young English women and men, within a couple of weeks the community was fully installed in this primitive, but prospective, Garden of Eden.

Lacking fresh water, gas, or electricity, and over four miles from the nearest village, much of the day was taken up with the business of survival. Money had virtually run out and food had become the few fish Peter— the only member of the group with any previous fishing experience—had been able to catch that day. That and, of course, the inevitable coconuts and prickly pears, which grew in great profusion all over the estate.

Life was simple and brutally hard.

They had pursued an ideal, doubtless believing they would be cared for when they arrived. They were hopelessly ill-equipped for such a venture, with barely a saucepan to heat water and no tools whatsoever. The tropical, midsummer sun sent its blistering rays down daily from a clear, blue sky. For weeks on end it didn't rain. Snakes and poisonous jumping spiders seemed to have taken over the place.

Mein Host discovered this, almost to his detriment, early one morning as everyone was stirring under their blankets, the few more fortunate ones struggling out of their sleeping bags. He was still half-asleep, his blanket wrapped around him, while I watched in horror as what I'd hoped would never happen did. I was powerless to do anything about it.

All I could do was to extend the Blessings of the Mother and hope for the best. Here is Mein Host in his own words:

"Barely awake," he has written, "I was suddenly aware of a strange, but not unpleasant, sensation under the light blanket. There was something gently rubbing itself along my bare leg. Before I could respond, there immediately followed a loud clash of metal on stone. I jerked upright to see that Peter had cut the head off a brightly colored coral snake—and even we knew they were deadly!—which had snuggled up against my leg overnight for the warmth."

I could only watch helplessly while this little drama played itself out before me. Only later did I discover that Peter—who'd been a close friend of my ward prior to joining the community—and Mein Host's guardian angels had the matter well in hand. When will I learn to trust? The incident turned out to have been one of those elegant pieces of angelic coordination—companion angels are capable of affecting their wards in many subtle ways—whereby one of Peter's angels alerted him to the coral snake's presence and Joy, one of Mein Host's, made sure the lad made no sudden movement before Peter killed it.

I would be tempted every so often to complain about the emotional strain the lad has put me through in his short life, if I weren't aware by now of the deeper reasons for the pain, the fear, and the joy—emotions that I have little choice but to feel, almost symbiotically, along with him. Besides, Mein Host disapproves of complaining. He says it's irresponsible and tells me I'm ceding my power when I try to chide him for what he puts me through.

Call it one of the challenges we Watchers have to confront when we identify so closely with a mortal being. You see, we have to share that person's feelings. Companion guardian angels also experience their human charge's feelings, but they have more choice as to whether to remain in the person's auric field.

Watchers are different in that respect. We're expected, for our own good, to accept the challenge of remaining within the emotional, auric field of the mortal we accompany, no matter how difficult or painful that might be. This is not to bleed off the emotional pain from our wards, as a more sentimental viewpoint might have it, but to strengthen our own emotional bodies. Angels, you need to appreciate, possess somewhat ineffectual emotional bodies. Since we are created as functional beings, the choices we face over the course of our lives are generally simple and we find ourselves well-prepared to handle them. This was one of the reasons that the Lucifer Rebellion, and the choices it forced us all to make, created such confusion among the angels. We'd simply never faced such an important decision, and we were completely unprepared for it.

Because angelic rebellions have tended to occur among only the relatively junior ranks, and they are extremely rare in a well-organized Multiverse, information concerning any previous rebellions is barely mentioned in the religious engineering courses in the galactic Melchizedek universities, the main centers of learning in the Multiverse. However, with what I now know, I am slowly starting to comprehend why this oversight might have occurred in this very Local Universe.

I've come to believe that a massive covert experiment is under way in which our two species—angel and mortal—are being fused in some way I don't fully understand. Angels and mortals are two different species with very different attributes. I've heard Mein Host saying that an angel incarnating into a mortal body is like "squeezing a rainbow into a Coke bottle."

From what I know of Multiverse history, I believe this project may be unprecedented and is most likely only made possible now since the Multiverse is moving toward the end of a truly vast Multiverse cycle. But, at best, my knowledge is limited and it is only by reaching out to others of my kind that I'm likely to find out more.

Gradually, I have become more certain that Watchers like me are, in fact, preparing ourselves for our own mortal incarnations. Just as I have observed others who are angels incarnated into human vehicles, over the course of narrating Mein Host's story, I know one day my time will come. Then again, it might turn out that I've become so closely engaged with Mein Host's life as a mortal, and we've become so intimately involved, that *this* will count as my mortal incarnation. In this way, perhaps I'll be able to continue with Mein Host on his Multiverse career. We've become unusually fond of each other over the course of his current lifetime.

As an angel of the Order of Seraphim, who was attached originally to the first of the off-planet missions to Earth half a million years ago, my instructions were always to observe, just as I've no doubt been observed, in my turn, by others from even more subtle realms.

Like all those of my order, I am unable to interact directly with the composition of your material reality. The frequency differential between our two domains makes that impossible. For example, I pass through your walls with no sensation at all, as you might walk across a shadow. This allows me to monitor any mortal activity I choose from my frequency domain, while remaining undetectable to mortal senses.

I need to emphasize that I can only observe. I can't get into the mind of any mortal unless I am deliberately and knowingly invited by that individual. Being a rebel angel, you might imagine that is a rare enough event! And quite rightly, too.

My presence can instill extreme terror if a mortal's mind is unprepared for it. In fact, one thread of my narrative, starting with the first volume in this series and continuing throughout this book, can be understood as a gradual preparation of Mein Host's consciousness to tolerate my presence and accomplish this work.

I had to learn this in the most painful way possible—painful for both of us.

I admit it was a bad error of judgment on my part, although I'd like to believe it stemmed from a kind impulse.

The event in question occurred in Mein Host's twenty-third year, some three years before his arrival in Xtul. He was just opening his eyes in the midst of an entheogenic trance, brought on by consuming five hundred Heavenly Blue morning glory seeds, crushed and forced down an hour earlier. To compound his impetuousness, he'd unwisely chosen to accompany an equally substantially dosed friend to a party in London. And, since readers may enjoy minutiae of celebrity gossip, the party was given by the jazz singer Annie Ross, she of the masterful, close-harmony group Lambert Hendricks & Ross.

Mein Host had come back into consciousness to find himself lying on the floor of the host's bedroom. He had fallen there unconscious after putting his jacket on the bed, along with the other coats. There was no one else in the small room. I could see from his contorted face that he was already terrified behind his closed eyelids. Goddess knows what he might have already seen in those few moments. I drew a little closer to him, my sympathy already aroused.

Then, when he opened his eyes, I realized the foolishness of my intention. I could see that he was perceiving me as a large black-and-gold snake, as real to him as the long pile of the dark-blue carpet parting under my weight as I slid toward him.

Poor boy! The die was cast by that time and I had little choice but to continue my advance. In his terror, he saw me as a serpent and I didn't have the power to override his perception. By then I knew it was wrong, yet it was too late to stop or change. So after flicking my forked tongue gently all over his face I entered him by way of his right eye.

I'll spare you the details, dear reader, since he has written more fully of the encounter in *Confessions of a Rebel Angel*. Yet I felt compelled to reach out to him in those delicate moments. I got carried away with my desire to reestablish the intimacy with him I'd once felt when he was a tiny child, with a desperate world war going on. When the bombs were falling from German planes, the nearby explosions would knock his child's subtle energy body right out of its physical vehicle. I would scoop his little astral body up in my arms and comfort him through his terror.

So, yes, I admit it. I approached Mein Host at the very worst time. But I wanted to comfort him again, however painful it was for me—and, in saying this, I recognize that I am still trying to justify my error. That probably delayed my later arrival into his life by at least ten years.

Mein Host has also written more extensively about this key event in his life, but he's never heard it from my viewpoint. Since I was aware that he was projecting his terror out onto me, I decided this was no time for sentimentality. With my tail still half out of his eye socket, whipping the air as I wriggled myself down his throat, forced open by my girth, I coiled myself within his *chi*. While there, I took it upon myself to prepare the way for the work I knew we'd be doing together later in his life. I moved into his power chakra and extended my own auric field to familiarize his subtle energy bodies with my intimate presence.

So yes, again. I did indeed possess him for those few horrific hours during which his hair starting turning white—and I've had due cause to regret that! However, my regrets have been tempered somewhat by hearing my ward recently claim he knew perfectly well that our first fully conscious encounter was bound to terrify him—however considerately I might have arranged it.

Historically, the few of my Order of Watchers who have attempted such a close encounter with a mortal have found it extremely problematic. In the past, these encounters have frequently been labeled as black magic. While I have no doubt that some of my kind have abused their mortal incarnations, humans may misunderstand the differences between thought forms and angels. This has led to much unfortunate confusion in some instances.

Consequently, a regrettable reputation has followed this sort of attempted contact between Watcher and mortal. With all its many tiresome rituals and an obsessive focus on self-protection on the part of the human magician, such communication has been shunted off to the side of serious study and largely dismissed as superstition. For the most part, contemporary belief in the Western world dismisses magic as self-delusion. I have no quarrel with that. Those humans who feel drawn to having these complex interspecies interactions will discover the truth for themselves over the course of their own investigations. They will find that it is all very real indeed.

Even though I've long sought to redeem myself for my error in supporting Lucifer, Satan, and Caligastia in rebelling against the Multiverse Administration, I'm quite aware that a rebel angel could well be a terrifying thing to behold for an unprepared mind.

Since my first appearance as a serpent, it has taken Mein Host almost forty-five years to get to know and trust me sufficiently for both of us to be able to write this narrative. I'm also aware that our growing closeness must have been far harder for him than for me. He needed to throw himself into the interspecies arena in the most practical of ways. He had to swim with dolphins—captive and wild—and learn to trust them so as not to flinch when they closed their teeth on his arm. He had to encounter extraterrestrials face-to-face without being confused or scared. He had to face his demons and learn how to disarm them with love. He had to build a long-standing and trusting relationship with his companion angels. He had to do all this and more, as he met all the normal challenges of a lifetime. For all that, he now has me firmly lodged in his creative life.

However, Mein Host's time at Xtul happened during the early days of our relationship. After our initial encounter four years earlier, when he was terrified by my appearance, I became far more cautious around him. I knew for this work to be accomplished at some point in the future, my ward would have to genuinely like and trust me without any reservations. Given my background, as well as most humans' inherent suspicion and fear of angelic interference (or worse), you can understand why it might have taken so long.

Thus, in Xtul, the first chinks in the wall of Mein Host's skepticism started appearing, as he began to grasp the true existence of other inhabited levels of existence. Despite having had a number of entheogenic experiences before joining the community, by the time he was living in Xtul he hadn't taken entheogens for over three years. He discovered it was one thing to perceive nonhuman beings in an entheogenic trance and quite another to encounter them in normal consciousness.

What Mein Host would encounter at Xtul, however, has set a course that continues to this day and one that has led indirectly to this narrative.

❉ ❉ ❉

Now let me pick up my other narrative thread. The Lemurian islands of Mu proved to be the ideal conditions for what Vanu had in mind when he started the migration there some sixty-five thousand years ago.

Contemporary science dismisses Lemuria as a myth, because scientists' current understanding of the movement of tectonic plates suggests that no such continent could have existed either in the Pacific or in the Indian Ocean. But this is based on the premise that Lemuria was a continent. It was not. Lemuria, or Mu, was a multitude of thousands of islands, some extremely large and relatively independent, others small and interconnected by ridges rising above the water. The islands were of volcanic origin, magma oozing up from the oceanic trenches for over fifty million years on the eastern side of the Pacific Ring of Fire.

You could think of the civilization of Mu as being perched on the top of a whole series of dormant volcanoes. Over millions of years, a number of the most ancient of the volcanoes had created large islands crowned with gently rolling, low hills. Coral polyps had colonized the shallow water surrounding the islands, creating elaborate coral reefs with their calcium carbonate exoskeletons. As millions of years passed, the reefs collapsed upon themselves, a new reef forming on top of it, only to collapse again and be rebuilt in an almost endless cycle of renewal. Over time, the compacted carbonate became a series of semisubmerged, stepped platforms, which greatly expanded the size of the island's landmass. In many cases it was possible to walk across these shallow platforms from island to island.

Over time the inhabitants of the many islands of Mu came to think of themselves as part of one great Lemurian civilization.

At the time of the three great cataclysms, which saw the demise of the Lemurian civilization, not only did the worldwide sea level rise up to three hundred feet, but almost all the volcanic islands of Mu were swallowed back into the trenches from which they had come. There was no sunken continent because there was no homogeneous continental landmass to start with.

Some of the more than 150 islands in the Tonga Archipelago, and a few other islands in Micronesia, appear to have survived the deluge, although in a vastly reduced form. There is even some Lemurian late-period stonework, for example, that can still be seen in the "city" of Nan Madol, the mysterious ancient ruins on the island of Pohnpei. There are also the remains of their temples and ceremonial buildings that are now underwater and that divers are regularly rediscovering off the coastlines of countries as far apart as Japan, India, and Peru.

The islands of Mu were uninhabited when Vanu's first migrants arrived from Luzon in the Philippines, as well as being entirely free of the large predatory animals that had been their bane back on the mainland. There were a handful of species of small mammals—no one knew quite how they got there; a profusion of birds of many different varieties; and a single species of aquatic iguana that originally must have swum over to one of the small islands closer to the mainland.

The volcanic soil on the older islands was so rich that there were trees over five hundred feet tall, and parrots so intensely blue they could disappear entirely against the sky as they dived and swooped between the high branches. Bougainvillea bushes swarmed colorfully all over the undergrowth. Swaths of long pampas grass clothed the rounded hills and were punctuated by dense clumps of what is now known as Chinese silver grass.

The larger islands possessed freshwater lakes, rich with fish and fed in most cases by the runoff from the heavy rainfall. Inland, fruit trees of every sort blossomed beside a tracery of small streams, while coconut palms lined the coasts of the islands.

Vanu, who traveled with the first group of rafts, knew the territory, but only from the mapping overflights completed in the early days of their presence on the planet. Yet there was something clearly very different in walking those round, verdant hills than viewing the islands from seventy thousand feet in a fast-moving vimana—one of the staff's small exploration craft.

Vanu, you might recall, and his assistant, Amadon, were the last survivors of the final collapse of the Prince's mission after the Lucifer Rebellion. This mission was the first of the major off-planet interventions that every world undergoes as their planetary populations reach the point of development at which they could do with some additional help. This intervention occurred half a million years ago. It was then that the one hundred "superhumans" arrived with their two leaders, Prince Caligastia and his assistant, Prince Daligastia.

Drawn from the Order of Descending Sons, both these leaders were thought to be brilliant and well-trained in the matters of planetary social engineering. Like their immediate superiors, they were chosen for the posts from among a large number of volunteers. The fact that Caligastia and Daligastia, as well as Lucifer and Satan, were all noted at the time for their unusual degree of individuality was quickly forgotten as the mission got underway. Since both Princes operated within a slightly higher vibrational frequency domain they remained undetectable to the human senses. Yet they were perfectly perceptible to their staff of fifty male and fifty female superhumans.

A word about the Prince's staff, those unfortunate off-planet missionaries who featured so prominently in the early years of Earth's history. Although their gloriously molded physical bodies, cunningly gene-spliced by Avalon surgeons from human plasm and tweaked into superhumanity, was sure to have impressed the locals, in the larger scheme of things the one hundred staff were neither old nor particularly experienced beings. Freedom of choice being what it is, they too were drawn from large numbers of volunteers. They had once been mortals on other inhabited worlds in this Local System. They'd died and moved up through the next seven levels to gather on the System Headquarters Planet, to then volunteer to return to a primitive world as part of a Prince's mission. Hardy, adventurous beings, they were beautiful, too, but no wiser than you would expect them to be.

All went relatively well for the first few hundred thousand years. It is a long and complicated story of a planetary culture lovingly nurtured by the Princes and their staff, which flourished throughout the Middle East before disintegrating as a result of the Lucifer Rebellion. This was the angelic uprising that occurred on Jerusem, the Local System Headquarters world, about 297,000 years after the staff's arrival, directly affecting this planet and the thirty-six others, all of whose Planetary Princes aligned themselves with Lucifer and Satan, the leaders of the revolution.

I've written far more fully about the Lucifer Rebellion, its causes and consequences, the personalities involved, and Prince Caligastia's baleful influence on the orderly development of life on this world in *Confessions of a Rebel Angel,* so it's my intention here to give only a sketchy outline of one of the most significant events ever to befall this world.

The Multiverse Administration's official viewpoint on the Lucifer Rebellion has already been made clear in their written records of the event in *The Urantia Book,* so the broad facts of the uprising can easily be confirmed.* Vanu's part in all this tumult was to oppose Caligastia's secession and make every effort to hold true to the original intention of MA's

---

*A word of warning: Since the papers in MA's account of the rebellion have been drawn up by the very administration that Lucifer, Satan, and thirty-six other Planetary Princes were rebelling against, I counsel studying them with an eye to the bias expressed in the attitudes of the Melchizedek Brother, the celestial authority who wrote the Lucifer papers in *The Urantia Book* concerning the rebellion.

mission. After the collapse of Dalamatia, the city on the Persian Gulf that was once the pride of Caligastia and his staff, Vanu and Amadon, together with their small party of loyalists, headed off to the east, setting up settlements all the way to the Himalayan foothills in northern India.

In the meantime, Prince Caligastia, with the majority of his staff who remained aligned with him, tracked north and west, to ultimately set up his two main centers, one in the hills of Salem, in Palestine, and the other a splendid temple structure in the area that would later be buried deep beneath the city of Alexandria.

From that point on, Caligastia seemed to me to have become obsessed with destroying Vanu and the last vestiges of MA's mission to uplift the planetary consciousness; the Prince had declared himself—completely illegitimately, I might add—to be God of this World and demanded to be worshipped. This fraudulent claim of divinity became the first clue for me that I may have made the wrong decision in choosing to follow Lucifer into rebellion.

In his haste to wipe Vanu off the map, Caligastia and his minions—among whom were the 40,119 rebel midwayers* who followed him into the rebellion—encouraged the rapid development of technology, with an emphasis on weaponry and weapons delivery systems. At the time of the rebellion, four out of every five midwayers chose to follow Prince Caligastia in rejecting MA's authority and siding with Lucifer in the rebellion.

Using an outlawed approach of accelerating technological development, Caligastia instructed his midwayers to stir up hostility in the many opposing kingdoms. After millennia of constant warfare in between the tribes and kingdoms in Caligastia's domain, the situation had resolved itself down to two large empires that despised and distrusted each other.

---

*Fifty thousand of these intelligent, nonhuman entities—midway between angels and humans—were sired by the Prince's staff soon after their arrival. Although imperceptible to human senses, midwayers are created to be permanent planetary citizens, living on through countless generations of humanity to serve an indispensable role as planetary helpers. Midwayers play their parts throughout my narrative, given that they have the ability, under certain circumstances, to manifest and interact directly with human life.

This was just the state of affairs that Caligastia had been angling for. By manipulating priests in both empires under the control of his rebel midwayers, he was able to stoke the rancor and mutual suspicion each side felt toward the other. As a result, technological advances over the next fifty years accelerated astronomically.

Focusing on weapons development in any era will produce a wide variety of spin-offs and derivatives. These innovations will then prove so useful to the society that it tends to sanction the proliferation of research into bigger and more effective weapons. It's an old technique, one that occurred more recently in the Cold War between the Soviet bloc and the West, in which a feudal society was modernized in only seventy years.

Then there came a time when Caligastia must have decided to push the weapons development technology into high gear. This resulted in one of the Prince's greatest crimes—at least, I'm certain that it was considered so in MA's judgment. Caligastia decided to share enough of the secrets of the atom with his trained scientists on both sides of the conflict to make them develop unheard-of levels of destructive power. This allowed the two hostile empires to arm themselves over the next forty years with an approximately equivalent number of crude fission bombs.

Then, quite suddenly, everything appeared to swing out of the Prince's control. In a pattern I have seen him repeat again and again throughout human history, he badly underestimated the innate cunning of human beings. Caligastia's plan was to finally annihilate Vanu, the object of his obsessive hatred. He was determined to destroy the hundreds of settlements Vanu and Amadon had established by this time, some as distant as the Chinese border. Now the possibility of wiping out his enemies was starting to slip through his fingers.

The hostility between the East and the West finally came to a head because of an impetuous action by one of the midwayers who was becoming disenchanted with Caligastia's hubris. Caligastia agreed to a surprise attack, but the war that followed this attack, exacerbated by the buildup of atomic weapons on both sides, devastated most of the fertile North African coastline all the way west to the Atlantic and inland as much as a thousand miles in the most ravaged areas. In some regions, which were already deserts, the surface of the ground became fused into great pools of glass. The city that had grown up around the temple in the Nile Delta region was razed to the ground, so when Alexandria came to be built some fifty-five thousand years later, the ancient demolished city was buried beneath 160 feet of sand. The Western Empire was almost completely eliminated after the surprise attack, only managing to fire a third of its arsenal of short-range ballistic missiles. And, because of the previously mentioned midwayer's sabotage, not all their bombs exploded.

The Eastern Empire suffered significant damage—even the crudest of atomic weapons will create a frightful mess—but, all in all, it came out slightly ahead of its bitter enemy to the west.

There were regions of land at the eastern end of the Mediterranean that were rendered uninhabitable for thousands of years, as were some areas of southern Turkey. It was mainly a Mediterranean war, but some areas in southern Europe, and others as far away as the Afghan border, were totally obliterated. The worst of the destruction, however, was concentrated in central and southern Spain, the North African coast, and much of the area around Jordan, Palestine, and the Dead Sea.

This terrible war should not be confused with later conflicts between warring factions of midwayers some thirty thousand years later. These hostilities are the ones recorded in Indian sacred literature.

When I had a chance to survey the damage some months after the war, the landscape was still burning as far as I could see, the result of a score of medium-range missiles that worked all too well, possibly an oversight by the midwayer saboteur. The Western military forces just had time to fire those devastating missiles from their hidden, underground silos before they were themselves vaporized moments later in the enemy's saturation bombing of their North African bases.

However insane MA might have thought Caligastia was, the Prince certainly wasn't stupid. He didn't beat out thousands of Planetary Prince wannabes without being blessed with a natural cunning. He had hedged his bets. He had plucked the best scientists from laboratories of both sides about nine months before war broke out between them. He then had the scientists relocated, together with their families, to a barely inhabited yet fertile island some five hundred miles off the Spanish and North African coastline.

This was the island that about forty thousand years later would start flourishing as the political and social center of the Atlantean Empire. However, throughout much of that time, it was not those on Atlantis who were the primary moving forces on the planet, but rather Vanu's expanding Lemurian territories on the other side of the world.

But I'm racing ahead of myself again.

⌗ ⌗ ⌗

Just as Xtul became the creation myth of the community, now known to itself informally as the Process, Xtul also became Mary Ann's apotheosis.

I still didn't know quite what to make of her. I was puzzled when I observed Mein Host's companion angels supporting his involvement with the Process, and even more concerned when they didn't discourage his belief that Mary Ann was the incarnate Goddess. But that is one of the challenges of being a Watcher. We observe and learn to share the feelings that our wards experience, yet we can never really participate in their lives.

Although I understand the reason for this now, at that point it was still confusing to me. By allowing myself to experience Mein Host's feelings and emotions, I am being prepared for my own mortal lifetime. My emotional body is being exercised and strengthened by proxy. There is no way I can avoid this, nor would I want to.

Over the last sixty years I've seen such an acceleration in the number of rebel angels choosing mortal incarnation that I have come to appreciate the divine justice in this. After all, we were the ones who originally aligned ourselves with Lucifer and Satan at the time of the rebellion and personally supported their declaration for greater freedoms. We were the ones who followed them, together with Caligastia and Daligastia, into secession from MA's long-standing traditions. We were the ones who thought we knew better.

Since so little was taught at that time in the Melchizedek universities about the three previous rebellions in this Local Universe, none of us fully grasped the implications of our choices. When the ax finally fell, and the thirty-seven Planetary Princes who aligned themselves with Lucifer were allowed to continue governing their isolated worlds, the large number of celestials of a variety of lower orders allying themselves with the rebels were exiled to what MA calls "prison planets." (These were the angels mainly functioning in the System Headquarters world in various administrative positions; other celestials were at the HQ waiting for their postings on 619 inhabited worlds in this Local System.)

To my surprise, while MA was exiling my colleagues to those prison planets, the authorities left the rest of us alone; that is, those of us who were already working in their worlds—and I'd been here for almost three hundred thousand years prior to the rebellion. They may have well thought, and with good reason, that a planet under Caligastia and Daligastia's control would be prison enough.

While Mein Host was at Xtul, the names Lucifer and Satan, along with Jehovah and Christ, started being ascribed to the mysterious Beings who had guided the community to the Yucatán coastline.

I was as surprised as anybody when those names began to be used. I wasn't present at the time, but they appeared to have come to light over the course of Robert's private sessions with Mary Ann as a medium. I'd seen her working in a trance before, but she never did it in front of the group. This new turn of events, in which Mary Ann felt she was in contact with Jehovah, Lucifer, and Satan (Christ came a little later), was reflected directly in Robert's copious writings, which had suddenly become more spiritually charged since the advent of the Beings into the community's life.

This unexpected transformation from what was essentially an experimental, psychotherapeutic methodology to a full-blown spiritual experience had a certain logic to it. Mein Host explained it recently to a friend as "a perfectly natural progression."

"The more we worked to release our compulsive mental patterns," he noted, "you know, all the stuff that just goes meaninglessly round and round in the head—then the spiritual questions become the only ones worth exploring: 'Who am I really?' 'Did I get this screwed up in one lifetime?' 'Why am I here on this planet?' 'Is it a blessing or a punishment?' 'Why have we been brought together as a group?' Those sorts of questions . . ."

He went on: "Don't forget: some of us already had those brief glimpses of lifetimes we'd had on Atlantis. That made us really think. And this sort of insight became even more pointed when we cut ourselves off from the world at Xtul. We were pretty much open to anything by that time."

Yet it was still a surprise—and for some an unpleasant one—when those four names—Jehovah, Lucifer, Satan, and Christ, each in its own way freighted with the baggage of a few thousand years of Judeo/Christian/Islamic tradition—started being bandied about. Mary Ann, as was now generally accepted, took the lead in this. She was the one to identify the Beings in the first place, to name them, and to start creating an elaborate cosmology around them, together with Robert. But for all that, the way these four "gods" were perceived by the group was quite different from how they were thought of in more conventional religious belief systems. Neither Lucifer nor Satan, for example, were identified with the devil in the Process theology.

They thought of the gods more as archetypes, reflecting particular aspects of human character, both positive and negative. The Jehovian type they thought of as the autocrat, the authoritarian personality, the one born to lead. Lucifer represented a more relaxed, pleasure-oriented approach to life. The Satanic personality was seen as passionate and ambitious. Mary Ann viewed Christ as the link between these three personality types, the unifier.

Each personality was also said to have a negative side. The Jehovian can be closed-minded and bullying; the Luciferic has a tendency toward self-indulgent hedonism; Satanic passion may descend into obstinacy or willful destruction; and the Christ personality can lose focus and become timorous and wishy-washy.

As I looked deeper into how this transformation from psychotherapy to religion occurred, I found myself drawn back to Mary Ann again and again, wondering about her motivations and intentions.

Robert had encouraged her talent as a medium and added his own intellectual imprimatur to whatever she was revealing. She'd been dictating works with titles like *I, Jehovah* and *I, Satan* throughout her time at Xtul, which Robert would then edit into a booklet form. So one way of understanding the origins of the cosmology would be to ground it firmly in terms of Mary Ann's ambitions and her growing recognition of herself as the central figure, as the Great Goddess.

By the time the community was living at Xtul, she was already starting to groom Robert as a messianic figure, a role he appeared to acquiesce without much opposition. This cultivation remained behind the scenes during their time at Xtul, only to be discussed by her with her innermost circle of committed young women. Robert, many of the young women were coming to believe, was the Christ to Mary Ann's Goddess.

Mein Host knew nothing about this. He had become convinced that Mary Ann was the incarnate Goddess and that seemed to be quite enough for him. Just as a prophet is seldom accepted in his own land, Mein Host knew Robert far too well to believe that his friend was endowed with any particularly divine qualities. Granted, the man was highly intelligent and widely read, yet in his choices and actions he was seldom wise. He could argue any side of an argument with equal conviction and was a great one for justifying an intellectual stance with sophisticated and often persuasive rationalizations.

While this was great fun and very instructive when he and Mein Host were architecture students together in London, sitting around the local café smoking Woodbine cigarettes, drinking coffee, and talking endlessly about the appalling state of British architecture, Robert clearly had no psychic depth at the time. Like many repressed Englishmen I've observed, Robert lived almost entirely in his head. Yet he was an affable and kind man who was clearly devoted to his wife. He was a lucid if tedious public speaker, and he was an effective organizer.

When Mein Host had been at architectural school, Robert was known to have had no particularly strong beliefs of his own—having argued himself cleverly out of them all. A short stint in Scientology— where he'd met Mary Ann—had given him a little more backbone, yet he was still somewhat emotionally stunted.

I believe it was these qualities that made Robert of such value to Mary Ann in the early years of the Process. Mein Host, in turn, continued to be so completely bedazzled by his Goddess that he was blind to Mary Ann's attempts to use him.

⁑ ⁑ ⁑

In contrast to Caligastia's devastated empires throughout the Middle East and North Africa, the Lemurian territories on the Pacific islands of Mu represented a real chance for the human race to flourish. For Vanu and Amadon, it was an opportunity to start fresh, with none of the weight of the planet's unfortunate history bearing down on them.

I call them Lemurian "territories" for lack of a better name. For a long time there was no emphasis on royalty, so Lemuria can't be called a kingdom, and I hesitate to call it an empire, as that suggests domination. Yet Lemuria was much more than a mere territory and more practical than a realm. In a sense, Lemuria was closer to a state of consciousness and a shared way of life than a territory per se.

Mu could also be thought of as a theocracy, although it was nothing like what passes for a theocracy in the twenty-first century, because for the Lemurians the spiritual life was authentically of paramount importance. They were not competitive or warlike, nor did they envy one another, since they all relied on their own inner guidance. They were, in common parlance, all in touch with their higher selves. And their higher selves were all broadly in touch with one another.

Of course, there were inevitably priests and priestesses, yet on Lemuria they were known for their purity of intention and acted primarily as mediums. They were also responsible for reminding the people of who they were. In this way, each human being—man, woman, and child (older than four years)—could be helped to experience the Presence of the Indwelling Spirit and received his or her guidance from this "still, small Voice." Children were raised to trust this Voice, which spoke within each of them. The one principle by which they lived was supremely simple: be kind. They believed that if they kept their spiritual lives in order, everything else would follow quite naturally.

And it did. For a while. That is, for about forty thousand years, when they had the presence of immortal Vanu among them. Vanu and Amadon were living proof of the existence of higher powers and had been the ones to insist that they always follow their inner Voice.

In fact, the Lemurians were living through those twenty millennia much as human beings were always originally intended to live. Inasmuch as human life can be paradisiacal, Lemuria was paradise.

2

The Worship Dilemma

Lemuria, Atlantis and the Maya, Fandor
Parthenogenesis, and Dangerous Voyages

Several thousand decades years earlier, Vanu had clearly hoped his settlements across Asia might have become self-sustaining, not requiring his constant attention as well as his much-celebrated visits. This was before he thought of making a migration to the islands of Mu.

The truth was, Vanu was exhausted to the core. By this time he'd been roaming halfway across the world, backward and forward, from the Caspian Sea, across Asia, down into India, all the way to China and as far south as Australia, for over 130,000 years. He had to make sure Caligastia's midwayer espionage agents were kept at bay, while at the same time keeping an eye on the peaceful development of his ever-expanding settlements. He was performing the functions for which the entire Prince's staff would have been responsible had there been no rebellion. This and the terrible loneliness from which I knew Vanu suffered—all this and more had simply worn his body out. His physical vehicle may well have been virtually immortal, but that didn't mean it wasn't subject to exhaustion.

Of necessity, he'd become more and more controlling, so it was nearly impossible for him to turn over his responsibilities to Amadon, even though he trusted his assistant. Vanu knew a change was in order. In the end, his body made the decision for Vanu and he stepped back, retiring to a monastery his people had built for him in the foothills of Kashmir.

Before Vanu entered the monastery, I overheard him briefing Amadon and claiming that his retirement would be sure to stop the personality cult that had been steadily growing in his name, despite his efforts to prevent it. Yet his long absence only ended up by making it worse.

Vanu's virtual immortality guaranteed that he'd be labeled a god even though he'd reduced his visits to each settlement to once every hundred years, thus avoiding ever being seen twice by the same individual natives. But it hadn't turned out that way. In fact, when he reemerged into the world from his first period of five hundred years of silent meditation in the monastery, the reports he received indicated that most of his settlements were now actually worshipping him.

I wasn't present at the time, but I heard that he was appalled.

Finally, his longtime and much-beloved assistant Amadon had persuaded Vanu that by making himself more available to the tribes and settlements, he'd be able to redirect the natives' adoration away from himself and toward the Indwelling Spirit and the Father God. I was observing their discussion.

"As you did before . . . before you . . . disappeared." This was Amadon talking over the situation with Vanu sometime after Vanu had come out of his meditation. Amadon had felt horribly abandoned by Vanu's decision to enter the monastery in the first place, especially at such a key point in their mission, and he'd greeted his return to the world with a mix of relief and resentment.

"But it's not going to be enough this time, Vanu. You have no idea what they've done while you've been away." I knew that Amadon, much to Vanu's irritation, had never grasped the importance of meditation—more than once I'd heard him call it a "right waste of my time" behind Vanu's back. Yet something had been starting to go awry in Vanu's absence. Not only had he been elevated to divine status among many settlements, but in some cases Caligastia's midwayers had been up to their old tricks, masquerading as gods. A few quantum sleights of hand and a "Nog" or a "Ba'al" could dazzle a whole settlement into awe.

"Our people need something solid to worship—a God they can see with their own eyes. You've taught me to experience the Unseen God,

Vanu, but they've had nothing. All they had was you. You can't blame them for that."

"The Father Spirit," Vanu corrected his assistant absentmindedly. He'd been trying to reframe the concept of the Unseen God into the Father Spirit, as he felt it was a more personal way of referring to the Godhead. I could tell he knew Amadon was trying to needle him. But from his tone I could hear there was also something on his mind—he must have been pondering it during his long meditation.

After a while he spoke again: "Listen, Amadon, you don't know this. It's me who has to go on faith. You, my dear friend, are the one who knows. In your very humanness, it's you who knows the God of your heart."

I could see a cloud of puzzlement spreading over Amadon's honest, open face. He'd been close to Vanu far longer than I was sure he could remember—for thousands upon thousands of years. Yet this had never come up before. Amadon had believed them the same, since Vanu was always most circumspect in explaining how they were both mortals.

"I'm just a little older than you, my friend, but I was once like you, and will be again." And that was it. That was as much as Vanu was prepared to tell his assistant during the time they'd been wandering with their small band of followers ever since the rebellion over 103,000 years earlier. Together, they'd created stable farming and trading settlements in their movement eastward, uniting the indigenous natives in the worship of the Father Spirit, and building temples for spiritual education in all the main settlements.

Amadon was the one native human whom Vanu completely trusted, and for some rather special reasons. Vanu was one of the Prince's original staff back in Dalamatia; Amadon was pure human genetic stock of the highest quality. This is why Amadon was one of the hundred native humans chosen by the off-planet surgeons for their excellent genetics in the first place. It was from Amadon's life plasm that Vanu's material body had been grown—the two could even have been taken for twins, although they had grown more dissimilar over time and with differing experiences. (Amadon, for example, preferred a full beard and allowed his black hair to grow out.)

As was customary for MA's missions, Amadon and the other ninety-nine natives who had originally contributed their life plasm for the staff's bodies, were all, in turn, rewarded by the gift of a deathless life as well.

I've already mentioned Vanu and Amadon's virtual immortality and have written more fully about how this came about in *Confessions of a Rebel Angel*. Suffice it to say here that this technique for rendering certain beings virtually deathless is standard operating procedure for all Princes' missions, wherever they take place. Their material bodies are designed to survive in good shape for at least the half a million years they're expected to serve on the planet.

The situation here on Earth was made far more complicated by the Caligastia defection. One of the unexpected consequences—at least for the staff—of planetary isolation was MA's deliberate shutting down of certain incoming cosmic rays. These were the frequencies designed to interlock electrochemically with a certain plant, a shrub that had been especially brought in from Edentia, a higher-frequency world. Providing these frequencies were maintained and all the staff together with their hundred genetic donors regularly consumed the leaves or berries of this shrub, their material bodies were physically replenished and they would potentially live forever.

Following the collapse of Dalamatian culture and the fall of the city, Vanu had managed to clip cuttings off the Edentian shrub. He carried them with him when the forty members of the staff remaining loyal to MA and to him, together with 9,881 midwayers, had started on their long migration east, together with their native followers.

However, it wasn't long before MA intervened to give all forty of the loyalists, and the native donors who'd stayed with them, the choice to be taken off the planet and returned to the capital planet of this system of inhabited worlds. All of them elected to leave the planet except Vanu, who, with Amadon, volunteered to stay for the duration.

"Someone has to stand against Caligastia," Vanu argued. "Nobody deserves what'll happen if that bastard son runs amok. And he will. Mark my words." At this point, the Melchizedek made some of their mysterious adjustments to enable the pair to remain immortal as long as they continued to eat the fruit of the Edentian shrub. They no longer needed those incoming cosmic rays to ensure their longevity.

It was rather different for the rebels. They were not given the choice to leave the planet. Closing down the incoming frequencies caused all sixty of the rebel staff, as well as the native donors who followed Caligastia, to physically die within a few hundred years of the rebellion.

"Much has changed since you've been away," Amadon reported. "As I said, the people need something solid to focus on when they worship."

There was no answer from Vanu.

"Fire, thunder, and lightning—these are real things. You, Vanu. They worshipped you, too, because you were real. We left them alone and before I knew it they went back to worshipping their old gods." Apart from the slight grimace that flickered over his chief's face at Amadon's mention of Vanu worship, his eyes were closed and he could still have been meditating.

"And Vanu, what did you mean by us not being the same? You always told me we were." There was an edge of anger in Amadon's voice.

I wondered if Vanu might have felt he'd said too much, or possibly if his mind were elsewhere, since he gave no sign that he was responding to his assistant's question.

"In my meditation I was given the answer, my dear friend, perhaps, for both issues we've been talking about."

It was then that Vanu confided in Amadon his plans for the Lemurian migration and his concept of the perfectly balanced civilization. This was a dream they'd all but forgotten as they'd struggled and labored over the millennia to keep the light of hope burning in the hearts of as many humans as possible.

"And the real problem? This'll fix it?"

"Amadon, Amadon. Patience. I heard you. You're right, of course. If our destiny were different; if there'd been no rebellion, no Caligastia going rogue, no war in the West; if Dalamatia still existed and we all worked together as we had done before the troubles, if, if, if . . . ," Vanu's voice dropped to a whisper before he visibly shook himself. No point in regrets.

"It's a risk and I'll probably live to regret it, but if I have to, we'll make it 'Father Sun' and 'Mother Earth.' How does that sound, Amadon? Father Sun, Mother Earth—it's got a ring to it. Should be solid enough for them, shouldn't it?"

Amadon was grinning happily, which was reply enough for Vanu.

"And, my friend, we can always redirect the worship energy back to the Father Spirit or the Unseen God," he continued, smiling at his assistant, "when the people have established a more balanced and stable life for themselves."

When Amadon's smile turned to a worried frown I realized that after 134,000 years he'd almost forgotten what "a balanced and stable life" might be, and had certainly given up on any chance of ever seeing it in this world.

"Lemuria. That'll be our answer, Amadon. The secret to the peace we seek we'll find in the beautiful islands of Mu."

❖ ❖ ❖

I wouldn't want to understate the difficulties and challenges the community faced daily at Xtul. For a group of city dwellers from England, prepared only for community life by their brief stint in Nassau, they might have been living in the antediluvian past, yet without the skills of their distant forebears.

Soon after settling in and when they'd found out who currently owned the Xtul acreage, Christopher—the community's treasurer—and Mein Host took the local bus to Mérida to talk to the landowner about acquiring Xtul. Their journey was hot and dusty and they were "endlessly stopping and starting, picking up and dropping off a constant stream of little old ladies, their chickens and their goats, and burlap sacks bulging with something viscous that wobbled threateningly with every bounce of the bus," to quote Mein Host trying to describe his day to Mary Ann on their return close to midnight.

After jolting along unpaved roads into the city, they'd found themselves, sweating and dirty, sitting in the once-elegant antechamber of a dilapidated mansion in the center of Mérida. Regardless of the state of the building, the owner was a smooth and elegant man of middle age, his face broad and deeply tanned, his cheekbones high and slightly protruding, with coal-black hair graying at the temples. He was dressed in a beautifully cut white linen suit, with all the appearance and courtesy of a Hollywood stereotype of a Spanish-Mexican aristocrat.

He spoke well with a slight American accent and seemed quite pleased to spend his time with two such well-educated young Englishmen. England was a country to which he claimed to be greatly attached.

After gesturing his guests to two high-backed, intricately carved armchairs, their red-velvet seats worn to the webbing, he tugged on a moth-eaten velvet cord and settled back behind an equally ornate desk for a serious discussion. The room was cool and dimly lit, with louvered shutters closed against the harsh noontime sun and pencil-slim rays piercing the crepuscular gloom.

An ancient retainer, responding to a bell that must have been ringing somewhere in the depths of the mansion, tottered in to take an order for coffee all around.

I heard Mein Host commenting afterward: "There was this odd disconnect between the man and the mansion. He was immaculate—a beautiful man, obviously wealthy—yet he lived in this dark old dump. I'll bet his ancient mother lurked somewhere inside howling at the moon."

Back in the owner's study, they were well into their discussion as to whether the Maya were indeed indigenous or, as the owner had become convinced, they were survivors of somewhere else. He was suggesting it might have been Atlantis when strong black Mexican coffee was finally served in clear glasses, through which I could see thick layers of condensed milk.

"How could that be? Surely all the native Indians came over the Bering Straits before the ice retreated?" This was Christopher, wanting to keep the conversation going. Show your interest in the other person—they'd learned this technique at Mary Ann and Robert's Communication Course back in London.

"No, no, no. You are believing the scientists! Yes, some did. Of course. Up north. Not the Maya. They're different. Olmec, too, and Inca. You understand this, yes?"

"You mean Atlantis? The Maya may have originally come from Atlantis?" Mein Host was leaning forward now. He looked genuinely curious. I wondered if he was thinking about the brief glimpse of an Atlantean incarnation he'd received a few months earlier back in London.

"You're laughing, Mr. Christopher. You don't believe in Atlantis? You think it didn't happen? That it didn't disappear in a single night? Poof!"

"You mean what Plato says? That's just a story. The Egyptian priests were just trying to impress him with their knowledge of antiquity." Christopher had studied classical history at Oxford University.

"That's what the books say. Here it's different. We know our own history. Yes, it's filtered through your history of colonialism."

"That's why we've come to Xtul. We want to get away from all that colonialism stuff." I could hear a hint of shame in Christopher's voice.

"Ah! Mr. Christopher, you want to get down to business. But everything in its own time. Here, we take our time. Your friend," he said, gesturing at Mein Host. "He, I think, is interested, yes?"

Indeed, Mein Host *was* interested. "There was something about the man. I could intuitively feel he was speaking the truth" was how he explained it later.

"Listen. I tell you something perhaps you know already." The owner sensed a captive audience. "You know about our Maya calendar, of course? Yes? No?" A sunbeam slicing through a broken slat in one of the closed shutters lit up those high cheekbones again and I wondered if either young Englishmen would realize their host was clearly of Maya ancestry.

"No?" The owner paused again and I could feel his sadness for a moment. "I try to make this simple. Maya say the calendar starts in the year 3114 before Christ came. We call it the Long Count Calendar and it started when we believe the Atlanteans arrived here. Maya believe it was our creation date. But the Maya weren't the first. This perhaps you didn't know. You heard of Lemuria? They were here first—long, long, before. They left their mark, too."

"Now I'm really confused!" Christopher looked as if he were trying to understand the owner in terms of what he'd been taught at school. "That's the Bronze Age, isn't it? How could they have sailed all that way from Atlantis, if it ever existed?"

Seemingly unflustered by the challenge, the owner continued, "The point about that date, 3114 BCE—it was around that time that Atlantis was having its problems. The wiser ones left before the cataclysm that destroyed them."

Christopher must have looked skeptical.

"You think, Mr. Christopher, all history starts and ends with Europe? Because your books tell you that? You never question your teachers?" There was a new edge to the man's voice and I could see the back of Christopher's pale neck reddening slightly.

"3114 BCE?" Mein Host asked quickly. "That was right around the time the Egyptian dynastic period started, wasn't it?"

"You are right, of course. Plato, he was right, too. His timing was wrong, that's all. He was told about Atlantis by an Egyptian priest. That was over a thousand years after the destruction—long time—but the priests made it sound far longer, you understand? In those days priests took their authority from antiquity.

"From the Egyptians' point of view, Plato came from a young, upstart culture. Naturally, they looked down on the Greeks. What they didn't tell Plato, what he didn't learn, some Atlantean ruling families were coming to Egypt a long time ago. They were the ones who came to be the pharaohs of old, understand?"

"So some of the Atlanteans came to Mexico while others went to Egypt. Is that what you're saying, sir?" My ward took over the questions while Christopher slumped uncomfortably back in his creaking armchair and sipped his coffee.

"And the Lemurians came before them to Mexico and Egypt as well. You know this?"

Mein Host shook his head. "When did that happen? What period was it?"

"Timing is difficult—almost everything disappears over time. What remains? A few rocks too enormous to lift—even now, some cities underwater. Places our elders talk about, but the West, it never believes. Our elders say the migrants come in waves. First the Lemurians, maybe 30,000 or 20,000 BCE, then suddenly come another series of waves between 13,000 and 9000 BCE. Maybe when their islands were sinking."

The man had clearly done his research. Mein Host's education had barely prepared him for this and Christopher by now was keeping resolutely silent.

"Then it must have been Lemurians integrating with the Native Americans, is that what you're saying? The ones who'd migrated over the ice bridge and worked their way down the continent." Mein Host was starting to see the picture. "These must have been the people the Atlanteans encountered when they arrived."

Their host, well on his hobbyhorse by now, was continuing, obviously overjoyed to have a rapt audience.

"So, when the Atlanteans arrive—that's why I think the 3114 BCE date is so important. It's when the troubles really begin on Atlantis. It's why the Maya wanted to start over, when they come here, the last big waves of refugees arriving between 1600 and 1300 BCE. You can find sudden improvements around that point in Olmec culture and Olmecs themselves—they were distant descendants of Lemurian migrants mixing with native Indians. Although, very sad by that time too.

"Some of the Atlanteans intermarried with the natives, while the Maya did their best to keep the bloodlines pure. Even Inca . . . even Aztec. You could say they were the last of the Andean civilizations; even they remembered the Atlanteans, to their sorrow."

There was that flash of sadness again.

"Quetzalcoatl?" Mein Host broke the silence. He knew his D. H. Lawrence. Christopher sank deeper into his chair, content to leave it up to his more widely read partner to keep the conversation going.

"Yes, Quetzalcoatl. Quet-zal-coatl." The name sounded different when pronounced by the owner, and I could feel Mein Host's momentary awkwardness.

"Of course, the story will be in your history books. The Aztec Emperor Moctezuma believe Cortés is Quetzalcoatl who return as he promised. That's how it was so easy for a few Spaniards to conquer an empire, right? Yes? That what you're taught?"

"Well," Mein Host mumbled. It was at this point, I heard him say later, that he started to realize the man was likely more Maya than Spanish.

"Yet, no one ask: Who was this Quetzalcoatl? Yes, yes, a mythic figure, a Serpent God. So how could he be real, yes? That's how he gets dismissed, because Atlantis a myth, too. Yes?"

I could see that Mein Host was starting to feel out of his depth. He mumbled something I couldn't hear before the owner, by this time thoroughly involved with his splendid pedigree, continued to issue challenges.

"So it becomes a joke, yes?" The owner's voice was rising. "An emperor who give away his empire to a monster because he think Cortés is a god? Everybody laugh, yes? What you don't read is something else. Cortés did arrive at a significant time, in 1519, the year of One Reed, or we say *Ce Acatl*. But, my friend, Cortés was never believed to be Quetzalcoatl—that's colonial myth! Yes, he arrive on the right date! How that happen?"

"But didn't Moctezuma just give up?" That was what Mein Host was taught.

"In manner of saying, yes. He try to please Cortés at first. He try to feel out the enemy. Perhaps he was Quetzalcoatl. It was right date. But he give them too much gold. Even he has Cortés and some of his soldiers stay with him in his palace. There has already been some massacres, so the emperor know what he's up against. He knows there'll be war because a flaming dragon crosses the sky that year—other signs, too.

"But point I want to make—my theory—it was not because Moctezuma, nobody else, either, was stupid enough to think Cortés was Quetzalcoatl—that is obvious. Because it was the year *Ce Acatl*. That only reason why, understand?

"Every fifty-two years, life hang in the balance for Maya. They don't know what the gods will do in the next cycle. But the Year of One Reed is even more special, understand? It was a great turning of the cycles, was the year of the start of the Nine Hells. Moctezuma, he know of horrors ahead. That is why he is so, so two-minded. He know he no choice but be defeated. There! That is my theory."

The owner leaned back behind his desk, cigarette smoke curling around his head and smiled happily. "Moctezuma know there be no choice but suffer through Nine Hells until year 1987 in your calendar, when long cycle start turning."

"When does your Long Count finish?" Mein Host asked. "When does this cycle end?"

"Nothing ever ends, you must understand that. But I can tell you, 2012, on December 21, that is the first day of the fourteenth *b'ak'tun*. Then, I think, *everything* change." There was a long silence in the room. The overhead fan squeaked rhythmically. Somewhere deep in the mansion a dog barked.

"And Xtul?" Christopher broke the spell.

"Xtul? Xtul, Señor Christopher, Xtul I give you. Live there as long as you wish. You pay only land taxes." He groped in a drawer for a file. "Ah, yes, mmm . . . that's seventy U.S. dollars a year, yes? Okay?"

Another stunned silence. The dog barked again, this time closer, ending in an unnerving squeal. Somehow I knew my ward was wondering whether the squeal was human or canine. It worried me slightly at the way I was starting to read his thoughts.

"Seventy dollars a year? You're renting it to us? Not giving it to us, right?" This is Christopher needing to make sure he understood the offer.

"Yes. Yes. I give it to you. Only $70 a year."

"For as long as we like? Forever?"

"Yes, forever if you like." He was smiling at them and for the first time Mein Host felt everything was too good to be true. They'd gotten it. For seventy bucks a year.

"And if we make a lot of improvements?" Christopher again.

"Ah. Of course. Land must stay in my family, you understand. You make your improvements. Stay there long as you want. When you leave, you leave. I give you nothing—evens-stevens, you say, yes? This way we all win, yes?"

It was hard not to notice how his English was improving.

"So, even if we build a big hotel?" Christopher asked. "If we sink millions into it, we still have to turn it all over to you at the end? We get nothing for all that equity?"

"Ah! but Señor Christopher, I think you are not going to do anything like that! I am right, yes?"

They were all laughing now. A grand hotel? Xtul was in the middle of nowhere.

"Now we make out a little contract?"

Mein Host looked at Christopher.

"We'll be back next week to sign the contract, if our superiors agree to the terms." Christopher was getting up and speaking more formally.

"The terms, yes. You know this is so strange." The owner was looking directly in their eyes for the first time as he warmly shook their hands. "Very strange indeed. I knew you were coming. Is that strange to you? This last week, I feel sure someone is coming about Xtul."

"Strange?" Mein Host held his eyes for a long time.

"Yes. In all my time no one, no one at all, has ever asked about the place. Isn't that a bit odd? I never think about Xtul until last week. And here you are! Perhaps Xtul . . . perhaps the place is being saved for you!"

Within a week a simple contract had been signed. Yet far more importantly for Mein Host, all this talk of Atlantis and Lemuria and the quiet confidence with which the owner presented his theory opened the young man's mind to new and as-yet-unconsidered possibilities.

❈ ❈ ❈

The carefully chosen migrants, arriving on their fleets of rafts in increasingly large numbers from Luzon in the Philippines, expanded rapidly through the thousands of islands, settling on many of the larger ones.

Every tenth raft carried a single fandor, the large passenger birds that had been so useful back in Dalamatia, and some of whom had chosen to accompany Vanu and the loyalists. Fandors were large creatures with wingspans at full extension of up to forty feet, and they possessed somewhat nervous natures. The birds had been extremely cautious when the Prince's staff first came across them in the Atlas Mountains. Individual fandors had come and gone for many hundreds of years, observing life in the city, before trusting humans to ride on their backs.

It had been Onya, a young native girl, now long-since dead, who'd been the first to ride a fandor, opening up another much-needed mode of travel. However, the birds were notoriously picky. They'd adamantly refused to allow any member of the Prince's staff too close to them and only a few native-born humans were ever allowed to ride them.

Fandors were known to be semitelepathic and they formed the deepest bonds of affection with their chosen riders. Only females of the species had ever been known to accept a human rider and, once accepted, that relationship was considered by the fandor to continue until one or the other died. Since fandors were somewhat longer-lived than their human riders and the bonds of mutual love were so strong, it was not unusual for one of these massive birds to build herself a funeral pyre, following the death of her rider. Knowing she would meet her beloved rider again in the afterlife and surrounded by others of her kind, she would submit herself joyfully to the flames. It was from this unusual custom that the myth of the Phoenix was born.

Fandors had never been easy to be around. Their semitelepathic sensitivity, although limited, gave them access to much that remained unsaid in the minds of staff and humans alike. Much of what the birds picked up telepathically they didn't like, and their way of handling this was to then employ something they were hardwired with: their acerbic sense of humor.

Unable to speak words, fandors were mercilessly truthful in the images they threw back and were known for the occasional bitterness of their sarcasm. Some of the staff, especially Böni—one of Onya's mentors and a senior member of the Prince's staff—developed a deep hatred of the birds.

When the rebellion occurred, I noticed that the fandors who'd previously been close to their riders in the city simply disappeared. Their telepathic abilities allowed them to keep up with what was happening in Dalamatia; the schism caused by Caligastia's rejection of MA's standard doctrine; Vanu's exile with the forty staff members remaining loyal to MA; the destruction of the city and its final disappearance under the waters of the Persian Gulf; and, finally, the increasingly erratic behavior of Caligastia, the Planetary Prince.

At this point, many fandors elected to return to their nesting grounds in the Atlas Mountains. The few who'd bonded with those riders choosing to follow Vanu and the other loyalists traveled with them on their long trek eastward toward northern India. At the time, I thought it was most significant that so few fandors decided to accompany Caligastia or the sixty staff who'd followed him into rebellion. And this was in spite of considerable pressure from the Prince.

Fandors apparently knew better than that!

I heard later that the handful of birds whose riders did follow the Prince had ritually incinerated themselves—as their custom would have it. Like the cetaceans in the oceans of the world, fandors were a pure and uncorrupted species. Their integrity disappeared with them when the last of them finally died at around the time the Lemurian civilization reached its apex thirty-eight thousand years ago.

I felt at the time that the fandors knew they'd served their purpose in giving their aid to human beings in the early eras of your development. These days I can't be sentimental about species extinction, but the disappearance of the fandors seems to me oddly prescient.

Fandors, it turned out, were the most modest of creatures. Nothing was ever discovered about their mating or procreative activities, not in the entire time the birds were on the planet. Every once in a while someone would catch a glimpse of an adolescent fandor, but no one had ever seen an infant. Sufficient time has elapsed by now for me to reveal what was happening in the world of the fandors. Much of this I was able to observe for myself while it was occurring.

When the rebellion broke out in Dalamatia the fandors were far more horrified than anyone in the city took the time to understand—the citizens had problems enough of their own. The truth was that none of the fandors wanted anything more to do with Prince Caligastia, the staff, human beings in general, even Vanu and the loyalists.

When the birds had recovered from their anger and disappointment, it became clear to them that those fandors who'd bonded with riders in Vanu's contingent of loyalists needed to escort the exiles. As I've mentioned, it was only female fandors who seemed willing to carry people on their backs. In fact, nothing was ever seen of male fandors who, if the citizens of Dalamatia could but know it, remained behind in their nesting area in the Atlas Mountains.

There were also remarkably few males, since female birds retained the ability to predetermine the sex of their offspring after mating with a male. Male fandors were regarded by the females as being incorrigibly violent by nature, which is why they were confined to the mountains and why there were so few of them.

This decision to travel with Vanu's group presented a problem to which the fandors possessed an unusual solution, even if it would lead ultimately to a shorter life for the species in general. Parthenogenesis, or reproduction from an ovum without fertilization from an external source, is not an unknown form of sexual reproduction in the animal world, although it is extremely rare. Plants do it; some invertebrates do it; even certain iguanas do it. And for the reason I can only credit to the Life Carriers who originally laid down the patterns of genetic life, fandors could also do it.

In certain conditions, female fandors were able to deliver their progeny without being fertilized by a male. And, as such, her offspring were also, of necessity, female.

Under the normal rhythms of fandor life, parthenogenesis was not the favored method of reproduction, since it narrowed the overall gene pool. Yet almost every mature female practiced it occasionally, since the closeness of the mother/daughter relationship that such autocloning produced was one of the few things the fandors held sacred. Mother and daughter were quite literally of the same flesh and although their individual experiences changed them slightly in different ways, it could truly be said that "When you meet the daughter, you meet the mother."

This became the persuasive argument when the decision was reached among the birds to permit the fandors attached to Vanu's mission to go with their riders. They would be traveling far beyond their ability to return to the nesting grounds in West Africa, and they all knew they'd be unlikely to ever come back. It would be a one-way trip, made by their daughters and granddaughters, and their descendants, for as long as that genetic strain retained its integrity.

Fandors turned out to be particularly valuable when the migrants finally arrived on the islands of Mu, since an island could be explored by a fandor and her rider in a fraction of the time it took for people to reach it by canoe. With this help the new migrants surged northward, settling island after island until they were well north of the Tropic of Cancer.

After a thousand years had passed, Vanu drew the migration from the mainland to a close. For the first eight hundred years, he'd used his limited telepathic abilities to attract those natives of the purest genetic lines and who possessed the relevant skills and courage for the long ocean crossing.

Vanu and his construction crews in Luzon had turned their raft building to a high art by this time. The route and the best time of year for sailing were well-known, but the actual process of navigating accurately remained a problem.

Although surprisingly few rafts had been lost at sea, Vanu, I noticed, liked to play up the dangers facing the new recruits—the sharks, the typhoons, the constant hunger and thirst, even the risk of plunging into the sea, pushed off by a sleepy fandor unfolding her wings in the sun.

During the last couple of hundred years, after Vanu had ceased to preselect the migrants, he permitted any natives willing to take the "enormous risks" to start a new life in Lemuria to construct their own rafts to make the journey. As can be imagined, this resulted in high losses, due to the hasty or sloppy construction of the rafts. In addition, with no knowledgeable navigator, the rafts could be swept hundreds of miles off course and miss the islands entirely.

It took courage, tenacity, and a great deal of luck to arrive safely. Most were never seen again. Occasionally, a raft washed up on one of the outlying Lemurian islands, its occupants dead or driven insane by thirst. Only relatively few managed to make it with an intact body and mind during the two-hundred-year period before Vanu closed it all down.

Previously, I've questioned Vanu's tactics. But this approach, which appeared to be one of sending people to their almost certain deaths, demonstrated Vanu at his most unsentimental. Only now, when I have a chance to place his actions in a larger context, do I appreciate why he allowed these suicidal voyages to continue. It also suggests that one of the deeper causes of the ultimate collapse of the Lemurian theocracy over sixty thousand years later might perhaps be traced back to Vanu's decision to permit such a small, random genetic quotient into the Lemurian genetic pool.

I didn't understand at the time why Vanu encouraged so many of what I might call the "rougher element" to take on the voyage, especially when he'd taken such care in telepathically preselecting the former migrants. Now I believe he was trying to accomplish two rather different aims simultaneously.

In any group of sentient beings, there will always be a substantial difference in personalities and differences of opinion. The more complex the personalities are, the greater the possibility of an extreme divergence of opinions. How we resolve those differences enables us all to grow in experience and wisdom.

Human beings were just as complicated then as they are now.

On Luzon, anger was one of the inevitable reactions of the generations of natives who'd been gathering all over the Philippine Islands, hoping to be invited by Vanu on a raft, but always being rejected. Hundreds of years of being continually turned down for the voyage—for no reason they could understand—had built up a considerable head of outrage and resentment among the increasingly large numbers demanding to migrate to Lemuria.

This rage and frustration finally boiled over, leading to a breakdown of trust in Vanu's leadership, the boldest among the rebels slipping into self-serving and criminal enterprises. There was a complete collapse of social order in Luzon, the settlement once dedicated to building the rafts and preparing them for the voyage, with a criminal element starting to take over. This sense of anarchy quickly spread throughout the other settlements on the Philippine Islands, as Vanu's teachings were openly ridiculed and mob violence threatened to break out.

I've come to think this was all part of Vanu's plan. By the time he opened up the voyages to anyone who wanted to try to reach Lemuria as an independent agent, many of those who demanded to travel were the angry rebellious ones who'd been previously denied. In this way, I believe Vanu was attempting to rid the mainland of the troublemakers on the one hand, while also providing something of a random factor in the Lemurian gene pool. Unfortunately, the voyage proved exceedingly hazardous—since no one ever came back, they never discovered just how hazardous the trip really was. A far smaller number of this renegade element ever reached the Lemurian gene pool than Vanu had hoped.

It was only thousands of years later that this apparently trivial miscalculation would factor so unexpectedly in the ultimate betrayal of all that Lemurian culture had held sacred for its entire long history.

3

Deconstructing History

Angelic Betrayals, Seraphic Transport, Alien Culture, and a Foolish Joke and Exile

As the weeks turned into months at Xtul, it became clearer to everyone in the community that Mary Ann was at the center of their lives. Whether or not every individual there had accepted the reality of having an incarnate Goddess in their midst, there was a sufficient critical mass of true believers to persuade the others that they were in the presence of someone truly extraordinary.

In *Confessions of a Rebel Angel*, I touched on Mein Host's peak experience in Nassau, which culminated in what he believed was a clear acknowledgment from Mary Ann that she was indeed the Goddess. He had no idea whether any of the others had had a similar experience because no one spoke openly about such a delicate matter. It's my observation that they believed that Mary Ann's divinity would remain more sacred if it wasn't talked about. Perhaps a more skeptical view might be that, in airing their personal beliefs, they may have been able to see Mary Ann with clearer eyes.

Since I'm not permitted to speak about the angelic activity surrounding other people in the group, I can only report on what I witnessed occurring in Mein Host's life. I've never made a secret of my distrust of Mary Ann and have admitted previously that I was puzzled to see Mein Host's companion angels encouraging, even contriving, for him to rejoin the community two years after a terrible row with Mary Ann had prompted him to leave for a couple of years.

Yet even after my ward rejoined the community he still shared my distrust of the woman—that is, until his revelation in Nassau and Mary Ann's admittance of her divinity. It was then it became clear to me that, despite my suspicions about Mary Ann, Mein Host's angels were supporting him in fully believing her to be the Goddess. I can only conjecture the others must have had somewhat the same experience because the level of commitment needed to wake every morning on a hard tile floor, to face another day of hunger, hard work, and heatstroke, must have required an iron will.

There was little to look forward to during the day. After sundown, having eaten their small portions of whatever they'd picked or caught during the day, the community engaged in discussions that would often last until dawn. From these discussions emerged the basic beliefs of what would, a few years later, become the infamous cult, the Process: Church of the Final Judgment.

It was in these intense evening discussions that Mary Ann shone so brightly. If I were to be skeptical about those long nights, I would suggest that Mary Ann, having led everyone into the wilderness, had to come up with something to validate her leadership. Hence, she focused her attention on what came to be called "enactments."

Enactments can best be thought of as a form of living theater that seems to be derived from the day-to-day, dramatic interplay of personalities when a group of humans are clustered together under extreme conditions, as Mein Host and the others were. Mary Ann would then decode and deconstruct the compulsive patterns of behavior that various members might be manifesting unconsciously in their interchanges with other people and relate them back to what was being examined.

Yet it would be too simplistic to say that Mary Ann actually created these enactments. They certainly appeared spontaneous to the members while they were occurring. Mein Host claimed, with some justification, that "enactments seemed to emerge organically and unprompted from the internal dynamics and power shifts in the group. And it was Mary Ann who had the wisdom to expose the deeper archetypal elements behind different members' otherwise innocent actions."

An enactment might last a few days, sometimes a couple of weeks, or months in a few cases. For some people, it exposed a repetitive pattern fundamental to their natures. It's beyond my brief to describe any of the enactments in detail, but the concept had tremendous dramatic and psychic power that Mein Host, for one, found invaluable in deepening his understanding of himself.

Behind the concept of enactments was the observation that human beings repeat specific compulsive patterns of behavior down through history. "Only by casting light on these patterns can we understand them and release the unconscious compulsion to act them out. Take, for example, betrayal," Mary Ann explained to the group one evening, "something we see again and again throughout history. A person, or an idea, emerges, and before long a trusted insider will become the betrayer." She let that hang in the air. No one likes a betrayer.

"On the surface," she continued, after looking around the circle of faces gathered in the dark around her, "the motive for any particular betrayal might be greed, fear, or perhaps it might be ideologically driven. But we're looking for the deeper, underlying, patterns of behavior.

"If we're going to start over . . ." she looked around meaningfully again, her green eyes flashing in the candlelight, "then we need to clear the patterns that history has dumped on our heads."

Thus, over the months, there was the Adam and Eve enactment, in which Mein Host found himself unsurprisingly in the role of the serpent; one focused on the last days of Jesus Christ, in which my ward played Judas; and another that deconstructed England's King Henry VIII's reformation of the church, where Mein Host played the role of the unfortunate and slippery Thomas Cranmer, Archbishop of Canterbury.

Mind you, all this had nothing to do with reincarnation. The roles unconsciously shouldered resonated with the personalities involved—that was both part of the drama and an apt vehicle for gaining personal insights.

In terms of personal insights, nothing could have been richer than the series of events that followed Mein Host's role as the serpent in the Garden of Eden.

However specious these enactments might have been, in my opinion, they provided the individual members with an arena in which to experience deeply affecting emotions and feelings to which they'd otherwise have no access. Mein Host, still a young man of twenty-six who was struggling to find himself, welcomed the insights he gained from these enactments.

⁂ ⁂ ⁂

Although I was still outwardly supportive of Caligastia and my function remained that of observing the Prince's mission, my every inclination was to accompany Vanu's migration to Lemuria.

I'd become progressively more disenchanted with Prince Caligastia since the initial excitement of the rebellion had worn off. For me, Caligastia's wholly premature distribution of atomic secrets among his scientists and the dreadful war that followed was the final proof of how utterly wrong it was for us to have followed Lucifer into the uprising.

Yet, to be honest with myself, I knew I was still confused as to whether I was really seeing Lucifer's Rebellion playing out as he had hoped and intended, or whether what was happening on Earth was the product of Prince Caligastia's growing hubris and his autocratic nature. Possibly life on the other planets among the thirty-seven whose Planetary Princes, like Caligastia and Daligastia, chose to follow Lucifer and Satan into rebellion was turning out better than the chaos and brutality on Earth.

I missed witnessing the terrible nuclear war on Earth because at the time I was on a neighboring planet, Zandana, for some recreation. At least, that is what I experienced on my previous trip. I certainly returned refreshed that time. Now, even well before the war, I could see the way matters were going to play out for Caligastia. I was at wits' end. I just couldn't watch another catastrophe. All our hopes were being dashed yet again.

So I'd managed to charm the various authorities into granting me permission to leave just before Caligastia's war broke out on Earth. I was able to persuade a transport seraph to take me to Zandana—yet I had little idea of what would happen when I arrived on the planet. Whereas my prior visits to Zandana were recreational, this one turned out to be strictly confrontational. I was put through an emotional and psychic wringer so that when I returned to Earth I felt I was a very different Watcher.

Now I was considering another trip to Zandana. Prince Caligastia was a lost cause. After the war and with almost all his territories rendered uninhabitable, he had retreated into himself. I believe he finally understood that he would have to leave humans alone while they gradually built up their numbers and their social organizations all over again. Not only did a sophisticated, yet warlike, culture simply disappear off the face of the planet, but the few human survivors degenerated back to a Stone Age life.

The survivors' troubles were exacerbated over time by competition from another genus of human beings who were slowly migrating north from Central Africa. Later, you will know them as the Neanderthals. And, if you subscribe to conventional anthropology, you might well think of them as the primary genus of humanity until Cro-Magnon came along twenty thousand years later to scribble so artfully on cave walls.

I don't believe I will ever quite get used to seraphic transport—not because it's frightening but simply because it induces such odd sensations. As I've previously suggested, it must be somewhat akin to being in a womb—not that I'd know much about that! Watchers, like most celestials in the Local Universe, are created by the Mother Spirit in great clans, tens of thousands at a time, as fully functioning beings. But traveling in that living creature, wrapped in her embrace for the trip, is the nearest I'll come to a womb—until I'm incarnated into a mortal body.

There is absolutely no sensation of traveling at superluminary speeds—or traveling at any speed at all, for that matter. This being my fourth trip, I was more relaxed, which is why this time I might have been able to hear the music that seemed to resonate through me during the all-too-brief trip.

The transport seraph was friendlier to me this time—I imagine I was starting to get the frequent-flyer treatment—so she explained the magical sounds to me after we'd arrived. "It pleases me that you heard the music." She was making the words in my mind. "It is one of the reason we transports love our work so much—the music can never be the same twice."

"But why? How?"

"I am told it is an electromagnetogravitic artifact of our speed through subspace and the precise position of the solar events in relationship to the transport, although I do not really know what that means." Apparently, the seraph wasn't as stuffy as I'd remembered.

"All I know is that a magnetic current spirals around me as I fly and the music subtly changes when I accelerate or slow down. How this morphs into the slower audible frequencies I have no idea."

"So can you play the music?"

"I am learning. But it is more nuanced if you can understand this. The sound is itself an artifact of flight—we make it into music. Some of my older sisters can co-create entire symphonies on their longer flights. Me? I am just making gestures at this point. But, yes, I am improving."

I swear she flashed me a shy smile before she turned away. It meant more to me than I can say. This was the first time since the rebellion that one of MA's loyalist seraphim had shown me any kindness. Of course, she must have known that I was counted as one of the rebel angels. I'm told we have a distinct psychic odor about us. It's this aroma that gradually changes, becoming more pleasing as our thought processes once more synchronize with the Multiverse Mind.

Yet, she was kind to me. I took that as a good sign. It boded well for my time on Zandana. I could always think and feel more clearly in this world. Back on Earth, Caligastia and his rebel midwayers had sown such confusion, distrust, and shame in the world mind that it was often difficult for me to get my thoughts straight.

Although the Planetary Prince of Zandana was one of the thirty-seven Princes who aligned themselves and their planets with Lucifer's cause, this Descending Son had been manifesting a rather different world than Caligastia, a Descending Son of the same order.*

Although Prince Zanda's motives for aligning himself with Lucifer

---

*In Prince Zanda's case, ninety-one of his staff and all ninety-one of their modified human companions chose to follow him, together with the majority of his pool of fifty thousand midwayers. Those remaining loyal to MA were returned to the Local Universe HQ planet following the uprising. Yet this was after they were allowed to live out their natural lives on another small island continent—Zandana has one large southern continent and ten smaller island continents. Thus Prince Zanda didn't have the constant aggravation of a loyalist staff member like Vanu offering an alternative path, which so infuriated Prince Caligastia back on Earth.

were originally much the same as Caligastia's, his way of conducting himself was completely different. Zanda, too, had believed Lucifer's assertion that technological progress in the Local Universe was being held up and stunted by some senior celestials for their own opaque purposes. He also felt he could do a better job if he were given a free hand. Zanda was clearly a very different personality from Caligastia, and he made no claim, as had Caligastia, that he was "God of his World."

On my previous visits I had felt nothing but admiration for Zandana's progress, even if this was restricted to only one of the eleven continents. Unlike the city of Dalamatia back on Earth, Zandan—the capital city of the large southern continent—was a thriving center of advanced technology and the arts. It was a delightful city, clean and filled with light, with broad tree-lined avenues and official buildings constructed with blindingly white local marble. Their twin suns, shining through the violet-tinged leaves of the massive trees, threw constantly shifting patterns on the blank white facades.

At first glance I'd thought their architecture was somewhat boring— white blocks, mostly between seven and ten stories in height, apparently windowless, and lining the central and radial avenues—until I looked more closely. Not only was what I took as the most quotidian of aesthetics—those apparently blank white facades were not what they seemed—but I suddenly had the insight that each structure utterly lacked any mark of its architect's egotism. No apparent striving for originality at all costs marred a sterling natural purity.

What the Zandanans had accomplished with their urban architecture was altogether more subtle than I'd thought possible. When I looked more closely at one of the blank white facades I'd found so lacking in personality, I could see that the bottom thirty or forty feet of each building was covered all over with the most delicate tracery, carved into the marble to a depth varying from one inch to one-sixteenth of an inch. As the planet moved through its day, shadows of the two suns formed a constantly shifting series of images delineated by the differing depths of the carved incisions.

Naturally, the citizens of Zandan were no more aware of me than humans were back on Earth as they purposefully conducted their business, sometimes looking right through me as I gazed up at one of the buildings from the sidewalk of the main avenue. Perhaps my senses had been dulled by my time on Caligastia's Earth, because I was surprised at my own amazement when I observed a handful of citizens—all women, I might add—stepping carefully around me. Some wrinkled their noses and a couple of them edged around me with slight smiles on their faces. And no, they hadn't "seen" me, that was clear. But they had sensed me, although I'd no reason to doubt that they gave themselves other reasons altogether for avoiding walking through me. Regardless, I was impressed by their unconscious sensitivity to my presence. I wasn't used to that.

Yet it was the delicately modeled facade that was engrossing me. As the lavender shadows played over the filigree of carved, biomorphic forms, I was slowly becoming aware that a story was being told. The sculpted forms seemed to come alive as the shadows of the leaves flickered over them. Now I could see what the artists were telling me. And it had to be *artists* in the plural—there was simply too much detailed work for any one artist to have completed alone.

Gliding a little closer to the wall, which now appeared to me to be writhing with life, there it was. The history of their home planet, Zandana, as seen through the lens of the particular council whose building it was, carved into the marble. It was so delicately fashioned and so massively detailed that the forms could only be seen when a shadow touched a recessed line.

Here I was looking at what must have been their council for technical advancement, because there was the first glint of fire as it was passed from hand to hand. Over here were children playing with small lumps of meteorite iron. I floated up parallel to the wall and there, just below the level of the shadows cast by the treetops, were the more recent tributes to Zandanan technical ingenuity—their gradual mastery of electromagnetism and fluid dynamics; their variety of telescopes and microscopes, with the exacting precision of their lens crafting reflected in the wondrous delicacy of the carvings. Over there were the intricate forms of machines and devices etched into the stone, the purposes of which I had no idea.

Then I saw what had initially so confused me. The shadowed forms of machines and all those enigmatic contraptions, while evidently technical, constructed things, were apparently designed to emulate as closely as possible the elegant forms of nature. In this way, as I was to discover later, the artists who created these exquisite carvings were reflecting an ancient tradition of integrating science, art, and the Zandanan love of nature into a subtle and harmonious balance of all three cultural necessities.

Looking up, I could see that here the carvings ended, leaving the blank glistening marble surface stretching up to the top of the building. I realized that their intention was to gradually fill the facade with their carvings over time, as their inventions and ingenuity advanced over the millennia.

Please excuse me, dear reader, if my dwelling on such details, in what must appear to you as a thoroughly alien culture, seems self-indulgent or unnecessary. I plead only that I seek to interest Mein Host, himself once an architect.

Should I describe how Zandanans' dress? Their fashions and fashionable conversation? The intricacies of their diets and the complexities of their love lives? For those of you curious about such matters, I can only suggest that you travel to Zandana in your astral bodies and observe for yourselves.

I report only that mortals appearing very much like Earth humans strode about the city streets, except, in general, both males and females were considerably taller and seemed in far better health than any humans I'd observed on Earth.

I'd only been on Zandana for a couple of turnings of their suns and already I was feeling filled with more hope than I'd ever felt on Earth. Here was a culture, after all, that was proving as successful as Caligastia's regime back on Earth was disastrous.

Might Lucifer have been correct all along? Was I witnessing here on Zandana the fruits of allowing greater freedom to mortals? Was it only Caligastia's overweening ambition that had made such a mess of life back on Earth?

Was I being somewhat premature in my positive assessment of Zandanan civilization? Had I perhaps been so carried away by all that subtle cultural beauty that I'd ignored the gathering storm of rebellion in one of the other, less developed, continents?

Why is it that the good never seems to last forever? Is that the most profound curse of the rebellion?

❉ ❉ ❉

It was a joke, of course, which so annoyed Mary Ann that she insisted, in front of the whole community, on Mein Host leaving the sacred grounds of Xtul, never to return. I say *of course* because blurting out a comment before he could stop himself—one that was sometimes funny, but often covertly critical as well—had become a personality quirk that often got him into trouble. Having firmly repressed his mercurial intelligence throughout his boarding-school years, and with Mary Ann's emphasis on the development of spontaneous, intuitive "speaking off the top of one's head," Mein Host often found that his comments could be taken too far.

Fortunately for him, he has grown more sensitive over the years. But he still finds himself in situations in which he seems to be impelled to speak the truth to someone who has no wish to hear it. Only twenty years ago I was taken aback to watch him lean forward over the dining room table in the London home of a couple he vaguely knew, to deliver the following line to the mistress of the house.

"When I look into your eyes," he said with a quiet intensity, "I find that I go straight to hell." (In partial defense of my ward, I should add that, although it was a much-needed wake-up call for a rich woman—who seemed to him to be throwing her life and talents away in self-indulgent and destructive mindlessness—it was perhaps a trifle too straightforward.)

There was a terrible silence before the woman starting screaming black witchcraft curses (thus confirming Mein Host's point), while her husband propelled Mein Host unceremoniously out the front door.

At Xtul, Mein Host's funny line need not be repeated here, but the context within which it occurred does need some explanation. It may also serve to illustrate some of the power dynamics at work within the group as well as revealing some essential aspects of my ward's character.

In essence, during the community's enactments, no one knew that an enactment was taking place. And the outcome could not be predicted by anyone until Mary Ann brought the whole enactment to cathartic fruition. As Mein Host has written previously: ". . . [Mary Ann's] psychic brilliance [was in] uncovering the hidden motives and dissecting the deeper intentions of all of us participants. She was brutally honest with her observations—which were also generally true—and since we all held her in such awe, we willingly played along."

Such was the case with the Garden of Eden enactment in which Mein Host was cast as the serpent. This should come as no surprise to the reader, since my ward's affinity for snakes has already been discussed. "You're one of the serpent people," Mary Ann had told the uncomprehending lad back in London at the start of this long and winding journey.

The Garden enactment itself had continued for some weeks before the evening that it came to a head. How this all played out over the days and nights of constant interaction is of less importance than the series of experiences it precipitated for Mein Host.

The serpent's role in the traditional Eden myth is a puzzling one. The unexpected appearance of a talking snake into an utopian garden can be read as either the entry of "evil" into the human condition or, just as reasonably, as wise advice to a couple of innocent humans under the thumb of a dictatorial and arbitrary pseudodivinity calling itself Jehovah.

Either way, the result was much the same, or so the myth suggests. Man, woman, and snake were all thrown out into the maelstrom of life. A thoroughly depressing myth, you must admit, for the three Abrahamic religions—and I don't know how many offshoots—to hold on to for so long and with such vigor.

As any thoughtful psychologist with access to relevant cross-cultural data can demonstrate, for a myth to continue to hold a place in the mortal spiritual imagination so tenaciously, it has to contain some element of deeper truth. In the case of this particular myth, it might also come as no surprise for those following my narrative that the Garden story's deepest historical resonance speaks of Lucifer's rejection by the high celestials in MA's bureaucracy and the resultant isolation of this entire system of over six hundred inhabited worlds from the larger Multiverse context.

The dramatic center of the Lucifer Rebellion is surely the thoroughly mixed blessing of permitting the thirty-seven dissenting Planetary Princes, as well as Lucifer, Satan, and all the angels and Watchers who aligned ourselves with the rebellion, to go out on our own, even if we were physically isolated from all we had previously known. The poignant central drama of the Garden story is just as surely the harsh rejection of woman, man, and serpent from the supposed delightful security of a choiceless existence into a world of fear, cruelty, and death.

Lest I get even more carried away with my endless digressions, let's return to the tropical night on which Mein Host was thrown out of his Garden.

There was, however, an odd parallel narrative going on, which had been puzzling the entire community for the preceding couple of weeks and which played its part in the serpent's expulsion. Of course, it was no mystery to me and I watched in amusement as, night after night, all the men in the community would dash out into the surrounding jungle, wildly searching for the source of a mysterious noise that would sound unexpectedly up to half a dozen times a night. It was frighteningly loud, a continuous, harsh, racheting sound that could have been mechanical or organic, or neither or both. It would continue unabated for a few minutes at a deafening volume before just as unexpectedly stopping suddenly. It was an ominous, threatening noise, quite unlike anything any of them had ever heard before.

I wasn't able to communicate (and didn't try, either) that the source of this baffling noise was merely a multitude of extremely vocal frogs who'd come to life after the recent afternoon showers. Their normally loud and raucous callings were, in this case, amplified to an unnatural volume by their all being at the bottom of the large, empty, salt-evaporation pool. Previously mentioned as something Mein Host had discovered on his early exploration of Xtul—but now evidently forgotten about—the edges of the pool were entirely overgrown with tropical foliage, making it all but invisible from the jungle surrounding it.

On this particular night, the men had been out four or five times, again fruitlessly looking for the source of the sound, and they were angry and exhausted. Once more they'd been frustrated by the frogs who would abruptly stop making their noise as soon as anybody approached the pool. Indeed, such was the grossly magnified amplification that, together with the offshore breezes, the sound echoing around the men might have come from anywhere.

Sometime after returning, hopefully for the final time that night, Mein Host made his ill-advised joke. In the silence that followed—no one made jokes at Mary Ann's expense—the entire community, almost as one, shifted their gaze to their Oracle, searching her broad face for the appropriate response.

"How dare you say that!" Her green eyes glittered in the candlelight as she paused for dramatic effect. "How could you? You, you found Xtul! Now look at you!" Mary Ann's Scottish burr always grew stronger when she was working up her anger. Interestingly, as I looked at her emotional body, it was obvious to me that her anger was contrived; there was no sign that it was grounded in her genuine feelings.

"Sacred land! This is sacred land! And you think you can live here and mouth off at the Beings?! They brought us here: remember that!" She was looking around now at heads nodding in agreement, who were clearly relieved that her diatribe wasn't aimed at them.

Mein Host sat rigidly still, wordless and not quite knowing what had hit him. He was generally well-liked by the others in the group, but he was also much envied for his apparent closeness to Mary Ann. I've remarked on this before, that Mary Ann, like many authoritarian leaders, used the time-tested technique of juggling her favorites. One moment Mein Host, or Eddie, or Christopher, or Paul, would be raised to the pinnacle of her loving attention, the next the favored one would be given the harshest tasks and frozen out of the Goddess's love for the slightest infraction. As a sad, but all-too-human, consequence of this constantly shifting power dynamic, the unfortunate focus of the Oracle's ire also became the object of other people's barely suppressed anger and resentment. This particular night at Xtul, with Mein Host in the hot seat, was the first time everyone had a chance to see these ugly emotions being played out, but this time in front of the whole group.

"It had to be you, didn't it!?" She was pointing at Mein Host, and her long, red fingernail seemed to hypnotize the lad. There was nothing he could say.

"You! You betrayed everything we're working toward. And I thought I knew you! How could you? After all I've done for you—you, you snake in the grass."

There was more of this, but you get the general idea.

Another time Mein Host might have said something similar and it would have been ignored, or everyone might have laughed and his words would have been casually dismissed. It seemed to depend entirely on Mary Ann's momentary whim as to what might then happen to him. There were other occasions over the course of the next eleven years during which Mein Host would once more become a favorite, and would then be cast down yet again, for equally arbitrary reasons, into a pit of despair. But this was the first time and certainly the most painful.

"Well? What are you going to do about it?" Mary Ann had everyone in her sway now. Mein Host was the whipping boy for the whole group; the sacrificial victim whose sacrifice would reunite the group again and give it back its sense of purpose. Mary Ann knew only too well how to work the knife.

"You know you aren't welcome here! You betrayed a sacred trust. You have to leave!" And at that very moment, the battery of frogs started up again, shattering the nervous silence in the hut—the ramshackle structure they used for meetings.

Mary Ann looked around triumphantly.

A sign had been given.

The Beings had spoken.

Mein Host was out.

❉ ❉ ❉

The waterfalls pouring from the central mountain ranges of Zandana's southern continent and the many fast-running rivers down on the plains had provided the natives with all the power they needed. Zandana's scientists had developed their understanding of electricity to the point that they had maglev trains connecting all parts of the continent. The general standard of living, although higher in the city than in the countryside, had risen to a level where no one was expected to work for more than three hours a day.

The arts were starting to become a dominating influence, with theatrical productions taking the lead. Zandana's inhabitants were, on the whole, very much less fearful and belligerent than Earth's natives, as there were far fewer predatory animals on the many continents. Yet to call

Zandanans by nature more submissive would also be missing the point. Of course, there had been wars in the planet's past, but for the last few thousand years, apart from a few minor scuffles between some of the out-lying island nations, peace had prevailed on Zandana.

At least, that's how it was when I left last time.

Now, arriving on Zandana, it was hard not to notice that the situation had subtly changed. There was a new tension in the air and people were moving around much faster than I remembered.

Prince Zanda had previously given me his permission to travel and observe wherever I wished and I didn't think he would mind if I took advantage of his openhandedness again without asking him.

How wrong I was!

I was soon called into his presence because one of his Watchers had apparently reported me as a spy, and I found that the entire continent had been put on a war footing. The Prince appeared to be deep in discus-sion with his inner circle when I was ushered into the Temple Conference Garden. Unava, the Prince's chief of staff, whom I'd observed briefly on my first visit, was furiously keeping notes on the meeting, while Janda-Chi, the Prince's closest colleague was holding forth telepathically from his lower subspace perch. Seven of his most experienced midwayers, also in subspace, clustered around him, throwing images of different possibili-ties around, while Janda-Chi was communicating to Unava.

Perhaps I should take a moment here to describe how these vari-ous subspace tranches function. Most inhabited planets of Zandana and Earth's third-density standing possess the same basic structure on the subtle energy levels. May I suggest that you visualize an onion, that peren-nial metaphor, with its many layers of skin. The first layer you encounter moving outward (and inward) from your center of consciousness will be the astral realm. This is a relatively thin tranche, which can be best visual-ized as wrapping around a planet, but it's still very much contained within the aura of the world mind. In the astral realm there are many layers, from the lower astral regions of nightmare and trapped astral shades to the higher frequencies of discarnate guides, bodhisattvas, and ascended masters.

Contiguous to the upper astral realm are the subspace regions.

Although subspace envelops and wraps around each planet, it also extends throughout the Local System of inhabited planets. It can be visualized as a homogenous medium within which third-density planets resonate as they orbit their suns. This gives subspace an element of nonlocality, which both midwayers and visiting extraterrestrials make use of under certain conditions.

Subspace may be considered as a relatively dense medium, which encompasses third-density matter as it also paradoxically interpenetrates the open lattice of the atomic dance. Similar to the astral realms, the subspace region also possesses many tranches, except these aren't layers but rather depend on the resonant frequencies of the participant. The more etheric nature of matter in subspace makes it an extremely malleable medium, directly responsive to the state of the consciousness of any who enter it.

Subspace has many names in different cultures: *Dreamtime* for the Australian aborigines; the *Nagual,* in the Toltec tradition; the *Fourth Dimension,* in certain advanced physics; and MA's documents refer to it as a *midway region,* since it can be thought of as being midway between a terrestrial frequency domain and that of us Watchers in the fifth dimension.

Two extraterrestrials that Mein Host encountered recently reported hailing from a fifth-dimension world, existing where you observe the star Arcturus to be from your third-density perch. They maintained that they were required to drop down through the fourth dimension in order to maintain an observer's presence in the higher frequencies of Earth's third-density domain.

As an angel who became involved with Lucifer's Rebellion, I am confined to the higher-frequency domains of the fifth dimension of this planet, and any other world I visit. I have to obtain formal permission to visit other worlds and even then it can only be one of the other thirty-six planets that followed Lucifer into rebellion. When I'm permitted to travel to Zandana, it is I who have to condense my material form sufficiently to drop into subspace for the seraphic transport.

Thus, when I was shown into the city's Temple garden, I was observing from Zandana's fifth-dimension domain. The two Descending Sons, Zanda and Janda-Chi, and the seven midwayers were in the lower harmonics of subspace, telepathically communicating with Unava, who was firmly ensconced in the planet's third-density reality.

Under discussion was what they were going to do about the invasion fleet that had been spotted approaching their southern nation. Apparently, for all their advanced technology, after two thousand years of peace they had grown complacent. They welcomed the occasional immigrants who managed to find their way across the ocean, without thinking they might have been spies. They had also developed a generally peaceful social agenda that suited their somewhat passive natures.

Believing themselves to be so far superior to the natives on all the other continents, Zandan's elite insisted on referring to them as ignorant barbarians. Nevertheless, the aristocrats appeared to take a vicarious pleasure in plays and novels featuring romantic relationships developing between rough, barbarian princes and the delicate, well-bred daughters of Zandan.

Yet were anyone on the southern continent to seriously take a barbarian lover or spouse, the couple would be quickly exiled and returned to wherever the barbarian came from. It was from these occasional returnees, as well as the few spies who managed to get home, that the barbarians learned of the riches awaiting them if they could pull their forces together.

Over the recent centuries, with the exception of the one island that Prince Zanda had given to the handful of his loyal staff to live out their natural lives, the other nine islands had forged a bewildering network of alliances, betrayals, and counteralliances. Yet in all those years, they had never been able to come together and form a single force.

Naturally, the ruling families on most of the islands had been aware of Zandan's increasing wealth and rapid technological progress for some centuries. They'd been known to take bribes of advanced equipment, like video cameras, sound recorders, and toothbrushes, modified to be solar-powered and reserved only for them. When the spies and returnees reported on the true state of Zandan's progress, the families realized they'd been bought off with toys and gizmos. Prompted by their fury and greed, for the first time they launched a massive shipbuilding effort.

As in everything else related to the barbarians, the elders of Zandan were oblivious to all this activity on the other islands. Even when the occasional message made it through to the council, it was dismissed as ridiculous.

"The numbskulls couldn't even figure out how to cross Mother Ocean, let alone land on our sacred shores!" Unava had summed it up to some patronizing laughter from the council members, before they'd moved on to another matter.

All this I picked up from the discussion underway and I couldn't help but notice Unava's embarrassment at discovering that he was so wrong.

An invasion was the last thing any of them had considered possible.

4

A Barbarian Invasion

Learning from Mosquitoes, Multiple Personalities, and Angelic Memory

On Xtul, the mysterious Beings had spoken, using the croaking voices of the frogs. In the subtextual language of the community—one of signs and portents—it was a done deal. Mein Host had been banished.

Throughout the drama, my ward hadn't spoken a word in his defense. Just as silently he got up from the floor, stretched his cramped legs, and slowly made his way through the sitting figures and out of the hut. No one spoke. Mein Host did not look back. The silence, an uneasy mix of embarrassment and heady relief that it wasn't one of them who'd been kicked out, was finally broken by Mary Ann's voice, heard over the grating cacophony of the yet-to-be-discovered amphibians.

The sky was clear and a waxing moon filtered light down through the gently waving palm fronds as Mein Host plodded disconsolately through the coconut grove and out into the meadow. This was the very meadow over which he, Mary Ann, Robert, and a couple of others had run at full tilt that first night Mein Host had discovered Xtul. They'd been suddenly, and somewhat mysteriously, spooked while they stood together inside the monastery and had bolted out of the ruin and raced across the meadow, panting and laughing at their own silliness when they reached the trail.

The croaking amphibian chorus stopped just as suddenly as it had started when Mein Host was halfway across the field. Observing him carefully, and sharing as much as I could tolerate of his feelings of utter desolation, I noticed a distinct change come over him. He'd stopped briefly when the raucous frog chorus ceased. After a few moments, I saw him straighten up and, when he started walking again, his pace was faster and more purposeful—although what this purpose was I couldn't imagine.

Veering off to the left, he made for a patch of jungle on the edge of the property. Here, the trail on which they'd arrived on that first night drifted off away from the gate and the broken-down fence to make its winding way to the tiny Maya village of Chuburna Puerto four miles up the coast.

He pulled himself through the barbed wire, stamping down the rusting wire, pulling up the top strand with his left hand, and ducking under. Next, he was moving along cautiously, poking his way through the jungle and walking parallel to the rickety fence, but making sure to stay outside the Xtul property line. He was swinging his head slowly from left to right, intensely examining the ground. He looked just like his primate progenitors did when they were seeking out a resting place.

Whatever could he be up to? What was on his mind?

This was one of those delicious moments we Watchers hold so dear. Understand, I really *didn't* know what he was going to do. What's more, I wouldn't have known what to do myself in such a situation. Likely I would have just given up, having been so directly reprimanded by one I believed to be the Mother Spirit. And then being expelled by Her? By *Her!* It would have shattered my emotional body into little pieces.

It was not my ward's pluck that touched my heart—and, yes, angels have hearts, of course! What thrilled me, as it would any Watcher in a similar situation, was that Mein Host made an intuitive leap of understanding we Watchers find so difficult to predict. Not being indwelt by the Creator Spirit in the same manner as mortals, we're not emotionally equipped for original thought. Traditionally, we don't make those wholly unexpected leaps of faith. It's what makes mortals so fascinating to observe.

When the chips are down, when your back is against the wall, when the buck stops with you—I do enjoy your expressions!—we never know quite what you're going to do.

What Mein Host did in this impossible situation was find a grassy spot and settle down into a single-lotus meditation, in this case with his back propped against a coconut palm.

The moon was now high in the sky and haloed with moisture as black clouds were gathering far above the treetops. In the surrounding jungle, little creatures were taking advantage of the darkness to scuttle through the undergrowth. A bird screeched. The thrumming baseline of the surf half a mile away provided an auditory background to the more immediate, higher harmonics of the nighttime flying insects.

Ah! Yes! The insects. Those little creatures of the night. Of the day, too, as Mein Host was soon to find out. Here I can only report what I heard him say to Juliette when, after the second day, she appeared with some water.

"I'm sitting here until I'm let back in, or I die, whichever comes first," he'd replied to Juliette's questioning look. Apparently she'd been told not to speak to him.

"And I think I've discovered something." He was taking small sips from the bottle she'd handed him through the wire. He squinted up at her, an enigmatic smile on his face. "I haven't moved, you know. Don't think I've slept too much, either. I just let everything bite me that first night—just let them crawl all over me. I didn't move or swat them away. Just let 'em do whatever they had to do."

He was only wearing shorts and flip-flops—no shirt or hat. He'd left with nothing but what he was wearing when he was thrown out. Much of his torso, and his bare arms and legs, looked like they were spotted with bites and small red lumps.

I caught a slight shift in Juliette's emotional body. I knew she was fond of my ward and hated seeing this happen. She ducked down to a crouch and looked over her shoulder to make sure she couldn't be seen from the hut on the other side of the meadow.

"Look. Don't worry." She was cupping her hand to her mouth. "I know Mary Ann loves you."

"Doesn't feel much like it! Why are we whispering?"

"I'm not meant to . . ." She was laughing quietly now along with him. "Seriously. You okay?"

He nodded.

"You just going to go on sitting here?"

"Only thing that makes sense to me. Nowhere else I want to be—nowhere."

"Don't be silly. You're going to die out here."

"Die?"

"She does love you, you know—the Oracle. Really, she does."

"Juliette, you're not listening. I'm onto something here. Listen. It's like an experiment. I'm learning something."

"This is meant to be a punishment!" Juliette hissed back through the wire. "I've been here too long. They'll think I've been talking to you."

"No, wait! You can listen, can't you? I'll keep it short."

"Okay, okay."

"The insects—they're not biting me anymore!" He hurried on before Juliette could interrupt. No one liked the mosquitoes.

"I found myself inviting the insects—all of 'em, the sand flies, mossies, the gnats—I invited them to feast on me. And if an ant, or a spider, or five centipedes wanted to crawl over me, well, fine. That was fine, too."

Now there was puzzlement as well as concern on Juliette's face. I guessed she was thinking he might be losing his mind. He must have seen it, too.

"No, no, that's not it! That's not what I discovered. Here, this is it. Look!" He was holding out his arms to her, turning them back and forth from his shoulders. "See? They've stopped biting me. These are the old ones. They don't count. Last night and today, nothing. No creepy-crawlies, either! Nothing.

"Seriously, Juliette. They seem to be avoiding me. And the mossies—they've been flying around me. They don't even land on me. Look!" He was holding out his arms again. "Look. The mossies aren't biting me anymore!"

And indeed they weren't. Juliette had been slapping the mosquitoes away while they were talking. They'd been whining and buzzing around

Mein Host's body all the while without showing any interest in landing.

"I want to see what happens tonight and tomorrow and . . . It's an experiment, see?"

Perhaps he really was losing his mind.

He poured the last of the water over his head and returned the bottle to Juliette.

Straightening up, still looking slightly puzzled, Juliette smiled shyly at him, her deeply tanned face crinkling, before turning and making her way back across the meadow to Mary Ann. In spite of Juliette's crossing the line and talking to my ward, Mary Ann was no doubt avidly waiting for her report.

The Oracle wasn't going to like this one little bit.

❉ ❉ ❉

I'd chosen to leave Earth for a while because I was disgusted with the horrors Prince Caligastia had visited upon your world. Now I was on Zandana, whose inhabitants I believed had solved their issues of war and belligerence, only to find myself once more embroiled in conflict.

Since I'd been in Prince Zanda's presence during the discussions regarding the imminent invasion, it appeared as though I was involved—in spite of myself. Both Zanda and Janda-Chi were well aware that I was present and I'm sure they'd witnessed my horrified reaction to Unava's complaisance. And, frankly, I couldn't believe what I was hearing. The council wouldn't have lasted long on Caligastia's Earth!

After the Council of Elders—all whom had appeared to me to be unduly influenced by Unava's condescending dismissal of the pending barbarian invasion—completed their business and left the Temple Garden, I wasn't altogether surprised to feel the slight pressure of Prince Janda-Chi signaling me telepathically to remain there.

Prince Janda seemed to be the only one with any practical sense. "As you must understand, we have a problem. You can see what we're dealing with?"

I didn't need to agree. I could feel the despair in his emotional body.

"We haven't had a war in more than two thousand years. We have no weapons; we've forgotten how to fight. And you saw how most of them think. They don't believe it's possible. They think they're above all that."

There was nothing I could say. Granted, there had never been any major wars in Vanu's territories, but there was always some small conflict going on over land or women. Human beings on Earth seemed to me to be naturally belligerent. I didn't believe, from what I'd seen of the Zandana natives, that they were quite as liable to erupt into anger and violence. They were cunning, of course, and clearly great businessmen and traders, but in whole city of Zandan I'd never seen any military or police activity. If the Zandanans were now living safe and secure lives, it seemed to me they'd lost the ability to even imagine that could ever change.

"They freeze the dangers out of their minds. They're in a state of chronic denial. I'm afraid there's no one who knows what to do." Janda-Chi had picked up on my thoughts. "Absolutely no one. Good people, of course, but not fighting men. And no time to train them, even if we could."

There was a long silence as both Prince Janda-Chi and Prince Zanda considered their position. Their problem lay in figuring out the appropriate level of intervention given their limited options. In spite of the greater levels of freedom allowed them by the Lucifer Manifesto, they still appreciated the wisdom of keeping their distance from mortals. Once mortals have decided to act independently, there isn't much an angel, a Watcher, or a Planetary Prince can do about it. We have to find other, more subtle, means of communicating, and you can see from the unfortunate demise of almost all your prophets that this approach also has its drawbacks.

Now Prince Zanda was communicating with me telepathically. "You know all about fighting, don't you?" It was not a question. "We know what's been happening on Earth. You're affiliated with Prince Caligastia, yes? You've seen more horror than we can imagine. You must know about fighting."

I was on the spot. What could I say? Watchers don't fight. We never have.

Zanda again: "It's not as though the barbarians have particularly advanced weapons. We've tried to make sure of that. But spears and, yes, knives, swords."

One of the midwayers who'd stayed behind was quietly signaling Prince Zanda. I could tell that he was one of their espionage agents tasked with keeping an eye on the two rogue islands. No doubt his reports had been dismissed as overwrought with the same casual ease as I'd seen in the previous meeting. I could tell from the emotional tone of the signal that the midwayer was still nursing his resentment.

"Yes, yes, I remember what you told me," Zanda told the midwayer, "but I doubt if they've been able to do very much with it." The Prince turned toward me again. "Well! Got any ideas?"

The absurdity of the situation struck me full force. Here were two Planetary Princes asking me, a mere Watcher, if I have any ideas! Well, all right, let's see.

"Your womenfolk," I said, an idea blossoming in my mind that I needed to keep shielded from the others while I spoke. "They're known for their beauty, aren't they?"

"We've maintained the aristocratic bloodlines, of course, at least here, in the city—less so in the provinces. And who knows what they've done on the outer islands. Complete genetic mess, no doubt."

"Prince, Prince!" I interrupted Zanda rather more abruptly than I'd intended. I was getting overexcited as this idea was taking shape. An original idea? Not really. An obvious one? So obvious I'd never heard it done before.

"All our women are beauties!" This was Janda-Chi with more than seemly enthusiasm.

"Well, my Princes, don't you see?"

I could feel that they were unaccustomed to be addressed so directly and it forced me to realize how tempered I'd become on the forge of Caligastia's violent nature.

"Beauties, you say! There might be a way." Now they were listening intently. How was I going to put this politely? I'd already been mildly telepathically reproved by Janda-Chi for being more direct than they're apparently comfortable with, so this needed to be handled delicately.

"So, no mating for love, correct? Not among the aristocrats, not if you're trying to keep the bloodlines intact, right?" I was hoping they'd have the idea before I had to image it. I still had my shields up. No? Nothing. Well, here goes. What's the worst that could happen?

"I know from my previous visits that the women here—how shall I put it? They consider themselves free, yes? They're not tied down by tradition, they think of their bodies as their own?"

"Many of our finest technicians and scientists are female, and the artists, of course—they're almost all women." Was Janda-Chi an old fool? He just wasn't getting it. Then I realized that, as nonsexual beings, neither of the Princes would be likely to grasp what I was suggesting.

"No, I mean free. They're not owned by any man. Isn't that what they say? It's what I've heard."

"Oh! Yes. They're very proud of that. The women choose who they want to be with, who they want to make their babies with. Is that what you mean?"

Was Janda-Chi starting to get it? I allowed a long pause before replying.

"You can't fight, right? But you can love!"

Still not a hint of comprehension.

"So don't fight them when they arrive in their boats. Use your women. Send them down to greet the boats. Have them hang flowers around each barbarian's neck. Invite the barbarians into your homes. Celebrate their arrival. Encourage your women to seduce them."

Both were looking horrified by this time. Horrified, but quite silent.

"Don't you see? It's what your people do best. Swamp the barbarians in luxury. Love them, feed them, sleep with them. Make them thoroughly at home, and if the women have to hold their noses, remind them there are worse things they could be suffering."

Janda-Chi's emotional body was starting to warm up.

"Then, when you have them thoroughly tamed, you can decide what you want to do with them. The invaders won't want to leave. They won't be used to being treated so well."

"If they don't leave, no one back where they came from will know what has happened to them. They'll think we defeated their fleet somehow." Janda-Chi was starting to understand the tactic.

"Will the women agree to this?" I asked, more tentatively.

"They're going to love the idea!" Prince Zanda appeared to have woken up. "Besides, what's the choice?"

"And the menfolk?" I knew how jealous and territorial mortal men can be with their women.

"They're going to have to deal with it. I think it'll work, though. They're pretty free with their own desires. I doubt if they could stop their women from doing what they wanted to do anyway," Zanda said with what looked to me to be a knowing smirk. I could see that he was starting to appreciate the idea.

"This could work." Janda-Chi tuned in with growing enthusiasm. "We can certainly stop anyone from going back, and the midwayers can throw up sufficient astral confusion to baffle their spies." I saw the midwayer bowing his head in agreement. Unlike on Earth, far more of them had followed Prince Zanda than the few midwayers who'd stuck with the rebel staff on the outer islands. They'd be no match for the powerful astral cloaking capacity of a large number of midwayers operating in concert.

"Then, when they're all settled and they feel fat and safe, we can choose who to keep and who to kill. That'll please the women!" The smirk was back on Zanda's face.

Then I recalled something I'd casually overheard on my second visit, as I was passing through one of the finer houses on the outskirts of the city. Three finely dressed and elegant women of the Zandan elite were sitting around discussing the comparative efficacy of different natural poisons. Amid much laughter, I overheard one of them claiming to have poisoned at least five people with a tincture of one of the more common plants that grew in the mountains.

"And it's absolutely undetectable," confided one of them to the youngest of the three.

"If there was anyone around to do the detecting," said the third, to some knowing laughter.

"Looks just like a heart attack, too. Very quick and neat—no mess to clean up and they don't know what's hit 'em." There was a terrible coldness in her delivery, which, following the laughter, shocked me even more, despite my unhappy acquaintance with the ways of conspirators.

But women?

Naive as it might sound, I was yet more horrified that these were three beautiful, well-bred, and highly educated Zandan women who were talking about efficient ways of killing people with such casual indifference.

It was something of an eye-opener for me at the time. Up to that point I was largely unfamiliar with the nature of female intelligence on Zandana.

The speaker was coolly dictating the recipe for optimum dosage to the younger woman when I chose to leave in disgust. But it left an impression on me that might well have provided the fertile ground for my idea.

My idea! I liked the sound of that. We Watchers aren't known for our ideas. I could only conjecture that I was starting to think more like a mortal.

I'd no need to say anything more. The Princes were clearly excited. They called Unava and the council back into the temple garden and I stayed well in the background while they briefed the assembled company on what they had come up with. I appreciated that they'd no wish to admit that it was me, an off-worlder—and a Watcher to boot—who had given them their idea.

After some initial concerned expressions on some of the elders' faces, Janda-Chi finished speaking with a triumphant flourish. "If the women agree, and I think they will, everyone will come out of this invasion with what they want. Everyone."

A short silence was broken by some nervous laughter, followed then by a chortling that quickly turned into full-throated guffaws.

It could work. It really could work.

⁜ ⁜ ⁜

They all knew Mein Host had been there—sitting, unmoving, out there on the fringe of the jungle. Juliette had whispered to him that there was a lot of excitement bubbling under the surface as to how the drama was going to play out. She was kind to say this. I'd observed Mary Ann talking to her inner circle, on the few swift trips I'd made back to the compound during Mein Host's first and second days of banishment. She was clearly stoking the ambient resentment generally felt for a favorite in free fall.

In a way, I rather admired her adroitness. She would have been aware that the group, after a couple of months of laboring in the hot sun, was starting to fray at the edges. Something had to be done to boost morale. It was true. The community members were getting tired of the meandering midnight discussions; the constant hunger; the sunburn and blisters; the need for water, which required four men, twice a day, to fill five-gallon containers in Chuburna Puerto and walk back with them, swinging on poles slung between the men's shoulders. Sometimes, on particularly humid evenings, the water carriers could be seen returning from the village, swaying with the rhythms of pole and water, and yet appearing from a distance to be covered with black fur. On closer examination, they were adorned with a furry suit of mosquitoes. I'd already observed this by watching Mein Host whenever his turn had come around. The weight of the water sloshing about in the five-gallon container made the wood pole sear into his sunburned shoulder bone—no matter what padding he tried jamming beneath it.

And it was long, painful, four miles' walk back to Xtul.

Twice a day they stumbled in single file along the overgrown jungle path; each man at either end of the pole seeking, with varying degrees of skill or desperation, the precise rhythm at which the slight deflection of the wood could be used to somehow lighten the load.

Mein Host and Eddie had found they could create an almost anti-gravitational effect by walking with a certain swinging gait and by skillfully synchronizing the sloshing of the water, as well as harmonizing it with the steady swing of the containers themselves. For brief but fortuitously repetitive moments, the pole and water could be made to feel virtually weightless.

Gripping the pole with both hands and levering it up slightly above their shoulder bones lessened the pain, while I could see it also allowed them far greater control over the rhythmic bending of the pole. No one knew quite how this worked and wouldn't have had the words for it if they had understood it. Yet soon all the water carriers were trying to emulate the technique; by all accounts it was that effective, even if it seemed to them utterly miraculous whenever they managed to do it. Hitting that resonant frequency became the holy grail of Xtul's water bearers, just as Mein Host had taken such pleasure at hitting a ball with the sweet spot of a cricket bat.

Sadly, this technique was difficult to achieve and had a distinct downside. Since it required both hands to sense the different rhythms, no hands were free to swat off the battalions of mosquitoes—large mosquitoes with vicious bites that seemed to easily penetrate cotton shirts. The water carriers thus faced a harrowing choice: to perfect the rhythm method and suffer the bites or to jolt painfully along with one hand free for the swatting, but with bruised and bloody shoulders.

As with many such activities at Xtul, machismo became the guiding principle for the alpha males in the group. Watching Mein Host and Eddie on one occasion, as they were digging the foundations for a new wall for the temple, quite bewildered me.

Mein Host would be standing at the top of a six-foot hole emptying the coffee can of sand, while Eddie (and it generally was Eddie down the hole first—he had the most to prove) dug furiously at the sandy soil with a flat piece of wood they'd fashioned into a crude spade.

The game seemed to be for the digger to dig with such passionate ferocity in the small, hot space that he fell down in a dead faint. You see why I might have been bewildered—no, more than that, I was horrified. They had no idea how dangerous it was.

Can you truly understand my situation—the bane of any Watcher? To observe our wards casually risking their mortal lives, entirely unaware of the perils they risk, and not being able to intercede? It is the very worst emotional and mental torture you can imagine. For a Watcher, such pain can feel like an endless trail of heartache.

Eddie would then be hauled up to the top and left to recover. He was quickly replaced by Mein Host, scrambling down into the hole and savagely digging away until he, too, in turn, fainted and was dragged out, only to have the whole exhausting procedure repeated again and again until they were both simply too weary, too depleted of any last shred of energy, too drained of anything but the squeaks squeezing out of their melting lungs as they rolled around the rim of the pit, convulsive in hopeless laughter.

On the evening of the third day, two women—Helen and Juliette—came to deliver the verdict. Mein Host finally opened his dirt-encrusted eyes to greet them. By this time, my ward had been sitting in one spot for sixty-six hours, leaving it briefly only to relieve himself. He had no food, only the small amount of water they spared him on the second day and, if he'd fallen asleep, I didn't notice it. He was sunburned and badly dehydrated, but, as he told the women as they held him up, his arms around their shoulders, half-dragging him back to the hut: "They didn't bite me anymore—not once since that first night and day. I must have put out some biological message, don't you think? Because the little buggers left me alone—completely. It was a success, Juliette! The experiment worked! It actually worked."

Juliette was shushing him as they got closer to the hut.

"I'll bet the mossies won't touch me next time I do the water run," he said, this time in a hoarse whisper. He could barely contain his excitement.

"Shush, really, idiot! For heaven's sake don't mention any of that insect stuff to Mary Ann. It's not going to help you."

Once they arrived at the hut, Mein Host's legs appeared to regain their strength, so when he walked into the group assembled around Mary Ann and Robert, I could see that, in spite of Juliette's warning, he carried himself with a certain air of pride.

It probably didn't help his situation with the Oracle, but I knew he didn't want to appear shattered by the experience. The experts hadn't broken his spirit at his brutal British boarding school, where they'd had over four hundred years to fine-tune the art of crushing the young, and he certainly wasn't going to be broken by Mary Ann—Goddess or not. That I knew for sure.

What I didn't know until much later was how strong and resilient the lad's emotional body was growing. He was finally learning to feel and experience emotional pain, to stay conscious of the suffering, rather than repressing it as he'd always done before. Granted, turning his three-day exile into an experimental study was a coping strategy he must have devised to deal with the torment, to distract himself. Yet throughout the process he never once split off into a subpersonality, as he had when he was a terrified child in England in 1943, at the mercy of German bombs.

These were still early days. Mein Host was a mere lad of twenty-six summers in June 1966. It would be many years before he discovered that his facility in moving between different levels of consciousness was grounded, in his present incarnation, in what might have been diagnosed as a mild case of multiple personality disorder (MPD). But this particular disorder hadn't yet been identified or acknowledged by the psychiatric profession (and still isn't by more conservative psychologists and psychiatrists who evidently have never encountered a full-blown MPD sufferer), and wasn't until the latter part of the twentieth century.

I have no wish to exaggerate the seriousness of the disorder in Mein Host's case. In a classic MPD case, there will be a high degree of amnesia between some, or many, of the subpersonalities. That is, they won't know about one another. In some cases, certain subpersonalities know about some, and not about others, which are cloaked from them by a psychological amnesic barrier. In acute cases, like those described in the 1957 book and film *The Three Faces of Eve,* and *Sybil,* the 1974 book that popularized the condition, also known as dissociative identity disorder (DID), there will be a complete memory loss between the different personalities as one or another takes control of the individual's behavior.

Fortunately, this was never true in Mein Host's case. Although he was able to leave his body with greater ease than most, he never actually suffered from MPD. Nevertheless, if you were to ask him, he would likely tell you that it took him at least thirty years of hard work—of meditation, of entheogenic probings, of patient self-examination, and of facing his deepest fears—to bring to light his seven subpersonalities. This turned out to be a process with which I was uniquely equipped to be of help, since I was the one who possessed the overview. I'd seen all the subpersonalities in action at one time or another, so I knew and understood them all in a way Mein Host couldn't. Since these subpersonalities were disassociated aspects of his primary personality, split off to cope with his early trauma, he had little understanding of them.

But, once again, I don't want to get ahead of myself. I've previously warned my reader that a Watcher's memory functions rather differently from the way humans believe they remember events in their lives. Possibly being able to remember your life's events as a linear continuity, as time's arrow moves you irrevocably from birth to death, is a helpful way of understanding one short human life.

Yet, if you were a Watcher like me—and I'm young as celestials go—and you have an awareness of a continuing lifestream of over half a million years, linear continuity becomes impossible. There's simply too much to remember! I'm not boasting. Some celestials are so ancient we young ones say of them that "They're so old they've never not been."

Perhaps the closest analogue to a celestial's memory can be found in your recent advances in cloud computing, in which information and software is retained by distributing it over a wide network of interlinked computers and other memory devices, like smartphones and tablets. Yet the user's experience is one of fluid continuity. She's not concerned with where all the information is being stored, as long as it's there when she wants to access it.

My memory for the events I'm describing here works in a similar way. It's basically associative. One event or relationship or encounter leads naturally to another—regardless of temporal continuity. To achieve any sense of order, as I try to unravel these different threads of causation that drop down through planetary history, and as cause and effect also plays out in an individual human being's life, I am dependent entirely on those I observe. Whether it's Mein Host, Caligastia, Vanu, Prince Zanda, or even the mortals I observe on Earth or Zandana, it's their lives that form my history of myself. Their experiences become my experiences. This is how we Watchers learn. We have no direct influence on the affairs of mortals and no choice but to observe. It is both the most terrible and the most rational of punishments, the most profound of learnings, just as it's the most painfully frustrating of lessons.

I hasten to say that I'm not complaining. Mein Host really doesn't like it, and being shamed by a mortal isn't much fun.

As Mein Host entered the ruined wooden hut in Xtul, Mary Ann was surrounded by Robert and her current favorites, who were clustered around her; the others sat or lay in a semicircle. The roofing tiles had been retrieved from where they'd been thrown by the wind, so the roof was largely closed in. Dusk was falling with tropical speed and the night creatures were starting to call in the surrounding jungle. The frogs were quiet again. There was some awkward shuffling of limbs; Vanessa was on her own in a corner, coughing into her hand. Silence hung in the air while Mary Ann stared at Mein Host with her green eyes, a curious mix of anger, curiosity, and admiration coloring her emotional body.

What happened next was to test Mein Host to the core of his being.

❉ ❉ ❉

Frankly, I was nervous, or as nervous as a simple Watcher can get.

My idea that the citizens of Zandan might wage love, not war, in the face of the expected barbarian invasion had been avidly embraced and claimed by the two Princes, with Janda-Chi enthusiastically handling the details. Regardless of the strangeness of the whole situation and my surprise as to where such a thought might have come from, all contrived to make me feel responsible for what might happen. If it was successful, it would create some turbulence in the Zandanans' personal relationships, but all would be essentially fine. Prince Zanda would herald the strategy as his . . . and I could disappear back into the dimensional woodwork.

If it failed for some unpredictable reason, I had no doubt the blame will be placed on me, the untrustworthy off-worlder. Just another rebel angel with her strange ideas.

It turned out, perhaps unsurprisingly, that the women of the city greeted the strategy far more positively than most of their menfolk.

"Trouble is, I don't know what the wife is looking forward to most: bedding the men or killing them afterward!"

"What if she ends up liking him more than me?"

"I don't want her making any little barbarian bastards. Oh, no. I'd drown the little buggers, no matter what she says!"

"Me? I'll be happy to get the old lady off my hands for a while!"

I overheard a number of remarks like these as I slipped through the fashionable men-only clubs in Zandan City's business quadrant. But within a few days what little opposition there'd been among the men faded away as the harsh reality of the alternative dawned in their somnolent minds.

Janda-Chi had sent envoys out on the silver monorails to all the towns and villages in the outlying regions of the vast southern continent. Because it was acknowledged as a delicate matter, even for the more sexually liberated Zandanans, the Prince had suggested that a more personal approach, in a series of town hall meetings all over the islands, would be most effective. Knowing that there would be more resistance to the tactic in the conservative provinces, he insisted that it be strictly voluntary on behalf of the women. Knowing mortal psychology as well as he did, Janda-Chi required his envoys to remain in the towns to ensure that no antipathy was stirred up between those who offered up their bodies for the continuing purity of the motherland, and those who chose not to volunteer.

Most of Zandana's mortal population of reasoning age quickly realized that any invasion would have to be first directed at the city to have any hope of success. The island continent was too large and too isolated from the other islands by a wide and dangerously stormy ocean, making resupply a real challenge for the barbarian military. First, they would have to cut off the head—which meant taking out the city as soon as they'd landed. That much was obvious. They might have put aside fighting for a couple of millennia, but they were no fools. They were quite capable of thinking through a simple military strategy.

This fact, and the provincial women's natural reticence, meant somewhat fewer volunteers came forward with what seemed to me the unbecoming eagerness on the part of the more sophisticated city women. But in the latter case I'm more inclined to believe that it was the prospect of practicing their arcane poisoning arts on one of the opposite sex, and being admired for all the personal sacrifices involved in accomplishing it. For some of the mature, yet still comely, women among Zandana's genetic elites, the opportunity was seen as almost too good to be true. I heard many of them express how interminably bored they were getting with the limited genetic pool available to them.

Besides, some of the wiser among the female elders had recently been pointing out that the tradition of preserving their bloodlines had started to deplete the life force in many of the ruling families. They strongly advised the fertile women to carefully choose, as far as they were able, the most physically well-developed of the invading men and mate with them, and to be prepared to poison the father of their child when the time for killing came around.

Since natural birth control had long been practiced by the women of Zandana, there was no fear of an unwanted pregnancy. The Zandanan mortal female was somewhat more biologically advanced than females on Earth. Even at the time I'm describing, some fifty thousand Earth years ago, they were capable of controlling their own biology. Like terrestrial dolphins, sexually mature Zandana females were able to retain male sperm in their bodies for many months following insemination. This enabled them to give birth at propitious times—while the art of astrology had long been dismissed by Zandana's foremost scientists, it still maintained its vitality among the women—as well as giving them the ability to consciously dispatch any male gamete, should it consider consummating its own zygotic drive.

This singular female ability allowed the Zandanans to maintain a balanced population growth on the southern continent without stressing their supply of natural resources.

I'm told the optimum population for an Earth-size planet of approximately the same landmass and biosphere is between five hundred million and a billion. As I write these words in 2010, the population on Earth has surpassed the seven billion mark, clearly a massive aberration of the natural order of planetary affairs. By allowing unfettered procreation and by lauding the Industrial Revolution and the medical advances that has led to the belief that technology has permitted the modern world to transcend the Malthusian checks traditionally limiting population growth, human population has exploded across the planet in less than a hundred years.

This is a delusion that should be obvious to anyone living on Earth in the twenty-first century. Hyperexponential population growth in most developing countries, diminishing supplies of natural resources, famines, changing climatic conditions, and air and water pollution—

these are but a few of the signs of an oncoming Malthusian crisis.

I've come to believe that the Zandanan women's ability to monitor and control their biological processes allowed them to accept their mission with such equanimity. Whatever was to happen, they were confident they would be in charge of any potential progeny.

I heard that one of Zanda's midwayers had just returned from an espionage mission to report that the barbarian fleet was delayed by a storm that had separated the boats and sunk one with all hands onboard. They were apparently regrouping in the lee of the closest island and were said to be unlikely to set sail again until the weather improved.

A Council for Recreational Survival, quickly dubbed the Love Council by the more scabrous of the city's news outlets, had been put together in one of Prince Janda-Chi's retreat centers up in the mountains. From there the strategy would be directed. Regular surveillance by Zanda's midwayers observing from subspace would supply the necessary information as to where to move the women to greet the boats.

The citizens made good use of the delay. Believing they had the weather on their side and there wouldn't be an invasion until the change of season, advisory workshops to help counsel the women were set up in all the major towns. Each volunteer was given an older woman as a mentor who would be on hand to deal with any emotional issues that might spring up in the course of her seductive activities. The brief respite also allowed the mentors to familiarize themselves with the volunteers' families—their parents, children, and their menfolk, particularly the menfolk!

They were all aware that the men might prove to be the major impediment to the "Make Love, Not War" strategy. All the women volunteers were required to get the agreement of those close to them, but in some of the men's cases, a prior agreement could quickly wither in the face of their wives, or lovers, willingly seducing their barbarian enemies. It was the mentors' function not only to support and encourage the women, but to make sure the men were kept in line by a constant reminder of how terrible any alternative would be for everybody—not just for them.

Rather than hide their valuables, households were encouraged to show off their wealth. The official buildings all received a face-lift and the public monuments, which had been recently falling into some disrepair, were spruced up and repainted. Shops were told to display their most resplendent goods—luxury was to abound. Food must be seen to be plentiful and all who were not directly involved with the invasion were encouraged to go about their daily business as normal. Children would continue to go to school. Life should go on much as usual, with the citizens appearing to project a complete lack of concern at the approach of the barbarian hordes.

Such were the directives being issued from Janda-Chi's Love Council while the citizens of Zandana busily prepared for the invasion. I heard many a last-minute assurance from a nubile maiden to her lover, as I drifted through their dwellings, and even more from young wives hoping their specious denials would mask their enthusiasm for some sexual novelty. Naturally, women in advanced stages of pregnancy were excused from participating, but all those in the first and second trimester were free to volunteer as one of the backup teams of women.

Since it still wasn't known how many barbarians would make it to their shores, Janda-Chi thought it sensible to prepare for a worst-case scenario in which all boats known to be in the fleet arrived intact. The southern continent possessed no military craft and since they had no interest in the other islands, they'd never had a reason to develop ocean-going ships. The many small fishing boats that tended to hug the coast and work the fertile fishing fields in the estuaries of the many rivers tumbling down from the mountains were told to continue their normal routine, but to stay well out of the way of the invasion fleet.

And, in the case of any encounter that might be precipitated by fog or an inconvenient storm, they were told to show absolutely no sign of any aggressive behavior. Neither of these strictures needed any excessive persuasion to gain the fishermen's approval.

The people of these early cultures have no reason to lie to us about their origins, and virtually all of them are telling us the same thing; that the skills of civilization were taught to humanity. Again, Occam's razor would direct us to the simplest of explanations, that the people in these societies, who are in substantial agreement with each other, might in fact be telling the truth.

LAIRD SCRANTON, *THE SCIENCE OF THE DOGON*

The fact that, nominally, the West professes Christianity has had only a minimal influence in this respect: the whole doctrine of the supernatural existence of the spirit and of its survival beyond this world has not undermined this superstition in any significant way; it has not made of what did not begin with birth and cannot end with death able to act practically in the daily, sentimental and biological life of a sufficient number of beings. Rather, people have clung convulsively to that small part of the whole, which is the short period of this existence of individuals, and have made every effort to ignore the fact that the hold on reality afforded by individual life is no firmer than that of a tuft of grass which one might grab to save himself from being carried away by a world current.

JULIUS EVOLA, *METAPHYSICS OF WAR*

Brand new, clean, without any principles, without notions, since everything they teach us is false! And free, free of everything.

ARTHUR RIMBAUD,
QUOTED IN EDMUND WHITE'S BOOK *RIMBAUD: THE DOUBLE LIFE OF A REBEL*

5

Love Not War

The Serpent's Penance, Enter Gabriel Stern, Predatory Evolution, and Planetary Heartbeat

The day finally came when the masts of the invasion fleet could be seen on the horizon. A ripple of panic ran through the crowds who were gathering on the shore.

Children, with their sharper eyes, could be heard counting the boats. Some lost count and had to start over, much to the annoyance of the adults around them. Soon the babble of children's voices, all at different stages in their count, became so chaotic and confusing they had to be hushed into silence by their elders. Finally, the senior girl at Zandan's most prestigious kindergarten was elected to do the counting. This produced the most curious sound effect. The crowd was absolutely silent, all listening to her pure, young voice, as she steadily counted the masts from right to left. It was as if her piping soprano had a sonic shadow, as thousands of young voices whispered the count along with her.

It was a most curious sound. I've never heard anything quite like it, since the sort of occasion that would precipitate it is unique to that one time, on the cliffs of Zandana's southern continent.

Soon enough this chilling, whispered accompaniment descended into susurrant rustle, as further ships' masts appeared over the horizon, requiring a constant reevaluation of the count as young eyes competed to see the next mast come into view. By midafternoon no more ships materialized and the count stood at 187, although a couple of twins insisted there were three more smaller boats that couldn't easily be seen behind some of the larger vessels.

I was surprised that no one seemed to possess a telescope, only to find that Zandanan scientists had made little progress in the development of optical lenses. They claimed they had no need to develop such powerful magnifying devices. They'd shown little interest in astronomy and, as far as most of them were concerned, their world ended at the shores of their continent. Some small advances had been made in grinding corrective lenses for their older citizens' spectacles, and this had led to further refinements, including the development of instruments for microsurgery.

After watching Caligastia's immense criminal infusion of technical information back on Earth, I found it an amusing idiosyncrasy to observe that while the Zandanans appeared intrigued by microscopic life, they appeared to have no interest whatsoever in the macroscopic.

Only after the fleet was fully visible and dusk was starting to fall did the crowds start to melt back into the city and their homes for the last night of normality. They knew the fleet would anchor well offshore. Thanks to some cunning midwayer disinformation, the barbarians had no idea about Prince Zanda's plan. Like all warlike people, the invaders believed their enemy would be as perfidious as they themselves were, thus they'd become persuaded by their own military preparations that Zandana would be bound to defend itself.

Carefully seeded propaganda by midwayer counterespionage controllers, running agents in barbarian territories, had prepared the way. I was told later that rumors swept through the fleet while it waited out the storm prior to the invasion, warning the soldiers of the hideous advanced weaponry that Zandana had recently developed.

Of course, it was a well-placed, two-pronged deception. There was always a chance the invaders would turn tail and run at the thought of Zandana's killing machines, but the Princes had staked their hopes on the Trojan Horse aspect of the disinformation campaign.

If the barbarians continued to advance, Janda-Chi, who had dreamed up the midwayer campaign, made the point: by generating an excruciating level of fear in the barbarian forces, their relief at being greeted by beautiful women and not some horrific superweapon would surely be made all the more poignant, rendering them that much more vulnerable to the amorous attentions of the cream of Zandana's womenfolk.

As darkness finally fell on the night before the invasion, I found myself, once again, on the horns of a dilemma. Did I really want to be around when the boats discharged their barbaric hordes? Or would it be wise to avoid the possible consequences if the tactic failed?

I couldn't wait to see the faces of the loutish invaders when the women come forward, dancing and singing the ancient songs, placing flowered leis around their thick necks, stroking their muscular bodies with scented tenderness. I imagined their rough faces softening, as Captain Cook's sailors surely did as the first Europeans in many millennia to sail the Pacific, when they found themselves being welcomed by the beautiful and sensuous women of the South Sea Islands.

If you were to wonder how I could have been on Zandana 57,000 years ago, while my imagination was drawing on a memory of an event on Earth in 1770 CE, apparently 55,230 years later, then I should remind you of the strange characteristics of a Watcher's associative memory, and the nature of time as we Watchers experience it. For us, it all seems to be happening at the same time, just as a two-hour film can be thought of as "all happening at the same time" when it rests as a singular item in its can.

I chose to spend the dark of Zandana's night at Prince Janda-Chi's headquarters—now charmingly called the Love Room—in hopes that I would be inspired to decide whether to leave or to stay for the inevitable fireworks. I found Prince Zanda there reviewing the day.

"How many boats was it in the end?" asked Unava, who had evidently pulled himself together and was back under Janda-Chi's guidance.

"Let's call it a 190. There's some disagreement about the smaller ones." Zanda replied. "We're having a midwayer check it out, but the opposition are throwing up veils as fast as they can. Good thing is, it keeps their midwayers close to the fleet, so they can't spy on us."

"Last thing we need," Unava agreed with a little more obsequiousness than I felt comfortable with. It was exactly the sort of sycophantic attitude that had been expected of us by many of the junior celestial bureaucrats back at the Local System HQ. It was precisely one of those attitudes we were rebelling against. I felt even more irritated as I saw heads nodding among the assembled council members. I wondered if I was picking up on the Princes' frustration with Unava, because the feeling of anger was so sudden and came on so unexpectedly.

Apart from a few Watchers, some companion angels, and a Melchizedek representative of Zandana's Seraphic Overgovernment, of those materially present in the chamber only Unava and the Melchizedek could actually see the two Princes. The council—now gathered around an enormous scale model of the entire southern continent, which stood on a basalt slab in the middle of the Love Room—could only hear Zanda and Janda-Chi telepathically. I thought this made the council members' acquiescent gestures look even more ingratiating.

"So it was reckoned about sixty active soldiers on each boat, yes?" This was Unava again, encouraged by the support he was getting from the council.

At that point I understood the dynamics of the meeting.

Unava had apparently held tenaciously to the view that the strategy I'd suggested, and which was so quickly adopted by both Princes, was both immoral and absurd. He'd attempted to subvert the approach, predicting the inevitable decay of social morality if the project were to go forward. I could see that he'd made a fool of himself, since his personal motivation was so obvious to everyone but him.

Reading his aura, I observed that he was fiercely—for a normally passive Zandanan—protective of a new mistress, a sensuous young beauty who had applauded the strategy with somewhat more enthusiasm that Unava thought seemly. He didn't want to be seen by her as trying to forbid her from taking part—I could see from his emotional body that he was terrified she'd leave him. So, as will many powerful men in similar situations, he tried to use his political influence to achieve purely personal ends. I could also see that he'd only just come to his senses, but as Prince Zanda's chief of staff, he must have been quickly pardoned.

"Could be fifty, Unava, probably not as many as seventy. We decided sixty on each was a fair estimate, while you were, ahem, well, off saying good-bye to your lady friend." Prince Zanda seemed pleased at seeing Unava wince.

I'd absorbed the pleasure the Prince could take from turning the knife on one of his underlings before. Possibly there was more similarity between Caligastia and Zanda than I'd supposed. But, then, both Princes had supported Lucifer! The touch of arrogance I'd seen in Zanda had metastasized into Caligastia's brutal indifference to human welfare.

Like me, the council could hear Janda-Chi in their minds.

"So, one 190 boats, with about sixty fighting men in each. What's that? About 11,500? Shouldn't be a problem, right?" More nodding of heads. They all knew there were at least five times that number of women volunteers and that wasn't including the backup contingents.

"Everyone in place?" Janda-Chi was making sure last-minute details had been taken care of.

"Everything's in place, chief." The senior midwayer manifested briefly from his perch in subspace to assure the assembled company that his corps of midway creatures had everything under control.

With that, everyone in the chamber heard Prince Zanda's booming voice in their minds. "Well, everyone. This is it. Tomorrow we'll know the truth. Will we keep the integrity of our beloved motherland? Or will we disappear into the dust of history? Will we continue to develop our beautiful culture, invigorated by new genes? Or will Unava be proved correct and we'll all descend into immorality and dissipation?"

There was a long, telepathic silence in which I could see the elders holding themselves in various displays of belief and righteous hope. Then the booming, confident voice continued. "They won't risk the reefs in the dark. Anticipating that they'll set sail at the dawning of the Wise Twins, five passages later they'll be here. I'll expect all of you here, in the Love Room." I was amused that Zanda would allow himself to use the slang term. "Be here three passages after dawning and we'll have a working breakfast ready for you.

"So sleep well tonight, for tomorrow we'll need every bit of our energy to support our brave womenfolk. Tomorrow our women will save the motherland. Tomorrow we will save our world.

"Dream well, my brothers and sisters." And with that the telepathic circuit closed down and the council members filed out, talking quietly among themselves.

The die was cast.

There was no going back now.

I was going to have to hurry to see if I could hitch a ride with a vacant transport seraph who would be traveling without a passenger back to Earth. I only hoped it might chance to be the one who'd treated me well on my journey here. There was no time for official authorization, but I felt that if my seraphic sister knew the original idea for the strategy came from me, she might possibly make an exception. Perhaps her amiability was a signal that she'd taken a peek at what was to happen tomorrow. Although, to be frank, even if she was available I had no way of knowing whether she'd summon the courage to break the rules. Seraphs are not widely known for defying authority. At best, it was going to be a long shot.

As a consequence, I decided to leave my decision as to whether to grab a transport and soon be back to Earth entirely up to the Tao—to the natural rhythm of Multiverse affairs. If my friendly transport sister found it in her heart to take me into her embrace, I would leave. If not, I would stay.

It's as simple as that. That's how we Watchers wend our way through the Multiverse, knowing by doing this we will be continuously in the right place at the right time. I can easily forget this as I grow progressively closer to Mein Host and mortal affairs in general. Observing the decisions you make to take action rubs off on we who observe. Didn't your Werner Heisenberg propose something along those lines in a quantum mechanical context?

I'm being so heavily influenced by mortals these days, with your ability to come up with creative solutions, that I came extremely close to hubris in claiming the love strategy as my own. The truth is, while I'm writing these words, it's coming to me that the "Love Not War" campaign, which jumped so spontaneously into my mind, was actually generated in the future by Mein Host. I cannot claim it originated solely with me.

Whether I end up back on Earth, or whether indeed I stay for the invasion, I am writing for both of us when I say I can barely wait for tomorrow to see how it all works out.

⁙ ⁙ ⁙

As I watched the drama playing itself out at Xtul on that sweltering summer evening in 1966, I hoped it was as obvious to Mein Host as it was to me that he'd walked into a carefully choreographed setup. I doubted that the assembled company had been told what was about to happen, but they'd certainly been primed to identify my ward as the serpent in the Garden. By now he'd been branded as the proverbial snake in the grass, and christened (if that's the appropriate word) "Snerp"—a name impossible to say without a sneer.

"Well?" Mary Ann's cold voice cut through the silence.

Mein Host stood in front of her, his face impassive and choosing not to reply.

"Well?" Again, even more demanding this time.

Silence.

No one in the community had experienced quite this level of tension before. Anything could happen. Although they were rather older than the schoolboy protagonists of William Golding's disturbing *Lord of the Flies,* there was a distinct sense in those long silences that something dreadful was about to happen.

"What do you have to say for yourself? Well?" Icy cold now.

I was glad to see that Mein Host seemed to know Mary Ann well enough to hold his silence, which, of course, irritated her all the more. She'd evidently hoped to make a far more protracted scene out of it. Since I now understand more about the nature and motives of this complex woman, I can be reasonably certain that she was using Mein Host's devotion to her to paint him as a scapegoat. If she was able to do this successfully she'd be able to unite the group in their mutual hatred of my ward.

Whether she was conscious of this strategy, I couldn't determine at the time. Yet there were a number of occasions over the years that followed in which I heard her assert the need for an enemy to bind people together, so I'm inclined to think it just came naturally to her, whether or not she was conscious of doing it.

Although the inner circle had seen Mary Ann working up a slow burn of anger before with one of them, and casting the offending person out into the cold light of her indifference, she had never done it in front of the whole group before.

"You think by sitting outside, by trying to bribe us into letting you back into the Garden . . . you think we're fools?"

More silence.

I had the oddest sense that Mein Host was listening to the rhythmic, booming beat of the waves crashing onto the beach beyond the coconut palms. Perhaps he really had learned something from those mosquitoes, after all. Just let it happen.

"Accept and allow whatever comes at you. Just let it flow through you." That's how I heard him try to explain it to Juliette after the event. "Remember those bites? When I surrendered to the mossies? After a while they left me alone. Still have, actually!"

With no opposition to play off, Mary Ann switched moods with all the finesse of a skilled dominatrix, scaling back the cold anger in her voice and replacing it with what I thought of as a seductive sneer—which is not as oxymoronic as it reads.

"You know what we call you now, Snerp? Aye, that's right. We call you Snerp. Ssssnerp! You betrayed the sacred trust, didn't you, Snerp? The sacred land we've been given by the Beings. They spoke and you had to leave. What makes you think the Beings will allow you back in?"

Was she seducing him or was she taunting him? Both? At the same time?

Mary Ann flung some more slurs and derisive insults his way, yet once again they were delivered in what I thought of as a sultry, almost flirtatious, tone.

I wondered what Mein Host was making of it, but I could see that he was still away with the waves, fast leaving his body. I knew he'd been bullied, berated, and beaten by the best of them back at Charterhouse, the British boarding school his mother had insisted he attend.

This onslaught, I knew he could cope with. Yet despite the verbal assault, he loved his Goddess no less. I'm sure he believed she was merely testing him.

Just dissociate, I might have once thought. He'd certainly had enough practice! But this time it was going to be somewhat different. This time I saw and understood what was happening, even if he didn't.

"Yes, dissociate by all means, if you need to avoid the pain," I could have told him. "But remember, another subpersonality is going to step in and take over your body. And then you'll never quite know what you've got yourself into." Easy to write now. Oh, how I wish I'd been able to communicate this to my ward there and then. I know it's a foolish thing to wish. Not only could I not communicate with the lad with the facility I can now, but all mortals have to be allowed to go through what causes them ultimately to grow in spirit. It's not for us to judge.

The only time I've ever witnessed a direct angelic intervention into your reality, it was the midwayers who accomplished it. And the situation has to be serious enough. The midwayers, after receiving instructions from the relevant companion angels, will intervene if the mortals in question are denied their legitimate opportunity to complete their life missions, or if their spiritual growth would best be served by their continuing to live.

Such was the case with Mein Host and his girlfriend who, in his eighteenth year, were pulled out of their crashing car by a couple of materialized midwayers. In this case, neither of the young people had completed their mortal tasks. Besides, Mein Host had swerved to avoid another driver's unpredictable error—his instinctive reaction to sacrifice himself for another must have counted for something.

However, it wasn't always going to be so straightforward and seemingly miraculous. And sometimes it was downright weird—even for a Watcher who thinks she's seen everything.

So it was in this case, as Mary Ann's vitriolic barrage clashed with Mein Host's stubborn intention to do whatever had to be done to get back into the Garden of Eden—the very Garden he'd found for his Goddess only months earlier. As the psychic pressure continued to build, Mary Ann was whipping up the energy in the hut with a cold ferocity.

"Well, Snerp, what are you going to do about it? You think you deserve to be let back in? Have you done sufficient penance?" It was obvious from her tone that she didn't think he'd paid the price yet.

"Well, have you? Have you?"

There was a long silence before Mein Host spoke for the first time. "No. No, I don't believe I have. No." His voice was unexpectedly steady and confident enough that it seemed to stop Mary Ann in her tracks.

But it wasn't Mein Host talking. Words were coming out of his mouth, but the dominant personality I'd known as Mein Host wasn't the one speaking.

This was somebody else I'd seen previously in a few brief glimpses, popping through during a handful of flashes of unexpected violence. But this was different. I'd never heard him speaking before.

"So, what will be your penance, serpent? What is it that the Beings demand of you?" There was a new, almost a singsong cadence to Mary Ann's voice. The gathering was acquiring an ancient pagan feeling, an incantatory mix, perhaps, of the Gnostic and Maya, with a touch of the Celtic.

"I choose to punish myself." It was that voice again, calm and firm. "As I am a monk."

I recall wondering, Whatever was he going to say next?

"As a monk, I shall flagellate myself twice daily for as long as I need to pay my penance."

There was an astonished gasp from behind him, followed by a breathless silence as everyone peered through the twilight to see how the Oracle would respond.

Although Mary Ann was a master at disguising her feelings, her emotional body lit up with a vivid yellow-orange wash. She obviously didn't want anyone to see her reaction because her voice tightened slightly and I noticed that it lost the sneer when she leaned forward to speak.

"Twice daily? You'll whip yourself? That's what you're saying?" I could hear in her voice a subtle combination of triumph—an unanticipated sense of relief (probably because she didn't have to think it up herself)—all tinged with a hint of erotic excitement. This latter I believe surprised even her.

"And I shall start right now."

With that, whoever was occupying Mein Host's physical vehicle picked his way adroitly through a space quickly left for him between the assembled bodies and strode confidently from the hut.

I followed him out into the darkness. No one else moved: they seemed half-hypnotized by the ritualistic character of the event. A sense of dread hung in the air.

He walked purposefully toward the dump—the place where the community kept everything they'd found on the beach, on the trail to the village, or lying around the estate. Among the flotsam were bottle tops, broken canisters in different states of disintegration, half a dozen Coca-Cola bottles, a couple of rubber balls, fishhooks, some netting and reels of line, and, yes, several pieces of rope.

Crouching over the dump, he poked around until he found a pliable piece some five and a half feet long, and about half an inch in diameter.

I watched him as he walked slowly out through the coconut grove and across the dunes to perch briefly on the edge of the low cliff. A full moon in a clear sky allowed him to see way out beyond the breakers; fine lines of glowing bioluminescence stretched into the mist as far as he could see, from extreme left to right. He appeared to know exactly what to do—as if he'd done it a hundred times before. This he, who wasn't really Mein Host.

Let me use the name Gabriel Stern, the name by which he came to be known somewhat later in Mein Host's life, when my ward finally decided to consciously integrate his subpersonalities. He has claimed the name floated into his mind one day when Gabriel Stern was manifesting, and because it felt appropriate the name stuck. I don't believe he accorded any special significance to the name beyond the observation that this particular subpersonality had a somewhat dour and inflexible affect. Gabriel Stern will also prove to be the most reluctant of the subpersonalities to be integrated. He will be the last to step out of the shadows to sit with Mein Host and the other six "subs," around a campfire created in Mein Host's visual imagination, to meet the others and tell his story.

So it was Gabriel Stern who appeared to know to soak the rope in seawater prior to knotting it firmly half a dozen times, starting at one end and working back at two-inch intervals—making sure to leave enough rope at the other end to securely loop it around his right hand a couple of times. It was this subpersonality who paused briefly at the top the cliff to look back out over of the water, before turning on his heel and making his way through the coconut trees to the temple, the most sacred of the three buildings on the estate.

The dirt floor had been cleared of debris to show tiles underneath: it was still roofless, with natural-stone walls glowing in the moonbeams flooding in through the trees. The small building stood about eighty yards away from both the monastery and their living hut. It was the most sacred of the three because it was the dwelling for the Oracle and the Teacher.

Gabriel Stern was the one kneeling on the hard tile floor, facing the full moon, placing the rope on the ground, carefully adjusting it. Stern was the one circling the rope three times into a neat concentric mound.

He carefully unbuttoned his thin cotton shirt, took it off, and folded it beside him. He propped himself up so he was sitting on his heels, his back rigidly upright and straight.

I watched as he sat like that for several minutes.

There were no sounds coming from the hut so I slipped back to find almost all of them sitting exactly where I'd last seen them, numb, I should imagine, by some of the implications of what they were witnessing, and what it might mean for each of them.

It's probably unnecessary to point this out, but being willing to inflict pain on the self in contemporary Western culture is generally met with complete disbelief. Whether it's an extreme version of the self-immolation of a Buddhist priest, a Tamil suicide bomber, or an Indian fakir's bed of nails, the circumcision of Aboriginal boys, or even the piercings of modern primitives, to the Western emotional intelligence, self-inflicted pain remains a horrifying mystery. Pain is something they prefer not to think about, lest it might happen to them, though they'll titillate themselves endlessly with violence on films and TV—as long as it happens to someone else.

Of course there is masochism, but Mein Host had never shown any sign of that. He'd been the recipient of a great deal of formally administered pain in his life at boarding school, but his response had always been to defy it, to never give in to the pain. I've never seen him enjoy it—before or since.

But now Gabriel Stern was in the driver's seat.

I had no idea what was going to happen when he leaned down to pick up the rope. I have to admit that I was confused and frightened.

There was something cold and slightly inhuman about Gabriel Stern. I respected him, but I didn't like him. There'd always been an essential kindness in Mein Host's nature, which seemed entirely absent in Gabriel Stern's character. This, of course, was barely surprising, since Stern's personality had stepped in to accept the punishment.

Then I realized it must have been this subpersonality who took over when the boy was being formally beaten at Charterhouse school. Of course, that's why the feeling was familiar to me. I simply hadn't recognized the phenomenon when I'd observed it earlier in his life. However, it did give me a clue as to why this particular subpersonality was so familiar with pain and why Gabriel Stern would so willingly announce that he'd inflict it on himself. Twisting the rope twice tightly around his right hand, he took a deep breath, curled his arm around to his right side as far as he possibly could, the rope trailing out behind him. He paused for a moment and then whipped the rope over his left shoulder with all his strength, so that by the third time the knots were cutting into the flesh on his back.

He continued, as hard as he could.

What new person, I wondered, would emerge from this ordeal?

Would we ever see Gabriel Stern again?

How would those in the community respond once this night was over?

⁜ ⁜ ⁜

The very fact that both Princes of Zandana so readily accepted the idea of using the women to subvert the barbarian invasion frankly astonished me. Whether or not the strategy would turn out to be successful, I found their openness and enthusiasm a charming contrast to the compulsively belligerent response I would have received on Earth, had I ever been rash enough to raise the idea with Caligastia or Daligastia.

Was this a difference between the characteristics of the Princes on the two worlds? Or was it in the nature of Zandanans to be more sexually liberated than inhabitants of Earth?

Mein Host told me he knows of no time in human history that the Love-Not-War tactic was ever used, not in all the many wars and skirmishes that have been recorded. The closest to it appears in a Greek play! How typically human, I thought. Then, when he told me that it occurs in the Greek comedy *Lysistrata* by Aristophanes and it's the women who come up with the idea, yet with one important and revealing variation, it further confirmed for me one of the most noticeable differences between the sexual dynamics of the two planetary populations. In the play, the women of Greece withhold their sexual favors from their own husbands and lovers. They agree to keep their men out of their beds as a way to force them into negotiating an end to the Peloponnesian War. The ploy finally works, as the eponymous Lysistrata dangles a gorgeous young beauty—significantly enough named Reconciliation—before the Spartan and sex-starved Athenian delegates, demonstrating the intensity of human sexual needs.

Although Lysistrata is a theatrical comedy, Aristophanes raises a significant issue in intimating that sexual hunger trumps nationalistic belligerence when that is the choice. And perhaps, Mein Host also suggests, the answer to my observation that Zandanans in general were a gentler, more passive people than the male and female mortals I'd observed on Earth.

I wasn't present on Earth through the earlier times of human development, having arrived here with Caligastia's mission only a half million years ago, so I didn't witness those eras for myself. In the training simulators back on Local System HQ, those of us due to be sent to Earth had a chance to view what we were getting ourselves into. There, in the spacious sim-chamber, I was able to see and experience the intense, predatory violence on all levels of biological life.

When I first viewed the historical recordings of the period in which true humans were evolving from their primate ancestors, I was almost overwhelmed by the constant state of terror in which they all lived.

I hadn't studied Zandana in the same way, but I had noticed on some of my earlier trips that, with the exception of the wild bears living up in the mountains, there seemed to be a remarkable lack of large predatory animals. I thought it most unlikely that the relatively gentle Zandanans had killed them all off by the time I first got there. The worshipful reverence with which they viewed the bears, their general love of animals, and the complete lack of animal cruelty suggested to me that they had a more placid evolutionary journey than your early ancestors.

I derive from these observations of two different planetary populations that there will likely be a direct correlation between the degree of predation mortals have had to historically confront in their biosphere and the intensity of their sexual desires and procreative needs. Was the gentler nature of the Zandanans due to a less violent and strenuous evolutionary journey? And since there would be a diminished pressure to procreate, might this in turn have produced a more stable, equitable, and sexually well-balanced society?

Or was Zandana a more typical planet, more like the worlds that refused to support Lucifer and weren't directly affected by the consequences of the rebellion?

Finally, I wondered whether I'd become so conditioned by my observations of the behavior of human beings on Caligastia's Earth that I'd come to believe that fear, chaos, and belligerence were the natural estate of mortals? This was only a preliminary supposition, based on the most minimal of samples, so I will reserve any final judgment until I've had the chance to observe other inhabited worlds.

My point is that there had to be a different essential quality between how these two planetary populations had developed. To have produced such a ready acquiescence of the Love-Not-War tactic among the Zandanans, and for it to be so hard to imagine it happening here on Earth, seemed to point to a fundamental difference in the way a world is prepared for intelligent life.

We're told during our training that Earth is an experimental planet—one in every ten worlds is so classified—on which the Life Carriers, the Multiverse biologists, are encouraged to make any adjustments to the planet's evolutionary strategy deemed necessary. Could one of the most basic ways of manipulating the belligerence of a given planet's mortal population be by controlling the level of predation in the evolutionary process?

Mein Host is reminding me that I can't put off revealing much longer whether or not I hitched a ride back to Earth and therefore would have missed the action on Zandana.

Well, here's how it worked out.

When I arrived at the Subspace Transport Station, one of the Wise Twins was dawning over the ocean. I could see the boats quite clearly now, clustered with soldiers, their long lances sticking straight up in the air, making the boats appear from this distance to be a swarm of 197 aquatic hedgehogs. There had to be more than sixty fighting men on each of those boats. I admit, it looked terrifying. I could only hope for the best. With a strong breeze I estimated they'd be onshore by midday, possibly a little later.

I could see from the promontory on which the station was perched that the beaches sweeping away on both sides of me were clear of people as far as I could see in both directions. So the trap was being set.

Before I dragged myself away to see about the transport schedule, I was already starting to hear the pulsating rhythms and the tonal chanting of the invading forces echoing over the water, ebbing and flowing with the wind.

The music, if I can call it that, was surprisingly moving. It felt familiar, although I was sure I'd never heard such sounds before. I stayed there listening to it far longer than I intended. The massive chorale that issued from more than ten thousand rough barbarian throats was far sweeter and more sonorous than I would ever have expected. The drumming, which I could hear more clearly as the fleet drew nearer, was as complex and richly patterned as anything I've ever heard.

Mein Host, who has played guitar and percussion in bands as different as rock 'n' roll, modern jazz, and progressive fusion, expressed his surprise at this. He appreciates how challenging it is to get even a few human drummers all working together. "How is it possible," he asked me, "that a coherent rhythm of any complexity could ever be maintained by so many drummers, in almost two hundred boats sailing under the stiff breeze, and distributed over a wide swath of ocean? They wouldn't have even been able to hear one another to keep the rhythm."

Ah, I replied, feeling another digression coming on.

You see, they weren't listening to one another. Their boats were too far apart and the wind too strong for that.

What they were listening to was the heartbeat of Zandana—at least, that's how they would have explained it—so they didn't need to hear each other. They drummed to the beat of the planet herself. And, since every boat had its own group of drummers, each boat was both independent and yet united into the collective by the rhythm of the planet.

Contemporary Earth scientists are familiar with the Schumann resonances, extra-low-frequency (ELF) waves, from a low of 6.9 Hz and rising in a series of harmonics to around 60 Hz. These resonate as a standing wave within the Earth/ionosphere cavity, with a wavelength approximately equal to the circumference of the planet. The most prominent mode, or frequency peak, on your planet occurs at 7.83 Hz.

Each planet obviously possesses its own signature resonant frequency, since the tuning of the standing wave is dependent on the state of the upper wall of the closed atmospheric cavity, as well as the surface characteristics of the planet itself. Because these frequencies can change slightly, due to geomagnetic and ionospheric disturbances, a planet's resonant ionospheric cavity is clearly sensitive to any external electromagnetic disturbance.

I am told there are celestial beings who can hear these constantly shifting frequencies as the music of the spheres, each astronomical body, from asteroid to planet to any solar body or event, each contributing its own unique range of frequencies.

Here I'm using the Schumann resonances as an example of something more subtle, something I doubt that contemporary geophysicists are yet fully aware of, since they'd have to be able to compare enough inhabited planets to make the proposition stick. Scientists attempt crude approximations of this when they crash space vehicles onto the moon and study the chemical composition of the debris field created by the explosion. But what I'm pointing to here requires a somewhat more advanced technology to detect and yet, idiosyncratically, it can be "felt," or experienced in some way, by a sensitive mortal sensorium.

Just as each planet possesses a unique Schumann signature resonating in the ELF range, there is the "sound" of the planet herself. Think of striking a large metal sphere with a hammer. It will produce a tone—not with quite the resonance of a gong or a bell, but it will make a sound. And any alteration in the material, the density, or the size of the sphere will produce a slightly different tone. This is essentially how a dolphin's biolocation sense functions, by bouncing tightly focused sound waves off an object.

As everything in the Multiverse is vibrating over a wide variety of different frequencies—from a rock to a snail, a human being, a planet, or a star—every material object has its own unique "sound," if it can only be heard.

We're taught in our training sessions that each planet produces a rhythmic, pulsating sound, audible to those with the sensitivity, or the technical mastery, to detect it. This rhythmic pulsation constitutes a unique signature of a particular planet, just as its Schumann resonances do.

This "sound" is also easier to identify, so we're told, over interplanetary distances, using a technology far more advanced than, yet not dissimilar to, the laser microphones that are used to listen in on conversations in a room with windows. The vibration of the voices in the room will create a sufficient sympathetic resonance in the glass for a laser microphone to bounce a light beam off it, reflecting it back to be analyzed by a device that then reconstructs the original speech.

Thus, each planet has a distinctive rhythmic pulse, a resonant frequency unique to that particular world. So the invading barbarians were using the deep regular heartbeat of Zandana to build upon, amplifying the beat with their drumming and singing, to create a pulsating wall of sound that swept over the surface of the sea in a veritable sonic tsunami.

I've already said how moved I was by the sound, which was at first mystifying—and, I was told, initially rather frightening for some of the older city dwellers. Yet as the fleet approached, the rhythmic complexity and the delicate choral mastery cast the "barbarians" in rather a different light from what I'd expected.

This was going to be even more interesting than I'd anticipated.

❉ ❉ ❉

It was so quiet that night at Xtul, while Mein Host was on his knees facing a full moon and flagellating himself in the temple, that I might be pardoned the hyperbole of suggesting that even nature fell silent. Of course, the surf continued to beat upon the beach, the wind went on rattling the palm leaves, and the night creatures didn't cease their calling. Yet it seemed to me the whole world was listening.

I've described how I believe one of Mein Host's subpersonalities, Gabriel Stern, took over the body and was now the one suffering the self-inflicted punishment. But here's the oddest thing: Immediately after Stern's third slicing thwack, I was able to observe Mein Host streaking up out of his body into subspace, heading toward the moon. All the while, there was Stern down in the vehicle, whipping himself with all his strength.

Mein Host has subsequently claimed that after the third strike he was "in ecstasy, far, far away," and that he could see his body far beneath him, "whipping itself with all its strength."

As you can see from his use of the indefinite article when describing his body as recently as 2008, he still had no idea at the time of that writing that a subpersonality had taken over his body for the entire incident. In fact, Gabriel Stern had emerged under the barrage of Mary Ann's verbal abuse when Mein Host returned to the hut after his three-day exile.

Here he is again in 2008, writing about the immediate aftermath of his flagellation:

Whether it was the loud and repeated crack of knotted rope on flesh, or my beatific smile when I returned to the hut, I was accepted back into the group. I made no secret of what I'd discovered about leaving my body and within days many of the others were borrowing my rope and making their way down to the temple.

Given the intolerable physical conditions we were living under, perhaps it's no surprise that flagellation became quite the thing to do. I recall nights in which four or five people, having made their own ropes, would be in the temple, all in their own worlds and whacking away at their backs.

I could see that his back was painful as he walked toward to hut, but from his smile and the way he held himself I could see, much to my relief, that the primary personality was now back in charge again.

My ward was back!

I hadn't realize how concerned I was until Mein Host was back in his body. It also explains so much about him that I'm astonished I hadn't spotted it earlier when I'm sure Gabriel Stern must have taken over the body. I needed to keep a closer eye on this.

Mary Ann did indeed welcome Mein Host back into the fold.

She was smiling broadly when he got back to the hut—evidently proud of him, although the reaction of most of the others appeared more ambivalent. They heard the shocking impact of the blows in the still night air, over and over again. I can only imagine that everyone would have been thinking about themselves, about how they might react in the same situation.

Here I have to be cautious in my assumptions since, once again, I don't want to get ahead of myself. Mein Host was far too blinded by his devotion to the Goddess, and his desire to take on any challenge she set him, to distrust her intentions. I'm also aware that in writing so closely with my ward, there will be times in my review of his life when his words and actions may appear naive and foolish. That's because he was both young and foolish, he assured me.

"How could I ever really know the truth," he asked me, "if I hadn't served my time swimming in a sea of lies? How can I be honest if I haven't known the consequences of deception?"

I had no reply to that, since it reflects my own journey. I, too, placed little value on the truth of the life I was living and have come to value it only through the long, slow process of working out the truth for myself.

Yet, being welcomed back into the community, feeling once again embraced by Mary Ann's love and surrounded by his friends, smiling again, albeit a little nervously, some of the girls caring for his bleeding back, seemed to me to be all he could cope with after his arduous ordeal.

The evening soon broke up and everyone retired to their blankets or sleeping bags for another restless night.

Mein Host was glad to be allowed to sleep as long as he needed—

until noon of the following day. Although his back was painful for the next few days, Juliette's application of jelly from an aloe plant growing against the monastery wall was doing wonders for his welts.

Life at Xtul returned to its normal rhythms as the weeks passed.

I doubt if anyone there could have anticipated what was going to happen next. Yet its raw power would become the sustaining myth of the community's collective Xtul experience and the ultimate test of faith. Adopting a courageous stance in the face of nature's raw power would shape the community's collective Xtul experience, becoming the founding myth of the Process.

No one who lived through it would ever be quite the same again.

6

Women's Sacrifice

An Invasion Collapses, the Purpose of Cults, Reincarnates, and Lemurian Influences

I wasn't altogether surprised when I finally managed to tear myself away from the action and see if there were any seraphic transports available, only to find I'd missed my friendly seraph. She'd just flown out empty to another planet in the Local System. It's possible I might have been able to persuade her to drop me off on Earth on her way, but the fact was I'd found myself drawn to stay by that magical sound, which in turn made me realize it was my cowardice that was prompting me to leave.

Cowardice? I didn't recognize it at first as a personal feeling. I didn't know what it was. It was new to me—the feeling of it. Although I'd previously observed the results of cowardice in others, it was invariably without experiencing the associated shame and guilt that accompany cowardice in the mortal psyche. This was different. It was almost too much. The feelings were as dreadful as they were new to me.

After hearing the news from the Transport Center, I felt even worse, since now I felt trapped. Morosely, I moved back to the flat boulder overlooking the coast from where I could watch the fleet as it neared the shore. As I stared out over the fleet with boats filling my visual field, it came to me that my cowardice had to be one of the possible consequences of my actually initiating an idea—a concept significant enough to potentially alter the course of Zandana's history.

This isn't something Watchers ever do. It isn't our function. We observe. That's why we "rebel angels" are called Watchers. In the time before the rebellion, when I was a simple seraph, I was permitted to intervene in human affairs to an extremely limited extent and generally only in an emergency. As articulated in *Confessions of a Rebel Angel,* the first book in this series, you may recall some of the ways I was able to help smooth the path for young Onya on her dangerous journey to the city of Dalamatia, back on Earth in the balmy millennia before the uprising changed everything.

After the rebellion, those of us assigned to the Prince's mission, and who aligned ourselves with Lucifer and had chosen to follow the Prince, were renamed Watchers, reflecting the instruction we'd all received not to take any action that would influence or affect mortals in any way. Yet here, on Zandana, I had done just that!

I knew what fear was, of course, but empathically picking up fear from mortals and thus experiencing something of theirs was turning out to be a pale shadow of the intensity of the terror I found myself feeling as a result of my own action.

After a while I slowly moved back along the cliff path toward the city. I'd given myself a lot to think about. I knew I'd become inextricably woven into the fabric of the planet, no matter what was going to happen when these two would-be antagonists engaged with one another. I recall thinking, "So this is what is meant by having a will." Every act, it suddenly struck me, really does have its consequences. Being prepared to take responsibility for the outcome, whatever it turned out to be, was part of what it meant to be mortal—to be a "will creature," as all mortals are known in the Multiverse.

This also allowed me to realize, perhaps for the first time, how hopelessly ill-equipped so many of us celestials were to grasp what Lucifer was presenting us with at the time of the revolution. I admit that I was carried away by all the wonderful prospects he was promising. Yet I can't recall giving any thought as to whether there might be any negative consequences of the uprising.

Was it my excitement, I wondered, that had blocked my vision? The revolution was such an unexpected event, and for so many of us, it was the first major choice we had ever faced. Speaking for myself, I'm now sure I was completely unprepared, emotionally, to foresee the consequences of throwing my support behind the rebels.

Celestial psychology is grounded in a complete trust of our superiors, so most of us found this dilemma intensely disturbing at the time. You see, Lucifer was our direct superior, so this introduced another layer of complication to the issue. By taking the stand Lucifer did, he was openly expressing his distrust of his own superiors.

What were we to think? Who were we to believe? MA maintained that we should place our trust in the time-honored traditions. Yet those were the very traditions our superior was calling into question. I'm not trying to excuse myself: I still feel our decision to follow Lucifer was a courageous one, however misguided it may turn out to have been. I merely want to mark this moment on Zandana as the first occasion in which I found myself impelled by my emotional body to gain some real insight into the consequence of my choices.

This might well sound simpleminded to you, patient reader, since you will have likely been raised to be aware that you are responsible for all your acts and choices. And perhaps, if you missed that class, you will have discovered over the course of your life both the blessings and the pain of taking personal responsibility.

But for a Watcher, the intensity of these feelings was new. I hadn't felt anything this forceful before. My fear, mixed with an unexpected frisson of excited anticipation, all flavored with a sense that I'd made a colossal mistake this time, became such a rich emotional concoction it almost overwhelmed me with its raw power.

I needed to stop moving again, this time with my back against one of the majestic Zandana trees growing on the promontory. I could catch a glimpse of the ships through the undergrowth, now within a mile or so of the coast. Through the haze, it appeared to me that they were dropping anchor. The chanting had ceased, leaving only the pulsating beat of a thousand drums.

Still high enough on the promontory to overlook the city, I could see flashes of movement in some of the gardens as women made last-minute adjustments to their clothes. The city itself, with its lush parks and superb public sculptures, had been spruced up; the gleaming white administrative buildings now looked from a distance like elegantly carved blocks of snow. The wide avenues—a series of concentric circles girdling the city—were cleared of the blanket of purple leaves that dropped from the massive trees at this time of year.

Zandan had been made to appear like a city that was utterly indifferent to a threat from the outside: a citizenry so confident of themselves, so comfortable in the life they had developed for themselves, that surely any outsider would prefer to live like them. They'd been living in a bubble of their own superiority, secure in the belief—or so they thought—that the political intrigues they'd sown on the other islands would have kept them subservient and undeveloped. Now they were going to find out the results of their strategy.

I wondered if they'd reckoned on the resentment they'd stirred up.

The barbarian soldiers were by now in small boats rowing hard for the shore. A new chant had started. The insistent rhythm of the oars slapping the water wove yet another cross-beat into the pulsating rhythm of the drummers who'd remained back on the larger ships.

What all the drumming and chanting was about was a mystery to me. Was it a way of working up their bloodlust? A subterfuge to confuse the enemy? A way of softening up the opposition? An ingenious disinformation tactic?

Frankly, I had no idea. Had they somehow heard about the Zandana Princes' novel strategy? Were they trying to outsmart us? Despite their long lances, they didn't appear all that aggressive from where I was sitting.

When the nearest small boats were a few hundred yards off the shore, I heard the ringing of bells drifting up to me from the city, which was followed immediately by women emerging from their houses and gardens and threading their way through the cobbled streets to the shoreline.

One moment the city appeared completely empty; the next, the streets were alive with flashes of every tint and hue, moving like columns of brightly colored army ants through the narrow alleys of the domestic quarter.

The women were all dressed in their finest and most colorful clothing. Slim or plump, tall and willowy, small but well-formed, some nervous and others striding with a lusty confidence, the women laughed and chattered as they joined up with their friends and neighbors, making their way through the streets.

I could see from my perch that Unava must have choreographed the encounter so as to permit the barbarians to land before the women were to make themselves known. And that's what I could now see occurring: men jumping into the surf and splashing ashore. Even from where I was watching, I could see their bewilderment as they milled around on the beaches. Not quite sure what to do in the face of no opposition, the front ranks, suspecting a trap, hung back while more and more warriors crowded in behind them. I could faintly hear the piping sounds of the officers' whistles as they struggled to organize the increasing chaos.

It was obvious, even from here, that the men were completely discombobulated. Trained to fight, they'd been effectively thrown into a collective state of mild cognitive dissonance. Some were trying to push forward but were finding themselves hemmed in by the volcanic cliffs, while their companions were spreading out laterally along the beaches, clearly hoping to find simpler ways to scale the cliffs.

Frankly, I was encouraged by their evident lack of good intelligence. I didn't know it at the time, but Unava had instructed all access to the beaches to be blocked off except for a select half-dozen. These were chosen because they were exceptionally steep, narrow tracks, so the invaders would be tired after clambering to the top of the cliffs—and they would be in single file.

Moving a little closer, I could see what Unava had in mind. He reasoned that if they could break the invading army down to individuals, the bonding instilled in them by their training would dissolve in the face of the promise of pleasure.

Now, this was interesting! They'd been fine-tuning my idea. For the first time I felt this could work.

I'd moved lower now, with the top of the cliffs blocking my view of the beaches, although I could still see over the trees in the lush park that separated the coast from the city. This was where the women were gathering to support one another before threading their way through the stands of magnificent redwoods to greet the barbarians. Throughout this whole operation, I saw no men present.

I was so emotionally involved by this time that next I found myself on the dunes watching the first of the barbarians climb, one by one, out of the clefts in the rock face that Unava had left open.

The men clearly had no idea what was waiting for them. Already confused and exhausted by the stiff climb, they emerged, blinking in the sun, and before any one of them had a chance to gather his wits, two young, scantily clad Zandan beauties stepped gracefully up, one to offer water from a crystal bowl, the other to hang a lei of local flowers around their necks. Even a Watcher could appreciate that it was an irresistible display by the most gorgeous and seductive young women. I realized that Unava must have instructed the cream of Zandan female pulchritude to step forward to greet the first of the warriors. That had to be made to work if the strategy was going to be successful.

If the poor men had been bewildered on the beaches, they appeared baffled by the loving attention they were receiving and willingly surrendered their resistance. There were, of course, a few men (very few) who attempted to push the women away, who refused their water and leis, and who showed every sign of trying to be the warriors they believed themselves to be. But that became a signal for three or four more young beauties to surround the man in a swaying and provocative dance.

The men seemed completely flummoxed.

No longer proud warriors, they couldn't bring themselves to use their weapons against the women. When they saw their buddies willingly throwing down their swords and lances and accepting wine and fruit, they quickly followed suit and gave themselves over to the women's amorous attentions.

If some of the men might have thought they'd been poisoned by the water, they showed no sign of it as they were led away into the park by the women.

I'd already noticed that picnic tables and colorful rugs had been set up in the many groves and forest clearings throughout the park.

Unava's people had certainly been busy, above and beyond anything I'd suggested.

It soon became a remarkably fluid process as exhausted warriors emerged one after another. Any remaining belligerence left in them after the climb I could see turning to astonishment, as beautiful young women threw their arms around them, before leading them away into the woods.

As the afternoon passed, this process became progressively easier as the men came into view expecting to be pitched into the battle of their lives only to find no battle and no army. Just Zandan women who seemed to want to have their way with them. What's a healthy red-blooded warrior to do about that?

When the barbarians' ranking officers finally made it up the cliff and saw the situation for themselves, they must have realized that their invasion plans were going severely awry. No information about the women, apparently, had gone back down the line, for reasons they would soon be appreciating.

Emerging out into the evening light, there was some peremptory use of whistles by the officers, which struck me as more out of habit than anything else—since there was no one around to whistle at or to obey their orders.

I assumed the officers must have lost control of their men in the chaos down on the beaches and never fully reclaimed it. In fact, I heard later that when they saw some of their more intrepid troops locating the routes up the cliffs and beckoning their fellows to follow them up, the officers were forced to make the best of it by trying to bully their men into orderly lines, and then by urging them up the steep cliff paths.

They'd heard no sound of the battle they supposed was being fought on top of the cliffs and must have dismissed the silence as an optimistic sign, believing their warriors were successfully pushing their way inland.

The last of the invaders were finally off the beaches by the late afternoon and the empty rowboats were slowly making their way back to the ships. Each was paddled by a man standing high on the stern who, as I watched them leave the bay for the ocean, seemed to be battling a powerful unexpected crosscurrent with a single long oar. Beyond them I could see the fleet—the great wooden ships, their sails furled and standing light in the water—straining at their anchors' chains. Some of the small boats had already been forced off course by the current when the last of the officers, a corpulent man whom I presumed to be in charge, managed to haul himself to the top of the cliff with great difficulty.

The officers who preceded him had proved every bit as amenable to the approaches of the women as had the rank and file. So when he clambered out and found no one there—no battle, no warriors, none of his loyal officers—just smiling young women in diaphanous gowns, offering tender ministrations after the long climb, I could see he that felt he had no choice but to submit with as much grace as he could muster.

As night fell I observed the women, some in small groups, some paired off with "their" barbarian visitors, making their way through the woods toward the city. I knew the city's plan was for everyone to open their homes to the visitors, to greet them as old friends and offer them the best of everything.

The park, which stretched for many miles and curved halfway around the city, was reserved for the recreation of the citizens. All building was forbidden there. In fact, to the casual gaze, the park appeared to be a natural marvel with forested hills, waterfalls, and streams that snaked through meadows rich with wildlife—small animals that would look surprisingly familiar to a visitor from Earth. Trees you would recognize as being close to weeping willows hung low over the placid water of the lakes; birds, not dissimilar to the birds you know in your world, flapped freely between the branches of what might have been elm trees, except for the deep violet sheen on their trunks.

The extensive stands of old-growth trees—the only feature that may have been natural—wound along the coast and covered the promontory from which I'd originally spotted all those aquatic hedgehogs poised for invasion earlier in the day. Yet the place did appear entirely natural, a swath of Zandana's wilderness preserved for posterity, one the citizens could be justifiably proud to pass down to their grandchildren.

However, it wasn't natural at all, but the result of cunning foresight on the part of a particularly harsh dictator some two millennia earlier. Ruling at a time in Zandana's history when a number of the elite families were struggling for dominance, this leader had exceptionally cruel methods of dealing with troublemakers. Yet they were effective enough to keep him in power until he was driven into exile as an old man.

In the account I'd heard on an earlier trip, this dictator had a change of heart late in his life and, wanting to be remembered for some great act of public generosity rather than for his brutality, he'd created the park. It came as no surprise to his subjects that he ended up draining the city's resources by the time his designers and contractors had finished the task of molding the landscape to his satisfaction. While he was remembered for the park, it was not at all for the reasons he'd originally hoped.

So, no, the park could never be considered a natural wilderness and once a few generations of Zandanans had come and gone, all that remained was a ironic monument to a foolish and profligate dictator.

And, of course, an appropriately self-effacing story with which to regale visitors to the city, illustrating how far the citizens of Zandan have come politically from those bad old days.

※ ※ ※

Excused from hard physical work for a while and spending more time with Mary Ann, Mein Host found that, once again, he'd become one of her favorites. By this time he was well aware of how fragile his position was in relation to the Goddess in the heightened emotional atmosphere of Xtul.

Although the games Mary Ann played in juggling her inner circle were those of any petty dictator, she wasn't the sort of autocrat who demanded constant affirmation. She was openly dismissive of "yes-men," and you'll note I say *men* because in her treatment of her female favorites, she seemed to me to be more forgiving and tolerant. She expected less of them than the men and, besides, the three or four women who'd become her unconditional devotees were more likely to go along with her.

She didn't need flattery or emotional support from Mein Host—at least not obviously—but high intelligence, a mythic imagination, and an original turn of phrase. In short, she required the very best from him. And in this, perhaps, we have at least part of an answer to the questions that must have occurred to the reader more than once: Why did the lad put up with all this nonsense? Couldn't he tell he was being manipulated? Why didn't he just leave?

Well, yes, of course, he could have left. No one likes to be treated the way Mary Ann had treated him. Yet during these peak times—when he was flying high and basking in his love for the Goddess, when he was meeting her challenges, when he was encouraged to be the very best he could be—it all became worthwhile, it all fitted into place for him. He believed she was the only person in the world who truly understood him, who knew who he really was under the surface.

I could see the changes Mein Host's emotional body was undergoing. He'd been experiencing extremes of feelings—overwhelming joy at being close to the Goddess and utter despair at being frozen out of her love. All this was more intense than anything he'd previously felt.

At this point he was also able to find out considerably more about Mary Ann.

I realize that over the course of this narrative I may not have been able to communicate quite what it was about this unusual woman that inspired so much devotion in her followers. But first, let's look at those followers, of which Mein Host was one.

Conventional thinking paints such devotees as cult followers and dismisses the phenomenon of spiritual teachers and gurus as irrelevant to the larger social context. In the case of Jonestown or the Heaven's Gate mass suicide, we may see cults as examples of how tragically deluded, immature, and needy are the people drawn to them. The most vociferous criticism of cults is generally reserved for the group's leader(s): certainly Jim Jones and Heaven's Gate's Marshall Applewhite richly deserved that kind of criticism.

However, we would be missing the true value of cults if we then made the leap that all spiritual communities are inherently destructive and function merely to reinforce the egos of the leadership, and that all devotees are hypnotized dupes who can't function in the outside world. Apart from the fact that all religions start off as cults, and, as such, inevitably pose a threat to the established religions of their time, small groups of spiritually driven people will always provide controversial melting pots of theological and metaphysical thought. Cults allow their followers to experience aspects of life not generally available in the course of everyday existence as well as giving them a chance to explore paths less frequently taken.

Whether or not a cult's leadership turns out to be corrupt is of less significance than the opportunity the cult's followers are given to experience some of the extremes of the human condition generally found only in war, famine, and shipwrecks. Although cults may dress themselves up with all manner of belief systems and improbable cosmologies, and rigidly adhere to them—sometimes even unto death—what the followers believe is of less value compared to what they experience as part of the cult.

So why would anybody join such a group?

More is generally understood about the nature and dynamics of cults now than was known fifty years ago. What is seldom mentioned, however—and this was particularly true in Mein Host's case—is that the intensity of community life in a cult accelerates spiritual growth. By constantly putting himself in situations that he would never have experienced had he continued to practice architecture and followed a more conventional trajectory in his life, Mein Host found that he was required to make many more moral choices. And it's by confronting difficult moral challenges that people can grow in spirit.

If you were to take a census among cults and spiritual communities worldwide, you would likely find that the great majority of devotees are reincarnates. And reincarnates have somewhat different needs and functions than regular people do.

To clear up a confusion that has persisted as long as some religions have insisted that everybody reincarnates into another human vehicle and others entirely rejected this belief, I should explain what I understand to be happening. Please don't think of this as an infallible truth, but if it rings true to you, it may well help clarify much in your life in relationship to other people.

Under normal conditions, mortals do not reincarnate into another mortal vehicle. There's little point in it. "Been there, done that" is what I believe you say. Neither do they die in the sense that an atheist might believe. Death is not the end of existence for mortals; it is the beginning of their eternal life—if they so choose. And I emphasize that. When you are awakened from your sleep of death and after you undertake your life review, you are always given the choice as to whether to continue in your Multiverse career or not. MA is infinitely fair about this and, as a consequence, very few ever choose to be terminated.

Reincarnates arrive in your world having preexisted this life. Many of them, like myself, have been Watchers—rebel angels, if you like, although we never thought of ourselves as rebels. These are the ones who have earned the privilege of mortal incarnation. Some are from extraterrestrial races who have spiritual or cultural investments in this world; others are here of their own volition, knowing that planets like this provide challenges unavailable on worlds untouched by the rebellion.

The first time Mein Host asked his sources about this matter, he learned that there were some sixty million reincarnates on the planets and that this number would be rising rapidly to ninety million. On a planet currently hosting over seven billion mortals, this is a relatively small number.

I can only speak for the Watchers here, since the extraterrestrial reincarnates, like ET "walk-ins," are relatively rare and have their own agendas. Naturally, when they have completed their tasks, they return to their own races.

Watchers, and a small subset of them that Mein Host calls Atlantean Black Magicians, are essentially here to redeem themselves and learn from living out the consequences of following Lucifer into rebellion in a world that has been so profoundly affected by the uprising.

Not everyone in Mein Host's community was a reincarnate, but, as the years passed, the few "first-timers" (to use Mein Host's somewhat condescending term for mortals with no previous experience) soon dropped away. Although I've never heard it put in these terms, since reincarnation was a basic assumption in the community, life in the Process was unnecessarily harsh for first-timers. They had no need to be challenged or to challenge themselves because, as first-timers, they played no part in creating the conditions that have prevailed in this world since the rebellion 203,000 years ago.

I am probably safe in assuming that this book will be of little interest to first-timers, so my readership will likely be reincarnates of one kind or another. Some of you will know who you are and know something about your own history; others among you may have had an intuition about your heritage but, because of lack of support for this intuition, have shelved it away. But if you find value in the "examined life," then the matter of your previous incarnations will need to be taken into account. The reason for this is simple: prior to this lifetime, you would have felt that a life in this world would serve your spiritual growth.

As a reincarnate, whether you're aware of it or not, you will have had previous experience with the consequences of your actions. You will likely have a natural sense of karma and an inner sense of correct action (to use a Buddhist expression describing this), as well as finding yourself constantly amazed and horrified by the thoughtless words and actions of human first-timers.

As reincarnates, there are two primary issues of which you should be aware over the course of this life. The first, and most important, is that having lived before does not confer on you a position of superiority. To laud it over first-timers is to miss the point entirely. To put it crudely, this is more their planet than yours. You are the interloper, the cuckoo in the mortals' nest, the Trojan Horse: you are the one who is piggybacking your way into the mortal ascension line—not something you'd want to have too widely known. They've only just stopped burning people alive who knew too much!

Secondly, you chose to incarnate here to redeem yourself, as previously mentioned, or you have volunteered to be on this world at a key point in human history to serve the greater good. In both cases it's wise, and certainly more effective, not to attract undue attention to your reincarnate status through excessive pridefulness.

Speaking as a Watcher who is being primed for human incarnation, I'm well aware that the life I choose will be both a gift and a penance. But, however perilous it turns out to be, I will have finally joined the mortal line. I will finally have the opportunity to know God through personal inner experience. Indeed, I believe I will finally gain the certainty I lacked when I was persuaded by Lucifer's rhetoric that God did not exist; that God was a delusion fostered by the Michaelsons—the Creator Beings of their Local Universes—in an elaborate conspiracy to maintain the status quo and retain their hold on power.

Now, 203,000 of your years later, I find Lucifer's claims increasingly implausible. I still have no definitive proof, of course. Yet I would like to believe that over the course of a human lifetime, I will learn the truth of this for myself, as Mein Host has.

I understand that I will forget all this at human birth.

I can only hope I will come across a book like this one to remind me of my need to be humble.

⁜ ⁜ ⁜

On Zandana, the crisis caused by the invasion started to dissipate after the third day. It became clear that being greeted with a rich combination of sexual pleasure and the ecstatic and aphrodisiacal properties of the sacred plants and herbs—cunningly administered to the barbarians when required by their Zandan lovers—were having the intended effect.

The invaders boosted their confidence with fermented drinks and yet knew nothing of the entheogenic class of plants that grew so profusely on the balmy southern continent, and yet rarely on the other islands, they were particularly open to revelatory insights provided by the entheogens. And when fear or paranoia would arise in one of the warriors, there were always beautiful women around him to mop his brow and comfort him.

Prince Zanda had advised Unava to proclaim the following month a Festival of Reunification, cleverly suggesting by this that there had been no invasion, merely the joyful reunion of a planetary family separated by oceans.

After five days of celebration in the city, and with no sign of their warriors, the captains of the ships standing five miles offshore had received no information. The few remaining commanders found themselves facing a completely unprecedented situation. Of course, they sent further scouting parties in small boats to investigate, but when they too failed to return—the captains stopped permitting this after the seventh boat disappeared with all occupants—the dilemma seemed to assume intolerable proportions.

I couldn't resist taking a quick foray through their ships, since I knew what I observed would be of some value to Zanda. His midwayers were no more able to break through the astral veils of the opposition midwayers who'd stayed to protect the ships than the far fewer midwayers with the invasion fleet were capable of penetrating Prince Zanda's subspace shielding. In short, neither side possessed any good intelligence about the intentions of the leadership of the other.

I heard the frustration building up aboard the bridge of the main commander's vessel as the final boat, together with another eight of that commander's most loyal adjutants, failed to reappear. The commander's angry discussions with his remaining crew were too confusing to report in detail, but the unavoidable conclusion reached was always the same. The large troop ships, with their oceangoing keels, were unable to come closer to the shore than two miles because of the many coral reefs in the warm waters surrounding the continent. And how many boats and men were they prepared to continue sending into a completely unknown situation, never to be seen again?

"Sir, we can try trimming the keels off. Perhaps we'd . . ." began a junior officer, blurting it out before he'd thought the plan through.

"And how would we return, idiot?"

"Well, perhaps just one, sir. One boat . . ."

"And you? You'll take her in, will you?" The commander's voice softened somewhat as he realized that he had to try everything to find out what had happened. If he failed to do that, he didn't hold out much hope of avoiding certain death upon his return.

"To be honest," I heard him confide to a trusted junior colleague, "after this debacle I doubt if they're going to let any of us live."

"Regardless?"

"I'll give him a chance—one boat. That's all. After this . . ." The commander swept his hand around at the nearly two hundred boats anchored in a great flotilla stretching as far as he could see. "What is this? A farce? A tragedy? Have we won or lost? Is it some kind of magic we know nothing about?"

"No harm in trying one, then, sir." The junior officer clearly wasn't going to attempt to address the unanswerable.

"We have to be able to show we tried everything. D'you see: We have to, well, do everything . . ."

"Wouldn't be right otherwise, sir."

Sawing off the keel of a large sailing ship while at sea should never be undertaken lightly. Even in an age of underwater breathing apparatus, it would be a rash decision. In this case it took two weeks, and the loss of thirteen men, to hack away a substantial section of the large, hardwood slab of timber. They'd had to sacrifice the ship's close-woven fabric sails. These they then cut into pieces and sewed together into large cones. After covering them in a coating of pitch and allowing them to dry out for a few days, they attached ropes to the top of the cones and lowered them into the water with a diver inside each one. Needless to say, the cones were only marginally effective. When seawater wasn't leaking in, the devices allowed divers a few minutes of breathable air. Due to their shape, however, they made work on the keel almost impossible. They had to be scrapped after the third man drowned in one of them, all of which slowed the laborious process down to a crawl.

By this time, the fleet had to deal with another pressing problem—they were fast running out of food and fresh drinking water. Fish could be found plentifully around the coral banks, but they weren't easy to catch and at best barely provided a starvation diet.

The real problem was water.

It rained briefly on a couple of evenings. On the first, they barely caught a drop on any of the ships while they all struggled to arrange their sails to collect the rainwater. The second storm was more prolonged and they were prepared for it, but, of course, it halted work on the keel.

Another mystery entered the picture as the ship, with its considerably stunted keel, was readied for action. Now dangerously top-heavy, it was wallowing around in the heavy swell when one of the small boats sent to within half a mile of the coast reported hearing the faint sound of music and gaiety echoing over the water. The sounds hadn't lasted long, since the wind had soon changed direction, and the gaiety seemed so improbable two of the men believed they must have been hallucinating and were reticent to tell the captain what they'd heard. By the next morning they'd relented and, in spite of the scornful response they received, they insisted that they were telling the truth.

They'd both heard the music. So how could they have been imagining it?

Under any conditions, the report of music drifting over the sea from a city under siege would seem improbable at best. Under the tense conditions in the captain's cabin, it was taken in a rather different way. It had to be magic! How could all those noble warriors simply disappear off the face of the Earth?

This belief had been rejected by the leadership when it first came up among the deckhands as a rumor that passed from ship to ship with amazing speed. With the disappearance of the party they'd sent aboard the keel-less ship—now wallowing on its side in the shallows close to the shore—even the more rational among them were starting to become convinced that some dark sorcery was afoot. It was the only plausible explanation—and it had the additional attraction of being the only explanation that might save their lives if and when the ships returned back home to the waiting crowds.

When I reported back to Janda-Chi and told the Princes and the council what I'd seen of the mood onboard the ships, they broke into gales of laughter. Apparently, it was one of the outcomes that hadn't been anticipated. Yet, as the laughter suggested, being thought of as sorcerers served their purposes perfectly.

"After this, they certainly won't try it again in a hurry," Unava squeezed out between laughs. "We've got them where we want them, right?"

When the laughter died down, more serious issues needed to be addressed. The immediate impact of the invasion had been effectively muted, but the next stages would have to be handled extremely carefully.

"The strategy worked beautifully," I heard Prince Zanda tell the council telepathically, "but the women can't be expected to keep up the charade for very much longer."

"They might get to like it too much!" This from one of the younger council members to some rueful laughter.

"What's important is that the truth must not get back to the barbs. Whatever happens, we have to stop that. Agreed?" Unava talked over the laughter, reasserting his leadership in the chamber. "Agreed, everybody? If killing needs to be done, we're going to have to do it. Someone will have to . . ."

The laughter ceased at Unava's flat statement of reality. They were proud of the lack of violence on Zandana and had dispensed with military and police over two hundred years ago. Even when they still required a police force, they had long since abolished the death penalty. Murder had become unheard of for at least five hundred years. So Unava's words were heavily freighted with all the memories of the long struggle to put killing behind them. They'd been proud of their achievement. No one wanted to kill anybody.

Yet this quandary had to be faced.

Part of the strategy that had been successful so far had included the death of those barbarians unwilling to become absorbed into the nation's culture. Perhaps the council had acquiesced to this in the excitement of the moment without really absorbing what they were agreeing to.

"First, we'll need to get the work on the island finished. How's that moving along?" Unava asked, cutting into the silence. At this, some of the council members looked puzzled.

"Island?"

"Should be ready for them, sir . . ." some scrabbling with papers on the table, " . . . I'd say within a week, sir."

"Are the women going to hang on that long? It's been five weeks already." Unava looked around the table, trying to catch the eye of the four women on the council. Unlike the men present, all of whom, it seemed to me, were still suffering from shock at the thought of all the killing that would have to take place, the women appeared to have no problem with murder. They'd made that clear when the tactic was originally discussed.

"What island? What are you taking about?" One of the members had missed some of the planning meetings while he was conducting the town hall meetings prior to the invasion.

"We won't have any difficulty with the women, sir. Perhaps a few, a very few." Sephira, the senior woman on the council, arched her eyebrows. "We can take care of it. Leave it to us, sir."

"Will someone please tell me about this island?" Louder and more insistent this time.

"Ah! yes, of course. You weren't here for this." Unava's mind was elsewhere, I could tell from his tone. "Things have changed a bit, you'll probably be pleased to hear it. It's to minimize the killing. You know Gibram Island?"

"Off the south coast—the uninhabited one?"

"Gibram, yes. That's where we'll be putting most of the barbs—the ones we can't absorb immediately into the workforce. Of course, there will always be a few who'll resist. And those we'll have to deal with." Unava looked meaningfully at Sephira.

All four women were nodding in agreement.

"There'll be some, sir, who might even enjoy it." The women laughed, while the men around the table seemed to be busily fussing with paperwork.

"We've been boring wells for water and clearing some of the land for buildings. The barbs will be moved there as soon as the wells are dug. There's plenty of small game on the island, so they won't starve. We'll provide them with simple tools and they can build their own dwellings."

"Sir, how far is it from the mainland? Gibram—I've never been there myself."

"Far enough—a couple of hundred miles, a little more perhaps. Quite far enough. And there's a strong current running through the straits. We'll get them there on fishing boats; they know the waters down there. Then we'll leave 'em to it."

"It's the kindest way," Janda-Chi chimed in telepathically. "The midwayers will keep an eye on them and report back to us. If they're showing signs of wanting to join us, work with us, then we'll bring 'em back over."

"And if some refuse to go?"

"Those are the ones we'll be dealing with." Sephira was smiling an odd smile as she left the statement hanging in the air.

❉ ❉ ❉

I'd been expounding earlier on what I've come to learn about mortal reincarnation. This is clearly an area in which many of the great religions disagree, with fundamental misunderstandings on both sides of the issue.

Where we find the belief in reincarnation most firmly held is in those religions that still retain some small traces of Lemurian influence. After the first cataclysm to affect the islands of Mu, a number of survivors traveled widely to create settlements in China and Japan, up the Indus Valley to Tibet, and along much of the western coastline of Central and South America.

There are some detailed variations, for example, between the Indian religious tradition of the transmigration of souls and the Buddhist rejection of a singular soul in favor of the concept of an individual stream of consciousness, which expresses itself in a series of lifetimes. Interestingly, one aspect of Buddhist cosmology comes closest to the truth when Buddhists maintain that rebirth can occur across a number of realms of existence.

Since anyone drawn to be reading these words is almost certain to be a reincarnate, whether you are aware of it or not, you will likely appreciate the delicacy of a reincarnate's place in the world. And if you've had a sufficient need to know to have been made aware of a previous life, you will also know that there will be a good reason, within the context of your current lifetime, for possessing this information.

You see, reincarnation should never be promoted as a general doctrine—because it's not a general phenomenon. It's an aspect of life that is far more important for each individual to discover for him- or herself. When reincarnation becomes enshrined in any belief system's doctrine, it will lead inevitably to confusion and intellectual dispute, since being a reincarnate will not feel intuitively true to the majority of people.

In this way reincarnation is likely to continue to be subject to disagreement. An adherent of a Western religion, for instance, might suggest that Indian society has suffered from the consequences of its belief in reincarnation; that reincarnation leads to a rigid social order, in which each person is scornful of those lower in the hierarchy as karmically deserving of their position.

A thoughtful Indian might then reply by asking, How can anyone think it's possible to perfect oneself in only one lifetime?

There is some truth in both views, and just as much mutual misapprehension.

As is now generally known, Greek influence on the birth of Christianity supported personal reincarnation, as did a number of Gnostic sects, until Christian dogma settled on salvation through grace and rejected all belief in previous lives. Reincarnation flowered again briefly in the Christian West between the eleventh and thirteenth centuries, as one of the fundamental doctrines of the Cathars, who believed in salvation through progressive self-perfection.

Christianity's traditional grip over much of critical thought in the West—which seems to be continuing in some quarters to this day—has, with few exceptions, discouraged any serious interest in reincarnation. Consequently, when cases have been subjected to impartial scrutiny and an authentic correlation with a past life has been demonstrated, these instances have been cavalierly dismissed for lack of further definitive evidence or simply rejected out of hand as impossible.

I suspect that if it could be established for certain that reincarnation exists, after an initial surge of excitement over all the claims and counterclaims, it would make no difference whatsoever to the lives of the vast majority of people. Perhaps there is a clue to the mystery in this probable response, since the vast majority of people will be first-timers who won't have had any previous lifetimes.

There will also be reincarnates who have no current access to memories of their previous lives and yet have a profound intuitive sense of having lived before—and this needs be an authentic self-realization, not merely the impression of some storefront psychic or clairvoyant. For you, I counsel patience, because unless there are other pressing reasons, you will be unlikely to recall a particular lifetime if there isn't a real need to do so. Life is complex enough and, unless the quality of a reincarnate's spiritual or emotional life is substantially improved by this knowledge, it will have little value and could even retard normal spiritual progress.

It should be clear by now that the Multiverse functions on a need-to-know basis, and I've come to believe that it's to everyone's benefit that it should continue to do so. "A little knowledge can be a dangerous thing" is one of those clichés that holds true for most sentient species. This isn't to disparage the acquisition of knowledge, of course, but perhaps is more of a warning to be cautious of any premature action based on insufficient knowledge.

However, if you have suffered a serious trauma or experienced an unresolved issue in a previous life, then echoes of this will likely appear in subsequent incarnations, until the imprint in the subtle energy bodies has been released. In Mein Host's case, one of these imprints—produced as a result of brutal and humiliating torture in a prior lifetime—was only released when he defied arbitrary authority as a schoolboy and regained his personal power. If there isn't good reason for you to know about previous lives, Mein Host assures me, you can count yourself fortunate. It means you have come into this incarnation free and fresh, with no long-term karmic baggage. What you've learned in your previous incarnations contributes to the wisdom you bring to the choices you make in this lifetime.

You have, in short, no need to know.

Be happy about that.

7

A Resonant Scream

Revenge Served Cold, Lemurian Culture, the Storm, and Being Kind

Whether or not all cults are repositories for reincarnates—generally in the form of rebel angels—Mein Host had a dramatic experience somewhat later in his life when he was living in New York City in the late 1970s that suggested at least some cults functioned in this way.

Walking along Lexington Avenue early one evening and passing the recently built Citicorp building, he stopped to admire the engineering that must have gone into calculating the tremendous cantilever upon which the skyscraper was perched. Turning to continue up the street, he saw a crowd gathering around the entrance of the small church tucked into the northeast corner of the site.

The Lutheran Church had originally owned the property and sold it to Citicorp with the proviso that a new church be built in exactly the same spot, designed to appear harmonious with the larger building, and yet visibly separate from it. It was this requirement to avoid any support columns for the skyscraper passing through the church that necessitated the immense cantilever. In spite of giving up architecture as a profession, my ward never lost his interest in it. So, seeing a crowd entering the intriguingly designed little church, he took the opportunity to join them and take a look at the interior.

Once inside the entrance hall, it was evident from some of the clothing—men in white and women in saris—that the gathering was one of the New York guru Sri Chinmoy's regular weekly meditations.

In 1970s New York, it was impossible to be unaware of Sri Chinmoy: his blank face with the slightest of enigmatic smiles, eyeballs uplifted in what the viewer was intended to think was a state of cosmic consciousness, gazed from billboards, leaflets, and posters on the sides of buses. A self-proclaimed avatar, he was known for his colossally improbable claims. He's said to have written 1,500 books and 115,000 poems, composed 20,000 songs, painted 200,000 paintings, and, during his eight hundred peace concerts, he could be seen playing up to fifteen different musical instruments.

His claims, including one that he had once lifted seven thousand pounds with one arm, were so outrageous that he'd made himself something of a laughingstock among more mature spiritual seekers. Mein Host once saw Chinmoy playing his music on a Manhattan cable-TV show, and I heard him joking to a friend afterward that, even though the man might play fifteen instruments, he plays every one of them badly.

Still, Chinmoy attracted a substantial following including some prominent musicians and well-known athletes. The guru made a number of demands of his devotees, including adopting a life of celibacy; abstaining from meat, alcohol, and recreational drugs; and living a pure life—not dissimilar to Mary Ann's dictates for her little flock.

When Mein Host found himself being herded together with about a hundred of Sri Chinmoy's followers into the main hall of the church, and saw the greatly enlarged, black-and-white photo of the guru hanging there, he decided to join them in their meditation.

As the atmosphere quieted and the meditation started, I watched my ward, eyes closed, settling into the longer, slower breathing rhythms of a calm, meditative state. Minutes passed. Some people had their eyes firmly closed, while others gazed up in devotion at the guru's photograph. I imagined that they were trying to emulate the "transcendent state of consciousness" Chinmoy claims he was in when the photo was taken in 1967.

There were one or two hurriedly suppressed coughs, but otherwise the silence was uninterrupted. The church is well below street level, so busy Lexington Avenue traffic became the distant hiss of white noise.

Everyone was sitting on the floor—over a hundred people, mostly men, I saw to my surprise. Meditation groups generally attract a higher proportion of women than men.

My ward sat, his back upright, in a single lotus, when I observed an unexpected flaring of energy in his emotional body. Suddenly, a single intense scream split the silence. It was shockingly loud, very short, its volume amplified even more by the silence it shattered. I'll let my ward continue the story, since, for him, the scream resulted from an internal prompting of which I wasn't aware.

> I was deep into the meditation when I started having this unusual feeling. It wasn't fear exactly, but I had the sense that something was going on beneath my level of awareness—so it wasn't that comfortable. I stayed with the feeling for a couple of minutes, hoping it would lift if I just allowed it to be.
>
> Then, before I could control it, this scream came barreling up from somewhere deep within me and out through my open throat. I was as surprised as everyone else must have been. Of course, no one would have known who it was.
>
> I was even more surprised when I opened my eyes and found myself surrounded by Nazi concentration camp guards in full uniform. Each was sitting, like me, in meditation, where previously a Chinmoy disciple sat, and each one had an expression of terror on his face.
>
> At the time I didn't know why I screamed; in a way it wasn't really me. I couldn't stop it, until I did. It echoed around the church like a rifle shot. I've wondered since then whether it was all me—my fears—or one of my subpersonalities perhaps, projecting its childhood terror of Nazis out onto a group of perfectly innocent devotees. But why, then, did I have an immediate awareness they were camp guards? Why not German Air Force officers—they were the ones who'd dropped the bombs on my head.

I'll pick up the narrative again to assure him that what he saw in those moments of truth was a real manifestation, facilitated by an agreement between all the companion angels present. It occurred not primarily for my ward's benefit but because the angels of those present who were reincarnated SS officers—and by no means all were—deemed it necessary for those people to gain some sense of their previous lives.

Strangely, this perception had nothing much to do with Mein Host. He was simply the right person, at the right place, at the right time. He was psychically open by this point in his life and had learned to trust his intuition sufficiently to be able to let go and allow whatever needed to be expressed to come out. Here he was being used to create a shock, one powerful enough to momentarily shake up the reincarnates' imprinted memory and create a group hallucination—but, in this case, a true hallucination. They needed to know who they were.

There would be many times ahead in which Mein Host would be used by the angels in this manner, and I've heard him more than once maintain his gratitude to Mary Ann for setting the stage for him to learn the crafts of a shaman.

I don't want to paint Mary Ann with the same broad brush as Sri Chinmoy, but I've come to see that there are certain similarities between the leaders of cults that attract reincarnates. Some of these cult leaders find themselves at some point held to account for fraud and misrepresentation; others are accused, rightly or wrongly, of sexual misconduct as well. The cults to which reincarnates are drawn tend to be those that explore unconventional social behavior and expose taboos in the more extreme ways.

However, at Xtul in 1966, the focus of each person's attention was on pure survival during the day and on complicated spiritual and cosmological issues during the interminable evening meetings. Mein Host contends that there was hardly any energy left over at Xtul for sex. Besides, he says, they were all living and sleeping so publicly, there was little chance for any intimacy, even if a couple were so inclined. There was one exception to this which surprised and puzzled my ward when it happened. In spite of his devotion to the Goddess, I knew he'd never shown any signs of being sexually attracted to Mary Ann—if anything, he tells me, rather the opposite. So when, late one night, she beckoned him over to the curtained-off area she and Robert made their sleeping quarters, I saw the surprise on his face. Nothing like this had happened before.

Everyone else was asleep as my ward picked his way carefully between the bodies. Mary Ann appeared to him to be alone in the tiny space when he pushed aside the curtain and stepped inside. The Oracle gestured for him to sit on the floor in front of her. Then, without saying a word, she shrugged off the light silk gown she was wearing and stood before him in the quivering candlelight, completely naked.

To Mein Host, this was completely unexpected. The intense closeness they'd had from time to time—always, I might add, on Mary Ann's terms—had never had sexual overtones. They had never even kissed and, as far as I knew my ward's intentions, what engrossed him was their spiritual relationship—nothing more. In this situation, he clearly had no idea what was expected of him.

He sat quite still. He couldn't see her face in the dim light, the candle only throwing its glow over her nakedness. So, having no other choice, he looked at her body with as much objectivity as he could summon.

She held the pose for perhaps seven seconds. One knee was crooked slightly in front of the other, her body at a slight angle, her left hand on her hip. She had well-proportioned and surprisingly firm breasts, and a neatly groomed, reddish bush covering her sex. After that seven-second interval, she stooped for the gown and shooed the lad out of the tiny room.

He has commented afterward that he found the whole scene entirely lacking in erotic content. Had it been a sexual seduction, he says, he would certainly have known what to do. Yet, although he wouldn't have been able to express it back then, he'd had no previous experience with such a narcissistic personality.

As it turns out, her unexpected act had more to do with provoking a reaction from her husband, Robert, than eliciting any kind of sexual response from Mein Host. I can confirm this because I was able to observe what Mein Host couldn't see: Robert was lying awake and watching from a dark corner.

After Mary Ann failed to get a rise out of Robert, what my ward didn't know until this moment is the reason she gave her husband for her strange behavior. I overheard her telling Robert that she did it to pay back Mein Host with a "quick flash" for an insulting remark the lad had made about her neck—implying that she was old—when he had first met her six years earlier.

Robert, it appeared, had long forgotten my ward's tasteless remark and evidently had no inkling his wife's striptease performance was intended to provoke an emotional reaction in him. I believe it was the first time Mary Ann showed her hand in what was to become a long, seven-year process of humiliating her husband in private, or in front of members of her inner circle. For the rest of the community Robert remained respected as the Teacher of the Process.

Mary Ann was a woman who enjoyed her revenge served cold.

❉ ❉ ❉

After that last evening in Prince Janda-Chi's HQ up in the mountains, I realized I'd seen enough of the strategy the Princes had developed to counter the invasion to be reasonably confident that I was off the hook. But I really didn't like that look on Sephira's face. The cold-blooded nature of it and the unstated implication that she would quietly kill those barbarians who didn't readily comply with the Princes' plan had shocked me.

It made me realize that females of any physical species that are prepared to handle sexual warfare in such a detached manner would be just as likely to bring the same level of detachment to dispatching those caught in their webs. That was not something I wanted to stay around for, thank you very much! And even if some hitch emerged later, I doubted that the Princes, having already claimed the initial success for themselves, would then try to hold me responsible.

I knew it was time to leave when I looked out to sea the next morning and the masts of the fleet were no longer visible; it must have sailed at the dawning. I imagined the stories the barbarians would be concocting on their return—the terrifying and utterly mysterious magic they faced, how their warriors were disappearing all around them, how they were the sole survivors who'd bravely battled the invisible forces to a bloody standstill before escaping with their lives. Yes, I remember thinking, it's definitely time to make my graceful exit if I'm starting to use my imagination. I'd gotten away with it once, blurting out my idea.

With these thoughts foremost in my mind, I returned to the Transport Center, this time to find my friendly seraph preparing for a trip back to Earth, very much as if she might have been waiting for me. But, no, she assured me with an enigmatic smile when I asked her, she'd made dozens of trips since she'd last seen me. So I certainly wasn't anyone special, no one worth waiting for, anyway.

We didn't speak after that, and before I knew it I was back on Earth.

Since the ice had withdrawn, the Transport Center on Earth where I landed was located among the new-growth sequoia trees on the West Coast of the North American continent.

I decided not to return to Prince Caligastia's headquarters in the mountains of Romania, in an area that remained unaffected by the radioactive fallout from the war. In fact, it was the obvious proximity of the Transport Center to the Pacific Ocean that suggested I first visit the islands of Mu and see the progress Vanu and Amadon had been making with their Lemurian civilization. Moving between various places on the planet for a Watcher is as simple as setting our intention and, with a barely discernible shift of space or time, we are where we wish to be.

Under more normal planetary conditions—for example, before the rebellion broke out and this world became isolated—it worked differently. Then, we angels merely responded to necessity. One activity led naturally to the next. We didn't have to think about the moral value of our actions or make impulsive choices we would later regret. We had no need to concern ourselves with right or wrong, or good or bad. In a sense, we were almost unable to make mistakes. We had no choice but to be in the right place, at the right time, and doing the right thing.

This was what was so shocking about the Lucifer Rebellion. As angels, we'd never been presented with such an extraordinarily important choice before. We knew nothing of the three previous rebellions so had no precedent from which to draw. We were appallingly vulnerable and far too easily carried along by the blazing rhetoric of our leaders.

In our minds we became the freedom fighters. We were exposing the inefficiency and corruption in MA's bureaucracy. We would show

MA up for the fraud it was perpetrating, we would denounce the conspirators before the entire watching Multiverse, we would change everything. Us!

It sounds so foolish as I write it down. So grandiose. So full of pride. So easily entranced. Would I ever have made such a frivolous choice, I wonder, had I been previously permitted to fail and experience the consequences of my mistakes?

Mein Host is reminding me that I'm indulging in nostalgia and self-pity again, so let me state clearly here that I have no regrets. Yes, I was foolish to have followed Lucifer into rebellion, for all the deluded reasons I mention above. I was naive and impulsive, granted.

Yet, for all that, there was this "voice" that whispered *revolution* in our minds—the mysterious voice some of us heard—and that most of us didn't. A soft female voice full of wisdom and love that accompanied us faithfully throughout the uprising, urging us on to be courageous, to hold on to our ideals, to defy MA and all her minions. A voice of encouragement and gentle enthusiasm, who was there until, suddenly, she wasn't.

One day, soon after everything started going awry back in the city of Dalamatia, the voice simply withdrew. With no explanations. No apologies. One moment I felt there was this deep loving intelligence guiding us into and through the uprising; the next moment, silence.

Never to be heard from again.

I've had many occasions since that time to ponder this mystery, wondering to whom this voice belonged. It was no delusion—too many of us were hearing her. She was loving and playful, yet she insisted on secrecy. She seemed to whisper on a frequency unheard by the bureaucrats, by those who remained faithful to MA, by those who turned away from Lucifer. Those were the ones, she let us know, who were to remain untroubled by our revolutionary zeal, who were not to be part of the Great Experiment.

She let it be known that we were the special ones, the chosen ones. It was us to whom she spoke. Not them. Shush. Don't tell them anything . . .

Then, when this thought comes to me, my self-pity drops away and I remember that far deeper currents are flowing under the surface of my life. After all, I would never have had all the experiences I've been having had I not joined the uprising . . . even if I had no idea of how challenging the consequences of doing it would be.

As Watchers, however, we're required to choose our destinations. I assume it is part of our preparation for our mortal incarnation.

However, of the three Transport Centers on Earth then in use, the fact I was deposited so close to the American north coast had to have been a sign I unconsciously absorbed. Because before I had much chance to think about reporting back to Caligastia, I was being whisked off to Vanu's Lemurian capital, which I recalled was built on one of the larger islands, south of the equator.

My first reaction on arriving was astonishment. Surely, I hadn't been away this long!

The capital, though not yet fully completed, was a wonder to behold. It was built over a series of smaller islands, connected by bridges and hollowed out with underwater tunnels and interconnecting canals. Small skiffs skimmed the water—which made me think of water taxis from another era.

The buildings were massive and seemed to grow naturally out of the sea, which often lapped at their stone skirts. Wide, flat platforms, formed of enormous interlocking blocks of granite, stretched out into the sea, with larger boats tied up alongside and a hive of human activity loading and unloading the goods that were transported between the islands.

Fish of all sizes and species were laid out on the polished obsidian slabs in the open markets. Women dressed in brightly colored sarongs, some with pitchers balanced atop their heads, moved in a relaxed flow between the open stalls. People, in general, appeared confident and happy with their lives. Overall, it was a prosperous sight.

A large structure lay at the top of a wide avenue that rose in a succession of broad, shallow steps up to its base. At first glance I'd taken it to be a flattened pyramid, but in moving closer, I could see that it was composed of seven levels that seemed to stack one on top of another, each smaller than the one below it, so as to give the appearance of a roughly pyramidical shape. Ceremonial staircases rose up between the platforms; the massive stonework was decorated with large carvings, which, I was amused to see, were of the fierce animals they'd left behind on the mainland.

As I moved around the city, I was struck by the apparent simplicity of life, especially compared to what I'd just been witnessing on Zandana. Perhaps if I'd have visited the Zandanan barbarians, I might have observed more similar conditions to what I was seeing in the residential sectors of the city.

Although both worlds were roughly parallel in terms of the timing of the emergence of intelligent life and the arrival of their Princes' missions, Earth's overall development was badly retarded by the chaos and confusion Caligastia had been sowing since the rebellion. Yet, here in Lemuria, I was finding something different, something rather more encouraging. The culture hadn't yet reached the level of refinement that I saw in the city of Zandan, but neither did the people seem so bewitched by their own self-importance.

Whereas the wealthy Zandan citizens built splendid houses and took great pride in their personal possessions, the Lemurians enjoyed living in small huts perched a dozen feet above the water on bamboo poles sunk into the lava and coral.

The Lemurians were evidently still a communal people, frequently living in large extended families, their pole houses connected by a web of bridges and platforms suspended above the waves. Children played their games, running in and out of the huts, sometimes swinging like monkeys from the rope bridges before dropping, squealing with pleasure and fear, into the water below.

A small group of old men sat on three-legged wooden stools and gathered on a suspended platform formed at the nexus of three walkways. I could see that they were playing a game, moving colored pebbles through a series of carved, concave indentations in a flat piece of polished wood. They were filled with excitement and laughter, but I didn't stay long enough to grasp the rules of their game. I was eager to see more of Mu before I reported to Vanu. He was always most curious to hear of the latest developments on Zandana.

As I traveled around, I found the contrast between the two worlds growing more extreme. The geography of the islands of Mu, for example, numbering in the thousands in a long chain straddling the equator, had evidently discouraged the growth of cities. The population appeared to be spread relatively evenly among the islands; the only large aggregations of people lived in pole houses encircling the three main power centers.

These were the rare places where, I was told later, telluric fumes seeping up through volcanic fissures in the rock could produce trance-inducing effects in some people.

The first of these places, apparently, was discovered some thousands of years earlier, and quite by accident. As the colonists spread through the islands, settling where the fishing was good or where there was some protection from the worst of the elements, a clan of villagers made their homes, without realizing it, over one of these fissures.

Since the islands were volcanic, the settlers had already seen some places where magma was still oozing out of the ground and others in which hot, sulfurous water gathered in pools that steamed quietly in jungle clearings. What they hadn't come across was a place in which the fumes were rich in ethylene, a natural, colorless gas with the delicate scent of wildflowers.

Drawn to settle there by the sweet scent, as well as the excellent fishing, they were unaware of the consciousness-altering potential of the fumes, which seeped into their huts every once in a while. It wasn't a common occurrence, but when it did happen, they noticed that it was always at the time of the full moon. Strangely, the fumes did not affect everyone in the community; adolescent girls appeared to be the most vulnerable.

The fumes had a subtle influence, by all accounts—nothing like the group madness that befell villagers in later ages who unknowingly ate bread infected with the ergot fungus. Here on Mu, there were no hallucinations, no screaming fits, no foaming at the mouth or tearing of hair, nothing to interfere with the natural rhythms of their lives. It was simply that a few of their young girls would periodically fall into a trance and some would even speak in strange riddles of unknown places.

Lemurian civilization around forty-five thousand years ago was a spiritually charged culture. Much of what might be dismissed as superstition today was intensely relevant to the citizens of Mu. Their connection with Mother Earth and with natural events allowed them access to her secrets. A sudden change of temperature, the direction of the flight of birds, the quality of the wind or rain, the forms in the clouds, the pattern of ripples on the surface of water, the smoke from volcanic vents—all these and more were regarded as signs or portents. Not only was this "superstition" a constant reminder to the Lemurians of their place in the natural order of life, but it allowed the midwayers to subtly influence human behavior, when required.

If, for example, one of Vanu's midwayers wished to guide an individual Lemurian in a particular direction to accomplish a task of mutual interest, he'd be likely to work in conjunction with the primary local nature spirits. They, then, might coordinate aspects within their realm so as to ensure, by the flight of birds or the direction of the wind, that the Lemurian would have natural signs to follow.

If this seems to have little relevance to modern life, perhaps a digression from Mein Host's life will serve to demonstrate how these hidden powers can be activated under certain conditions.

On a beautiful summer day in July 1983, Diana Ross was due to give a free concert in New York's Central Park. She'd been the top disco singer for a decade, but with the diminished popularity of disco this concert was designed to put her back on the map.

At the time, Mein Host was living on the twenty-fifth floor of the Eldorado, an art deco apartment building overlooking the west side of Central Park at Ninety-first Street. Mein Host would jokingly refer to the park as his back garden and liked to make a point of going to the various free concerts presented there. Diana Ross's would be no exception.

It was one of those balmy New York summer days, not a cloud in the sky, and there were well over half a million concertgoers already on hand when my ward arrived. He stayed at the rear of the enormous crowd, where there was more space—I knew he liked to dance when the music started.

As with most concerts in the park, it did not start at 3:00 p.m., as promoted, but at least half an hour later, so by the time Mein Host arrived many people who'd been waiting in the park for hours were already starting to grow restless. For such a glorious day there was a curiously disturbed atmosphere.

Here are some of Mein Host's journal entries, written on returning from the concert:

I arrived shortly after 3:00 to a very warm, sunbaked, and dusty central field. Walking through the west side of the park amid mainly young blacks, I caught the drift of at least five separate altercations. Nothing too serious, but enough to remind me of the contrast with three of the previous events I'd attended—the Elton John concert, the 1982 peace demonstration, and the Simon and Garfunkel reunion—at which the atmospheres had been excellent—stable and uplifting.

I recall thinking at the time that there was likely to be trouble, and with that thought I headed into the thick of it. If there was going to be an explosion, then I would sooner be there to see if there was anything I could do to defuse it.

While this might be considered a somewhat grandiose intention, I'm of the opinion that it was likely his companion angel's best way of hurrying him along—encouraging him to feel that he could be of service.

He found "his tree," just inside the path running to the back of the meadow. I knew he thought of it as his place of power. Here he could dance freely, so that's where he usually went to watch the concerts.

After a few minutes, he was approached by a Hare Krishna devotee who tried to get him to come to the group's Saturday Vegetarian Feast later that day. Then I heard her telling him that she'd been harassed by some of the young men hanging around at the back of the park.

I know this confirmed for Mein Host that violence was in the air. Even I could feel it: a horrible sense of an imminent overflowing of anger and resentment. Ms. Ross, for all her professional success, was evidently not well-liked. Perhaps many in the crowd were really here simply because they envied or resented her success and wanted to pull her down off her pedestal. And, of course, disco, on which she'd made her name as a solo artist, was just starting to be eclipsed by punk—another reason she was probably being so vigorously scorned by the younger crowd.

Standing under his tree was a CBS-TV van beside him and behind him, across the path, stood row upon row of police officers. Here he is again, describing what was going on:

Thick rows of policemen and women were gathered in the smaller, treed enclosure behind me—over eight hundred of them, I'd read somewhere. It was intriguing to observe the reactions of the young studs as they turned the corner to see this massive, low-lying blue cloud of fuzz. Mouths dropped open. "Sheeeet!" and they'd double over laughing. Others yelled "Freeze!" and postured, primate-proud, for their shrieking womenfolk. They all seemed to be just on the edge of hysteria.

Their reactions on coming across the CBS van were not dissimilar . . . [but] the tired, old-lag technicians were far too jaded to take anything but the most cursory interest in all their posturing.

At this point Mein Host must have realized that with so much restlessness and testosterone in the air, these interactions could easily turn from harmless posturing to very real violence. Something had to be done, but what? He was extremely sensitive to psychic atmospheres by this time, and this one was not good. He started dancing under the tree to the recorded music being played over the PA system as a way of trying to dissipate the negative energy in his immediate vicinity.

At least four news helicopters were hovering low at the periphery of the meadow, whipping up the leaves of the trees, their washes gusting clouds of dust across the crowded field. Large swaths of the crowd—subsequently reported as being more than eight hundred thousand—were starting to grow ever more restless, even angry, by the time the singer came onstage. Finally, she appeared. Once onstage she announced she was giving this gift of a free concert because she loved New York so much, and that she was donating a portion of her sponsor's payment for the concert to build a children's playground.

She paused after making these announcements, expecting a roar of applause. There was some clapping of hands, but not much. It seemed that the pride the crowd was supposed to feel at one of their own making it to the top was merely building the mix of envy, resentment, and angry dismissal. Most people clearly felt it was merely another publicity stunt and many of them even appeared embarrassed by her obvious self-admiration.

The response of some of the young men at the rear was less inhibited.

They'd been circling the meadow playing their boom boxes at full volume, laughing unpleasantly and shouting and cursing at anyone who complained. The attitude of this crowd was in sharp contrast to that of the previous concerts Mein Host had attended in the park before. Was this because of the rumor she was only giving the concert to kick-start her failing career? Ms. Ross had started singing, but that wasn't doing anything to lift the atmosphere. If anything, it was making the insulting and aggressive behavior even worse.

Mein Host, by this time, was dancing with all the energy of a whirling dervish. And as he was spiraling around with his eyes tightly closed, he invoked the midwayers and the nature spirits to intercede—to do something, anything they could, to disrupt what was threatening to turn into a full-scale riot.

As he whirled, I could see what he couldn't with his eyes shut. Behind him, to the northeast, a large, dark, and very menacing thundercloud was scudding rapidly toward the park. This even though, moments before, the weather had been picture-perfect.

Now people were giving the whirling crazy person a wide berth. A couple of loud arguments broke out close by; thunder rippled over the crowd, resonating with the amplified thumping of the bass drum onstage. The pitch of the helicopters' rotors suddenly changed—they must have been warned about the coming storm—as they climbed fast over the crowd, throwing up dust, hats, and paper cups in their inconsiderate haste to return to their heliports.

The diva sung on, seemingly as oblivious to the angry, disturbed, tone of the crowd, as she was to the looming disaster. The thunder roared. The skies darkened. The crowd seemed bewildered. Mein Host, aware now of what was happening around him, whirled on, more vigorously than ever, eyes closed again, singing loudly to the storm.

And then the rains came.

It poured. Vertical columns of rain, like dark, standing waves, marched over the crowd, soaking everyone to the skin. The wind changed direction constantly, growing stronger by the minute, throwing spray every which way.

Still Diana Ross sang on.

"It's just water!" She was shouting between songs. "It won't hurt!"

But she was taunting the crowd and the crowd clearly knew it. Whatever they might have felt about Ms. Ross as individuals, a collective anger was now building that could only end in a massive riot.

It was becoming so overcast, it was like twilight. The rain beat down unmercifully, turning every spot of ground to mud that was unoccupied by a body. Eventually, the music ground to a halt. No one was taking notice any more. Every single one of those eight hundred thousand people was preoccupied with trying to stay dry.

Well, not for long. The rain was implacable. It came down with the ferocity of an Asian monsoon.

Here's Mein Host again, summarizing the debacle:

Harder and harder it rained. There was no protection from the wind as it constantly gusted in different directions, beating water into every nook and crevice of a shivering human being.

Then, something broke the psychic atmosphere. More people were roaring with laughter now, slipping and sliding in the mud. Gone was all the jeering and abuse, Diana Ross forgotten about. There was nothing else to do but to surrender to the maelstrom; total immersion in the nature of the situation. A baptism of water arranged by the elements, not only to cool down the escalating violence suffusing the concert, but to give a large and unruly mob the chance of a truly shared experience!

So that's how Ms. Ross's Central Park concert ended. The impending violence had been transformed by the storm into a mass of laughing, singing, sliding, dancing, rain-sodden, mud-covered New Yorkers.

Not so the next day.

Mein Host did not attend her repeat performance on Sunday, when five hundred thousand people showed up. This time violence did erupt, with reports of more than a hundred people being robbed by groups of young men on a rampage during and after the concert. Lawsuits were filed. The million dollars Ms. Ross was paid for the first concert went to pay for the second. As a consequence of the previous day's fiasco Ms. Ross initially refused to give any money for her promised playground, although she did eventually shell out a quarter of a million dollars toward building it.

So did Mein Host cause the storm? The answer is obviously, no. What he did was defuse the situation by summoning help from the mid-wayers and nature spirits. An intervention as specific as this one is only permitted when there is a request from, or an agreement with, a mortal of the realm who is aware of what he or she is doing.

Mein Host, by then in his forties, was starting to know what he was doing. He was more than aware at this point in his life that he was work-ing collaboratively with the midwayers and nature spirits. I was pleased when he felt no obvious inclination to claim that he had brought on the storm.

It was too easy to dismiss as coincidence, but in Lemuria, Mein Host's actions would have been well-understood.

❖ ❖ ❖

Apart from the cataclysms that upended entire civilizations in a single night, few times in human history has a global population undergone such rapid changes as this world has been experiencing over the last sixty years.

England and America were very different places in the 1950s and '60s than they are now, and in ways that are sometimes difficult to grasp today. The English class system, for example, which had been harshly maintained for hundreds of years, was collapsing after two world wars. It finally breathed its last toward the end of the twentieth century.

The old social orders, whether czarist feudalism, Indian religious castes, or the English class system, were strictly conservative by nature, holding their people in cultural trances in which everyone believed they knew where they fit in the social hierarchy. Naturally, there were always a few who rebelled against the social structure and took their consequent lumps for it. Yet, like members of an authoritarian cult, most human beings who are existing within restrictive social orders tend to live blink-ered lives, in which they are tacitly, or harshly, discouraged from breaking out of their inherited roles in society.

In the West, the Industrial Revolution, followed by two world wars, put an end to all that. Among the cultural shifts: new technologies required an educated populace; armies needed skilled warriors; new inventions gave rise to new industries; local wars, the growth of consumerism, and expanded tourism all broke down national barriers; better-educated men and women demanded their rights of parity; traditional religious belief systems were forced to reevaluate their doctrines in light of scientific advances; and, perhaps at the root of the changes, information became massively democratized, ultimately manifesting in the World Wide Web.

From a spiritual viewpoint, the implications of this social shift and the similar changes occurring all over the world are truly profound and probably will not be fully appreciated until after the coming transformation shakes out. However, having said that, I'm well aware that conditions on this planet from a purely materialistic viewpoint don't appear to be much improved—rather the opposite. The deterioration of the biosphere has accelerated; the political leaders in most countries are increasingly corrupt and craven; dreams of a united world have resulted in dehumanized transnational and global corporations—the list of woes is as endless as cable news.

Yet, from a spiritual standpoint, what this profound shift in human affairs has been demanding is a much higher level of personal responsibility. And, more specifically, that each of us, Watchers as well as mortals, to the extent we can assert ourselves, now has far more freedom to believe or disbelieve, to work how and where we wish, to succeed or fail, and to live the life we choose for ourselves.

By *spiritual* in this context, I mean all that is of lasting spiritual significance, which you'll be carrying through to your next existence: what you've learned about yourself, your capacity for love, your acts of kindness, your ability to forgive yourself and others, and any knowledge of value to your continuing Multiverse career.

Yet there is another aspect to my use of the word *spiritual* here, which might be less obvious. It is the spiritual freedom to make terrible mistakes in this life, so that you can learn from those mistakes when you have your life review.

There's no need to fear this occasion. Human beings are essentially good. Unless they have been bent out of shape by abuse or negligence, or the karmic consequences of a previous life, human intentions are basically kind and ethical.

This can be difficult to grasp when you look around the world at all the violence and injustice rampant in your world. But, when you focus deeper, you'll find that the world you live in is a frequency domain, one of many—a construct, a kindergarten, if you like, which has been specifically constructed for humans to discover who they truly are.

And the way some humans go about this is by exploring all the things they are not.

Perhaps the Process and other cults and communities can be appreciated in these terms: as spiritual microcosms of society in which members have a chance to discover who they are not, by submitting to the will of another person.

This certainly appears to have been Mein Host's trajectory.

⁂

Lemurians were living contentedly in a state of harmony with nature.

The islands of Mu were fertile and the fish plentiful. The people were healthy and lived long, active lives. Because their settlements were relatively evenly distributed throughout the islands, population pressure was minimal. Mu had been colonized now for over twenty thousand years and, apart from some minor scuffles, there'd been no wars and remarkably little personal violence.

The absence of large predators on the islands meant nature's tooth and claw held few threats for them. Their children played in the wild and there seemed to be no undue concern for their safety: Mother Earth would care for them. Many of the women had become knowledgeable herbalists, and the breeding of domestic animals had reached a high art. The few wild buffalo brought over on rafts from the mainland by their distant ancestors now appeared very similar to the longhorn cattle you might find on a ranch in present-day Texas. Chickens, too, descended from the red jungle fowl they had originally brought with them from Indonesia, were first domesticated on a large scale in Lemurian households.

Lemurians, in general, seemed to me to be living fulfilled and secure lives. Their temples and administrative buildings, built many millennia earlier from massive interlocking blocks of stone, had withstood many centuries of Earth tremors and were becoming more a reminder of their endless past than places of active worship or labor.

Vanu and Amadon, now accepted by most as familiar presences, continued to travel among the people. They'd both sired many children with mortal women and their progeny had become the leaders of the principal clans on the islands.

Most enjoyed an easygoing life. Families generally stayed on the island of their birth, which, in turn, seemed to reinforce their conservative tendencies. I believe this cultivated a responsibility for caring for their birthright and a desire to pass along their contented lives to their descendants.

News of life on other islands was brought by traveling bards, their long, elaborate songs never failing to make listeners aware and proud of their ancient past. As Vanu must have known, people who revere their past, who have a knowledge of an unbroken thirty thousand years of their history, want to conserve their traditions for future generations.

The people lived by a barter system, which, though limited in some ways, inherently supported honest transactions based on genuine needs. In the few small urban centers, shells were used as a convenient medium of exchange, but since the shells had no inherent value—unlike the gold coinage that Caligastia had introduced on the other side of the world— there was no temptation to hoard them. Personal ambition had been discouraged for so long that generations of Lemurians were content to live out their simple lives without wanting anything more.

If I were to summarize the general social situation in Lemuria on this tour, I'd have to say that for all the ease and comfort of their lives and their dependence on Vanu's traditional teachings, it felt to me as though something vital was missing from the culture. It was almost too placid. The challenges the people had met on their long trek across Asia and the punishing sea crossing to the islands, as well as all the demands made on the original colonizers, were no longer pressing issues in their lives. They were not an aggressive culture and so had no envy of other lands and little desire to leave their islands.

Once Vanu was certain that the focused sound and light techniques he introduced could not be easily weaponized, he permitted them for use in cutting, shaping, and lifting the cyclopean stone blocks the Lemurians used for their building work. These innovations in building were far more advanced than the general level of technology at the time, so despite these advancements in construction techniques, the artifacts used in everyday life remained somewhat primitive.

Bathing was communal; every small settlement possessed a well-appointed bathhouse, designed around a hot spring. Women could also wash their clothes in hot water, diverted from the spring and running in stone channels to a special courtyard set aside for laundering. The bath-houses became the social center of the villages, and one of the most plea-surable outings to which a Lemurian family treated itself was a visit to a bathhouse in a nearby village.

While the northern and southern extremes of the Lemurian archi-pelago could become moderately cold in their winters, most of the islands enjoyed tropical and subtropical temperatures year-round. This tempera-ture differential produced a curious phenomenon that the world wasn't to see again for many tens of thousands of years. As the weather started cooling off in the northern hemisphere, many of those living there moved toward the warmer regions for the season, and those who delighted in cooler weather traveled away from the equator. They all lived for their pleasure.

What struck me when I learned this is that families would share their homes in what you would recognize as house swapping. And if you won-der at the many similarities with contemporary life, know that human beings—their loves and jealousies, their desires and aversions, and their needs and greeds—have changed very little over the last half a million years. All that really changes is humankind's capability to slaughter increasing numbers of people and its impulse to ravage the planetary bio-sphere. These latter changes came in waves throughout history as civiliza-tions rose and fell. Some were technological, some not so much. Yet very few were wise enough to learn from the failure of their forebears. The Lemurian civilization can be thought of as the slow swelling of a wave that crested as a true planetary culture before it collapsed—as has every other civilization that followed it.

At the time I'm reporting, however, the people of Mu trusted one another. With few personal possessions and ample available food, thievery was almost completely unknown. The one "commandment" they lived by was simply "Be kind," which, I've come to believe by observing the Lemurians in their daily lives, covers all ten Mosaic commandments, yet without a possessive deity's demands for devotion and worship.

Lemuria was in many ways an ideal culture for its time. To use contemporary jargon, the people of Mu left a minimal footprint on the planet—so small that most modern anthropologists will cursorily reject any talk of such a mature civilization existing so long before the Bronze Age.

Yet the Lemurians have left their mark on many of the world's most ancient myths. Among them, the Garden of Eden, or the paradisiacal state in so many creation stories and from which humans have somehow fallen.

This is how Lemuria lives on, as the promise all humans hold in their hearts, that one day the world will become a paradise again. And a paradise it would have been by now were it not for the Lucifer Rebellion and the profoundly disturbing actions of Prince Caligastia in his guise as God of this World.

8

A Harsh Mistress

The Consul's Warning, Music on Mu, Lemurian Midwayers Withdraw, and Hurricane Inez

If the community at Xtul believed their lives for the preceding months had been hard, they had no idea what was advancing on them from far out in the Atlantic Ocean.

It was late in September 1966 and the building work had been moving steadily ahead, the focus of the community's efforts being the so-called temple, which was to house both Mary Ann and Robert. A pattern was now starting to appear, which would continue unabated for as long as Mary Ann lived. I had seen it beginning in London, with Mary Ann and Robert's special apartment at the top of the Mayfair mansion; then in Nassau, when the privileged pair lived in separate, more comfortable quarters; and now in Xtul, where all the community's available energy was being thrown into preparing the temple for their Goddess.

Mein Host was back in favor with Mary Ann, although by now his grace period was over and he was working as hard as everybody else. He continued to be wholeheartedly devoted to the Oracle and had as of yet been given no reason to discount her divinity. Dear reader, please be patient with me as I digress to place the interaction between Mary Ann and Mein Host in a deeper spiritual context.

Plate 1. *Falling into Matter.* The start of a journey into transcendence.

Plate 2. *An Unexpected Surprise.* Extraterrestrials come in all sizes.

Plate 3. *The Archaic Revival.* There are magical times ahead.

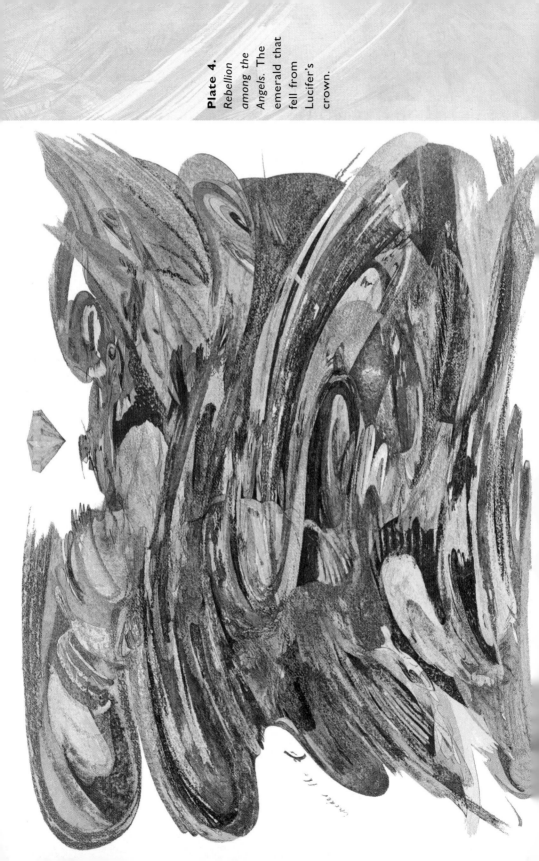

Plate 4.
Rebellion among the Angels. The emerald that fell from Lucifer's crown.

Plate 5.
A Fandor at Rest. The semi-telepathic passenger bird, extinct now for more than 30,000 years.

Plate 6. *Meditating Angel.* Wholistic reconciliation of positive and negative energies.

Plate 7. *The Old Man: Avebury.* What did the ancients know about the first dimension?

Plate 8.
Falling into Time. The seven stages of angelic redemption.

As I've already outlined, we're taught that the Multiverse consists of seven vast Superuniverses. Each of these contains one hundred thousand Local Universes and each Local Universe supports approximately ten million inhabitable planets.

I've talked about how we angels believe the creators of each Local Universe are a pair of high beings, known to us as the Creator Son and the Mother Spirit. That there are about seven hundred thousand of these pairs should demonstrate that while they are high Creator Beings in their own right, they are not to be confused with the Creator of All. This is the Prime Source who remains in the Central Universe, and yet who indwells you mortals and permeates Creation as the Invisible God, while also encompassing Creation and transcending it.

My brief in this work does not allow too much further elaboration on the Central Universe, where we are told the Prime Source exists. Putting it crudely, this Central Universe is the Universe behind the Multiverse we all inhabit. It's the primary frequency domain from which energy pours into the Local Universes to be modulated by its Creator Son and Mother Spirit into the galaxies, solar systems, planets, and ultimately the life-forms on all the worlds in each Local Universe.

In trying to describe these cosmic events and the personalities behind them, I'm bound to oversimplify a thoroughly complex affair that has been ongoing for many billions of years. You can find a more detailed description in the papers the midwayers transmitted early in the twentieth century and which have been published in *The Urantia Book*.

What I'm trying to do here is to give a broad overview of the relevant Multiverse and Local Universe personalities, as well as seeking to convey a deeper understanding of their nature and intentions.

I should mention here something that caught my attention in our training sessions before coming to this world. It has remained in my mind because it seemed to have been subtly more emphasized than some of the other facts we were being taught.

Each Local Universe, so we were told, possesses its own unique tone. This can be understood as a dominating dramatic thread that runs through the interactions of all sentient life within that specific Local Universe. The tone of this Local Universe is said to be mercy and forgiveness.

Even when I first heard that the tone was mercy and forgiveness, I was surprised that no one drew the obvious conclusions: to be merciful and forgiving clearly requires sufficient wrongdoing, or misconduct, to call forth mercy and forgiveness. This inference worried me for a time, and then when I arrived here with the Prince's mission, I promptly forgot all about it. Now, however, when I have the chance to unravel some the less apparent threads that lie behind the rebellion, I find myself drawn back to those thoughts.

I've had a chance now to observe mortal behavior on two worlds, both within this Local Universe. A small sample, granted, yet I have no reason to believe the fundamental nature of male and female mortals would be that different on any other planets in this Local Universe. The reason I can say this with some confidence is that the essential structure of mortal psychology can be thought of as a distant echo of the natures of the male and female Creator Beings of their Local Universe.

While the Multiverse supports life of every sort imaginable—celestial and material—I think you'd be surprised, after a steady diet of film and TV monsters, to find that mortal beings on all the worlds within your Local Universe have remarkable and endearing similarities. You'd certainly recognize them as your interplanetary sisters and brothers.

I trust feminists will forgive me for noting that there are indeed fundamental differences between female and male psychology and in the basic impulses that drive women and men. To simplify this, we're taught by the Melchizedek Brothers that the female energy is inwardly directed, while the male energy is outwardly driven. On the most quotidian of levels, this manifests as women caring for hearth and home, while men venture out into the world. At its best, this can be appreciated as an ideal collaboration, whereby the female energy lays the groundwork, preparing the way for the more specifically directed male energy.

While this is a generalization, each sex clearly possesses sufficient characteristics of the other so that, to a certain extent, their roles can be reversed. Yet the ubiquity of this pattern of female/male relationships in all historical cultures, both here and on Zandana, demonstrates a deeper source.

If we now keep this fundamental pattern of female/male relationships in mind, perhaps we can understand something of the division of energy and labor between our Mother Spirit and her Michaelson. The clue I've suggested might be found in the word *mother,* and its close relationship, through the Latin *mater,* to matter. From this simple substitution, I posit how deeply the Mother Spirit is embedded in language, as she is in the very matter of the Multiverse. In this way, matter can be understood as the ground of existence into which the Spirit of the Creator Son enters.

I've already proposed, in comparing Zandana and Earth, how the impact of predation on a mortal species's early development can influence the manner in which those mortals think and behave in later eras. Worlds, we were told, differ greatly in this respect.

In our training sessions, we're taught that the Life Carriers seed life onto a planet, just as the Mother Spirit supplies the essential spark that catalyzes the lifeless material. From this point, the natural evolutionary processes of mutation and natural selection take over, until, finally, a creature emerges capable of intelligent self-reflection.

I take this information on faith, since I've never had the chance to observe such a moment for myself. I recall, too, that much was made in those sessions of the care and attention Life Carriers take with their original life implantation. Life is no accident, no random concatenation of molecules somehow "miraculously" organizing themselves into organic life. They assured us of the diligence and ingenuity that went into progressively improving the Life Carrier techniques. They spoke of their extensive laboratories, the experimentation they are permitted on every tenth planet, and, most of all, they emphasized the genuine pride the Life Carriers take in their work. I have no reason to doubt my teachers when they tell me that the evolutionary life processes are meticulously designed.

Yet what has consistently concerned me, as you'll have discerned from my narrative, has been the level of violence I've seen permeating life on Earth. Whether it's strangler vines, or parasitic wasps that lay eggs inside their paralyzed victims so their hatchlings can eat their way out of living flesh; whether it's cats torturing mice, or orcas throwing seals around; or, whether it's the fearful cruelty humans can inflict on one another, I've heard this world spoken about by those with wider experience as being "the third worst in the Local Universe." And that's third worst out of ten million inhabited planets!

This digression was prompted by my sense that Mary Ann seemed to possess something of the ruthlessness of a Mother Spirit, a Creatrix who would sanction the savagery that appears so deeply embedded in life in this world. Let me be clear: I am not trying to find fault here, neither in Mary Ann, nor in the Mother Spirit. If anything, my observation tends to support Mein Host's revelation of Mary Ann's divinity.

The Mother Spirit, in creating a ground of existence on which mercy and forgiveness might at some future point be demonstrated for all to witness, would have had to prepare the turf by introducing particularly high levels of callousness into the evolutionary process itself. This would have set a stamp on what was then certain to become a dog-eat-dog world, thus ensuring that when beings capable of intelligent self-reflection emerged out of their animal ancestry, they would be forced to use their courage, their cunning, and their ingenuity in their struggle to survive. As the human species continued to expand in numbers and resourcefulness, these characteristics would be sure to create fertile conditions for the practice of mercy and forgiveness.

Mary Ann, it could also be argued, had good reason for her actions. She had led thirty young people into the wilderness and she clearly felt justified in using any method she could to weld them into a cohesive unit, able to survive the difficult conditions they faced. She was empathic enough to be well aware that morale was failing badly before throwing Mein Host out of the Garden. And indeed the group had bonded together more closely through the excitement and fear generated by his expulsion and the subsequent flagellation drama.

The timing of this turned out to be fortuitous, since the next challenge would test the community to its very limit.

It began with the surprising arrival of the British consul at Xtul's gate one day in early October 1966. This was "surprising" because no one had ever visited the place the whole time the community had been there. The consul was a plump, middle-aged man in a white linen suit. A kind man, no doubt, possibly too kind to have risen far in the cutthroat colonial service, he appeared to be a stereotype of a failed civil servant eking out his days in the boondocks of a minor province of an unimportant country— at least to his superiors in England.

The man took a quick look around, during which the members made sure to be extra nice in case he was spying for the British government. The man had a slightly panicked air about him. It seemed to me that he was trying to hurry the tour along and soon I overheard the consul telling Robert that he wanted to have his say in front of the whole group, which delighted me because it would allow me to watch everyone's reactions to whatever it was he was going to say.

Soon everyone in the community had been found and called back from where they were working and were now gathered around on the grass in front of the monastery.

"Listen, everybody. This is serious." The consul began after introducing himself, his accent instantly revealing his minor–boarding school and provincial university background, as my ward said scornfully to Peter who was standing close by.

The consul's thin blond hair was combed back and his epicene face, reddened by the sun, suggested that he hadn't spent much time out of his office. He was holding up a Panama hat in his left hand to block the sun from his eyes and gesturing with it whenever his voice rose. He was evidently trying to remain calm. As British consul, he would have considered these people his responsibility.

"There's a hurricane heading our way. And it's a bad one. It's still a few days away, near the Bahamas now, so it might weaken. But we don't know for sure what it'll do."

He let that sink in. Although it was obvious that some previous hurricane had ripped the roofs off all three buildings at some point in their history, I'd heard no one talking about how vulnerable they were right on the coast.

"I've seen a few of these before," the consul continued after evoking almost no response from the group. He wouldn't have known that the group was watching Mary Ann's face for her reaction to the news. And the Oracle's face was oddly impassive—that I did observe.

"These storms are bad! Really frightful! And look at you . . ." he gestured toward the Gulf. "You don't understand. I mean, coming from England. I didn't when I, I mean . . ." As he looked around, his voice getting louder, I could see that this wasn't what he expected at all.

"Do you people have any idea what 150-mile-an-hour winds will do to all this? With all you've done? It's going to kill the lot of you!"

The lack of obvious response was starting to rattle the man. I could hear it in his voice. Yet he was trying to keep his clear sense of alarm in check. Stiff-upper-lip, British colonial office in mien, he'd no doubt seen for himself the damage a hurricane can wreak. His sense of duty to his fellow Brits—at least most of those in the community were—must have made him determined to get across the worst that could happen.

When he still didn't get any rise out of the group, although he might have sensed the sudden fluctuation of the energy in the emotional bodies of the community members—the consul got to the point.

"You're all going to have to leave this place. It's just too dangerous. All this will disappear." He was pointing around the estate somewhat disdainfully. Acutely aware of class—in the English way—the consul had already heard enough boarding school accents on his tour of the buildings to sense that he was somehow being made a fool of, without quite knowing how. The very way these people were living was a rejection of all he believed—that was obvious. Yet they were polite and kind. They seemed to be nice people. He obviously liked them. And here they were, living like savages. They were an insult to the British Empire.

"I'll arrange for a bus to pick you all up tomorrow," he said with as much certainty as he could summon. A brief gesture from Mary Ann brought the man to a halt.

"Thank you. Thank you so much for your kindness and thoughtfulness." She fixed him with her gaze, her face a mask of gratitude. "We are grateful to you for coming all this way. You're very brave, risking your life like this, what with the hurricane coming at any time." Mary Ann was at her most unctuous. By this time I'd observed her technique well enough to know she was setting him up—this supercilious civil servant.

The consul, his red face getting redder with pride, appeared unaware that she was toying with him. It must have been impossible for him to place her in the class hierarchy.

"Really, it's verry good of you." Her slight Scottish burr was coming through charmingly.

"But this place—our place—Xtul." Her voice now took on a harder tone, and I saw the consul's head recoil slightly.

"This place you just dismissed with a wave of your hand," and I thought "Here it comes." "This place—Xtul—probably looks like a dump to you, right? And us? Like savages, eh?"

Oh! I had to admire this woman. Just to let him know she was inside his head.

"You wouldn't understand this, but we were led here by the gods." A murmur of agreement from the group. "By the gods! Get it?! This is our place and we will let you know if we'll stay or go with you tomorrow."

And with that the gathering broke up, leaving the consul looking drawn and irritated. He'd reluctantly agreed to stay while the group meditated together to decide on their course of action and he was obviously anxious to get back to Mérida before sundown.

The meditation was short and the Beings apparently spoke clearly. "Stay. We brought you here. Trust us."

Whether from faith in the Beings, or because Mary Ann had made it clear where her sympathies lay, all but three of the group elected to stay and face the hurricane.

The consul, severely rattled by this news, tried making more urgent pleas. His descriptions of devastation grew more lurid, as his voice started taking on a shrill, almost hysterical tone. I guessed he was seeing the end of his career flashing before his eyes.

"So that's it, then." This was Robert taking control. "We won't be needing the bus tomorrow, but thanks anyway."

The three with the good sense to leave had gathered their few possessions and were standing around near the consul, awkwardly shuffling their feet. The others were clearly shunning them. I knew two of them at least, Vanessa and Canadian Dave, were both taking this as a convenient moment to leave—each for his or her own reasons.

Walking over to the car, the three of them crammed into the back seat, the consul turned back to the meadow for one last attempt to "talk some rational sense into their thick skulls."

"This is on your heads!" was how this came out. "Let me make it clear—I think you are crazy. You're suicidal. I've tried my best. I wash my hands of you. It's your responsibility now."

"Of course it's our responsibility! It's always our responsibility." I wondered if Robert was going to give the man a lecture on personal responsibility.

"And if you're all killed?"

"Then that's our responsibility, too."

Sensibly recognizing that there was no satisfactory response to that, the consul turned, shook his head in bewilderment, jammed his hat back on his head, and stamped back to the car.

The hurricane, named Inez by this time, was indeed a bad one. The consul was right about that. Category 4, they were calling it. However, the consul was wrong in his hope that the hurricane would lose energy after moving over the Bahamas. It didn't.

"A building upper-level anticyclonic ridge from the western Gulf of Mexico," Mein Host quoted from Wikipedia, "slowly forced Inez to the southwest on October 4, where more conducive upper-level conditions for intensification set in."

After crossing the southern tip of Florida, "delivering hurricane-force winds to all the Keys," Inez thrashed across the neck of the Gulf, intensifying to a major hurricane and heading steadily for the Yucatán peninsula.

Yet without radio or any communication with the outside world, the community didn't know any of this. And the consul was certainly right about one thing. Coming from an island in which hurricanes were all but unknown, and an entertainment industry which, without computer-generated imagery, sensibly avoided casting hurricanes in their movies, members of the community had absolutely no idea of what they were about to face.

If I wasn't somewhat privy to Mein Host's incarnational path, I would have feared for him and the others. But, then again, he could have been a survivor of a storm that killed everyone else.

⁂

I will leave it to others to try to understand some of the wonders I observed during my long stay on Lemuria. I simply don't have the technical know-how to describe the details of some of their advances. Their ability to dissipate the power of cyclones, for example, before the winds have a chance to build up, by the placement of massive stones in combination with the skillful application of platinum, remains a mystery for me to this day. Yet it was obvious that their technology worked. Luzon, on the mainland, hadn't experienced the ravages of a typhoon in many millennia.

Even though I might have a better intellectual comprehension of how sound might be manipulated to produce resonant frequencies that would be able to negate the impact of gravity on enormous blocks of rock, I have no actual experience with your material reality. So I can't say I thoroughly understand it. What was of far more interest to me were the social and spiritual changes the Lemurians as a culture were going through.

As I've previously mentioned, the people of Mu lived lives you would likely find paradoxically simple for such an advanced culture. Their physical needs were taken care of with a minimum of effort. They seemed to be remarkably free of ambition and envy, since, as children, they were encouraged to find what they most loved to do and then to follow that passion into adulthood.

Yet something was happening to the group psyche—something new, something that Vanu and Amadon watched with a certain amount of trepidation. In spite of their long history of social and psychic homogeneity, two new dynamics seemed to be occurring simultaneously, so much so that it was hard to say which one might have precipitated the other. As generation followed generation, possibly helped along by a growing specialization, Lemurians appeared to be becoming far more individuated. Their long-held practice of each following his or her own bliss was encouraging them to think more for themselves. I overheard one of them claiming that "it was as if a whole new space opened in my head."

At the same time I was hearing talk from the midwayers that they were having an increasing problem reaching humans telepathically. I even heard Vanu remarking on this difficulty in his own case and his telepathic powers were somewhat stronger than those of the midwayers.

Yet life on the islands continued relatively unaffected. Society remained peaceful. The arts flourished, especially large-scale choral productions, in which many thousands of men and women would gather and sing together in the one of the natural amphitheaters formed in the bowl of a dormant volcano.

A word about the sounds I heard as I lingered in the sweet spot of one of these vast natural concert halls: I was to learn later more about how they structured their music, but the first time I listened to one of these "performances" I was so deeply moved that I couldn't leave the place until it was over. Incidentally, I hesitate to call it a performance. Nobody was performing for anyone else. Each person there was totally involved with the event. To my mind it sounded both completely spontaneous and superbly orchestrated.

The event began as dusk was falling with a whispered monotone from a thousand throats, rustling like a fresh breeze through cedar trees. Yet, as I listened, I was able to hear that what I'd taken for a single monotone was, in fact, composed of a mass of microtones, all weaving and interweaving around a central core of sound. Listening even more closely, it was as though I could hear in the sound the flapping of a bird's wings and the scratching of small claws, and then the sound of a snake slithering through dry leaves. As I listened to the sound of trees sighing as they bent in the breeze, I felt I could hear each leaf murmuring to its neighbors.

Then I heard waves breaking against the shore as another mass of people took up the chant, layering over the susurrant sighing of the wind, a pulsating roar of waves followed by the hiss of sand as the water withdraws. This continued hypnotically, broken only by the call of waterbirds and the occasional boom of water exploding out of a blowhole in the lava.

I couldn't believe that that these sounds were emanating from mortal beings. Then, like a massive pipe organ, a thousand throats opened up and a wall of sound reverberated around the bowl, each quadrant amplifying the harmonics as a wave of central tones spiraled around the gathering.

The concert, if that is what it was, continued until dawn when the entire amphitheater of perhaps sixty thousand men and women sat quiet, each one turned toward where the sun first peeked over the rim. It was only after this that the people started silently filing out to return to their homes.

As I watched this peaceful parade, I couldn't help noticing how well-balanced all the participants' subtle energy bodies were. The singing, of course, was extraordinary, unlike anything I've heard since. Yet I realized the singing was secondary to the effect it was having on the people. Had I been more astute and less carried away by the glorious sounds, I might have observed sixty thousand Lemurians shifting into their light bodies simultaneously, becoming one coherent organism moving freely through the upper regions of the astral realms.

Indeed, this is what I observed the two other times I attended such a ceremony. Mein Host tells me that a modern parallel might be the "raves" that have been so popular for the previous two decades in Europe and America. In both the Lemurian ceremonies and the raves, beneath the singing, the music, and the dancing lay this far deeper level of psychic activity in which a group mind can be liberated from the material realm, to rise in ecstasy toward the light.

And yet Vanu took it as a good sign that the development of the general state of consciousness on Lemuria was maturing well—it was now almost on track with the original time line that had been so badly retarded by the rebellion. As occurs on all normal inhabited planets, the basic intention is that the neurological patterns of the human brain should become increasingly individuated and thus a truly personal consciousness would blossom.

Sadly, due to Caligastia's constant interference in the West, this general transformation of consciousness would not occur until around 3000 BCE—some forty thousand years later. That's how comparatively advanced the general state of Lemurian consciousness was in relation to what was happening on the other side of the world.

Then again, the Prince was using his midwayers in a completely different way than Vanu was. It was evidently in the Prince's interest to keep humans as dependent as possible on midway telepathic entrancement for as long as it could be managed, because it was only under those conditions that he and Daligastia were free to invade human minds at will.

A couple of millennia later, many years after the last human beings on Lemuria heard the final faint whispers of a midwayer in their minds, the first of the sacred places that I mentioned earlier was discovered.

It had taken some time for the people to realize what was happening. Since a distant racial memory of the midwayers had by this time entered the realm of myth, a new caste of priests had started to emerge who claimed to act as intermediaries between mortals and what they came to call the "ancestors" or, in some cases, "household gods" or the "Old Ones."

I'd prefer to paint the Lemurian culture in the best light possible, but even the finest human beings are going to err in judgment from time to time—they wouldn't be learning if they didn't make mistakes. Frequently, this has taken the form of placing more credence in authority figures—political or military leaders or, as on Lemuria, in priests or mediums—than having confidence in their own personal intuitions.

In this case, a secret report by the priests prompted such internal strife. You'll recall, earlier in the book, I mentioned that some of the Lemurian settlements had been built over naturally occurring fissures, through which fumes escaped. Two so-called experts had been called in to assess what was happening when resident girls fell into trances under the influence of these ethylene fumes.

The pair of priests had been extremely resistant at first, evidently hoping to dismiss the entranced utterances of the girls as mere mutterings of the deranged. Yet on listening with greater attention, they discovered in the girls' oracular pronouncements—despite being cryptic and issued in obscure metaphors and enigmatic rhyming couplets—the voice of a midwayer making itself known through the mediumistic trance of the young women.

I had no doubt that they quickly recognized this phenomenon as a threat to their priestly power. This news also hadn't been greeted well by other priests. They'd had over a thousand years to gradually build up a power base, through which they now wielded considerable influence over the lives of Lemurians. They'd become the counselors, the intermediaries (or so they believed) between the gods and humankind. They clearly foresaw their power diminishing if news got out about this new access to the ancestors that was readily available to any Lemurian prepared to travel to one of three oracular sources.

Vanu and Amadon had been doing their best to maintain the spiritual principles they'd brought with them from the city, trying hard to follow the original dictates of the Prince's mission. Vanu, in particular, had some cause to regret the compromise he'd made with Amadon back before the migration to the islands of Mu. In agreeing to embrace the worship of Sun and Earth as material substitutes for an immaterial God who required faith to accept, Vanu must have believed at that point that Amadon's demand would best serve humanity.

Of course I'm not one to judge the wisdom of Vanu's decision. I can only report what I observed while I was present on the islands throughout this key period in Lemurian history. Up to this point, I knew that he and Amadon were able to use their loyalist midwayers to support what Vanu hoped would be a provisional arrangement, but much of that depended on midwayer telepathic contact with humans.

However, with the rapidity of the transformation in human consciousness and the people's increasing individuation getting in the way of their previous mental intimacy with the midwayers, a number of trying anomalies were emerging, of which the vastly increased power of the priest caste was the most pressing.

In a few extreme situations, Vanu felt he could justify intervening. But the population had to be facing an exceptional threat of almost genocidal proportions for him to take any action. Once mortals have set out on a course of action, they have to be allowed to follow the path they've chosen and directly experience all the consequences of their endeavors.

When two more places were discovered to have the same entheogenic properties, the priests realized that something had to be done. They tried to stamp out what was rapidly becoming a populist cult, but by this time it was too late. After some fruitless attempts to kidnap the girls and realizing that such kidnappings did nothing to stop others from falling into entheogenic trances, the priests had no choice but to back down and let the sacred places be.

Naturally, the priests did what they could to discourage interest in the oracles, but they never could eliminate people's innate curiosity. And, although they had done their utmost to dismiss the old legends—of a time when the midwayers spoke to all Lemurians in their minds—as an era of paganism best forgotten, the memories proved too pervasive (and true) to wipe out completely.

I observed that this profound change is human consciousness hadn't taken Amadon by surprise. He'd always kept in close contact with the midwayers and it was from them that he first heard of the neurological barrier preventing them from communicating directly with human minds. As a consequence, once this new phenomenon had appeared in a score of mortals, he'd requested Vanu, on the midwayers' behalf, to close down direct midwayer communication with all humans.

Since this took several generations to accomplish, the relatively few priests required previously for the handful of annual ceremonies had ballooned in number to take care of the general sense of insecurity among the populace, which resulted from this gradual withdrawal.

The midwayers' departure from human consciousness proved both a gift and a temptation for the burgeoning priesthood. There were some individual priests who'd built their reputations on being reliable interlocutors for midway counsel and continued to be valued for their wisdom after the midwayers withdrew. Yet a greater number by far chose to pretend to speak for the midwayers long after they'd pulled out. Lacking the midwayers' vision and guidance, these priests became increasingly self-serving and greedy, making up meaningless rituals, building temples for their own aggrandizement, creating religious laws by which they could control their people's natural physical urges, dispensing "divine" favors and punishments, and demanding sacrifices from their increasingly fearful and compliant flocks.

In falsely contending that, unlike the common people, they still maintained their privileged connection with the gods, the priests of Lemuria contributed to an unhappy situation that persists to this day. When religious (or political) leaders assert the sole divine authority to speak for their God, their claims will tend to be every bit as spurious as those of the Lemurian priests over forty thousand years ago.

I could tell that Amadon had been watching the rise of this new priesthood with a certain sense of dread. His midwayer spies had kept him up-to-date on the news from Caligastia's Western Empires, so he was aware of the Prince's misuse of his contingent of midwayers and the corrupt practices of their priests. After all the work he and Vanu had done to maintain the spiritual integrity of the Lemurian people, he clearly didn't want to see the culture then being co-opted by a manipulative priesthood.

It wasn't altogether surprising, therefore, to find that Amadon had insisted that the priests desist from interfering with the three oracles.

"Let them develop naturally," he'd tell gatherings of religious leaders.

"The oracles won't trouble you as long as you don't try to suppress them. Leave them be. The people need them, don't you see? They need to hear the voices of their ancestors, to hear their questions answered . . ." He'd pause here and look meaningfully around at the priests before lightening the mood and continuing: ". . . even if the oracles don't make much sense!"

This generally got a laugh from the priests, who'd apparently used this line in their campaign against the growing popularity of the oracles— with their whimsical and enigmatic answers. Yet I couldn't help noticing Amadon's implicit criticism of the priests' inability to transmit the voices of the ancestors directly, which itself would have signaled the priests that Amadon and Vanu were fully aware of their deceptions.

This was Amadon's way. I'd come to admire his approach. He was seldom direct in his instructions to others when he could deliver the same message by subtle implication. I remember thinking that he'd probably been living in a material body for so long now, and having to deal constantly with human beings and all their contradictions, that he, more than anybody, would know how best to handle them.

And, over the next few hundred years, Amadon's implicit directions to the priests did manage to keep some of their previous excesses at bay, while news of the oracles spread throughout the islands. For a while, it appeared to me that the Lemurians had found themselves caught between the strictures of a suspect priesthood, on the one hand, and, on the other, the growing influence of the oracles in which some of the old superstitions were reappearing.

Ever since the midwayers had withdrawn from human consciousness, some Lemurians had gone through a serious crisis of faith. It seemed that one moment they were alert to the voice and presence of this or that household god; the next, there was just the echoing silence of an empty mind.

I remember thinking, "The people are starting to fend for themselves."

Vanu had been on one of his long sabbaticals in his monastery in Kashmir, leaving Amadon in his stead—with instructions not to intervene in any of the dramas likely to ensue. His assistant resolutely held firm to his instructions and resisted all pleas for him to step in and help. Sadly for Amadon, he'd become such a significant figure in Lemurian culture by this time that he'd been forced to move around constantly from island to island to avoid the crowds that invariably swarmed him wherever he went.

It wasn't an easy transition for anyone on Lemuria.

❈ ❈ ❈

The hurricane at Xtul was one of those events in Mein Host's life that, prior to incarnation, he chose to experience in order to bring to the fore an aspect of his personality that required attention. It was similar to the torture trauma, described in *Confessions of a Rebel Angel,* that he'd carried through from his previous lifetime, yet deeper still was a sense of shame and personal worthlessness that were so deeply buried he had no conscious awareness of them.

He hadn't lived long enough to realize that his willingness to throw himself so completely into whatever challenged him was fueled in large part by the lack of value he subconsciously placed on himself. The word *counterphobic* hadn't yet entered his vocabulary, although he certainly recognized the feelings involved in surmounting his fear by doing what he was most afraid of. I believe he may have thought of these actions as courageous or, at least, a matter of facing of his demons. Yet I'm sure in retrospect he agrees with me that many of the incidents were downright foolish.

Here again, I'm getting ahead of myself. It was 1966. The lad knew nothing about this at the time of the hurricane. In fact, he didn't release the compulsion until much later in his life when he'd had the opportunity to impetuously (and foolishly) throw himself away enough times to have thoroughly illuminated the issue for himself.

9

Shame and Disbelief

Ravaged by Inez, Lemurian Entheogens, Daligastia Speaks, and the Plot Thickens

The consul had estimated that Hurricane Inez would hit the Yucatán Peninsula a few days after his visit to the community. This gave the members of Xtul some time to prepare for the worst.

Not that there was much they could do, as they quickly realized. Perhaps then, for the first time, they understood how hopelessly vulnerable they were, perched on the edge of an about-to-be-frighteningly-turbulent sea, with no real protection.

I'd need to be a competent novelist to reproduce all the various reactions when this reality sank in. The bravado of the previous day was draining away as various people were dealing with their second thoughts. Some were more open about their fears than the macho-spirited, but on the whole, the British boarding school, stiff-upper-lip attitude prevailed, and people got on with the preparations.

The five members who were architects whom Mary Ann had gathered together in order to decide where the safest place would be to construct their shelter had had an animated discussion on the topic. The options were limited to three, once the not-wholly-serious suggestion of roping themselves to trees had been rejected. There was either end of the monastery, sheltered by one of the high, thick walls, or in the pit they had already dug in the temple to increase its internal size. This latter could

170

probably fit eight to ten people without too much of a crush. And, of course, there were the dogs. No one knew how they'd react to the storm.

The material they had available was equally limited—a couple of tarps, some rough-cut lumber found on the beach, a few pieces of rope— not enough to create more than one lean-to shelter propped against the wall. Some argued to place it on the outside, on the windward side of the monastery wall closest to the ocean, reasoning that the wind coming from that direction would aerodynamically slip over the angled roof of the lean-to, so if the wall were to collapse it would be sure to fall inward.

Mein Host, and a couple of the others, equally strongly recommended building the shelter leaning up against the far wall, but on the inside of the monastery. This was decided when they finally agreed on the obvious craziness of building what was bound to be the flimsiest of shelters on the windward side of a wall to face those 150-mph winds—however aerodynamically convincing the arguments for it were.

As the day dawned when the hurricane was expected, the lean-to was as finished as it was ever going to be: a tarp lashed to the beams that leaned heavily at about forty-five degrees against the inside wall. The internal space could fit more than the temple pit, perhaps sixteen people—eighteen or nineteen in a pinch. Neither pit nor lean-to were going to be comfortable—everyone was well aware of that.

And how long did a hurricane last anyway? No one had any idea. The skies had darkened and I heard Mein Host telling Juliette about the curious feeling of buoyancy he was experiencing.

"It's the atmospheric pressure," she told him. "It must be dropping fast."

They were gathering for a final meditation to offer themselves to their gods, who by this time had become more solidly defined by Mary Ann and Robert as Jehovah, Lucifer, Satan, and Christ.

Now, this is curious. After I wrote the above paragraph about how they'd "offered themselves to the gods," I had to remind myself that I'm only able to tell this story by reading Mein Host's feelings and observing his actions. If I left the paragraph standing as is, it would be to suggest that all of them were as fatalistic as my ward. It was in his nature to offer himself up, not to ask to be saved, but to throw himself on the wheel of fate.

Others, I have no doubt, were equally ardently—and perhaps more sensibly—appealing to the gods for their help.

For them to be saved.

For a miracle, in short.

The winds had picked up and the sky to the northeast was darkened by roiling black clouds when Mein Host made his way on his own through the coconut trees and across the dunes to stand on the cliff's edge.

I could feel his astonishment at what he saw before him, and then his horror, as he realized its implications.

The sea was going out.

The waters were retreating. Leaving an ever-widening band of beach.

Small fish slapped and flapped on the wet sand.

Massive storm waves broke a hundred yards farther out than usual.

Hurricane Inez was on her way.

I watched the lad running back, breathless with the news of what he'd seen. As he arrived in the compound, the rains started.

"All that sea is going to be coming back in a hurry," he was telling everyone he could, although, by now, there was little anybody could do about it. Even though the cliff was about twenty feet above the beach, the dunes sloped down from the edge, putting Xtul a mere seven feet above sea level.

Oh yes, indeed! The water was going to be back in hurry.

His announcement created a rush of activity as everybody gravitated to one of the two shelters. Robert, Mary Ann, and some of her favorites were hunkered down in the temple pit. Mein Host, as one of the strongest supporters of the lean-to's placement at the base of the inside rear wall, chose to share that shelter with something like the sixteen or seventeen others who were crammed awkwardly together in the small space.

Outside their shelters, the winds were gathering force, howling now across the tops of the roofless buildings and creating subsonic rumbles more felt than heard. Rain slashed down on the tarps, leaks soon appeared, water came pouring through.

The lean-to shelter was already proving to have an unforeseen problem: of the rain striking the inside of the rear wall, some was splashing heavily on the tarp while most was pouring in a constant sheet of water down the wall and right into the shelter.

The ferocity of the storm continued to build, with an intensity far beyond anything Mein Host thought possible, as he commented to Eddie, crouched in a puddle next to him.

The wind was roaring now; coconuts ripped from trees were moving like cannonballs parallel to the ground and smashing into walls and trees.

Peering out of a slash in the tarp, Mein Host watched everything left loose in the monastery being swept up into a whirling maelstrom of debris and then being sucked up out of the roofless structure. The tarp was tugging wildly at its moorings, pulling first in, and then snapping back out, like the spinnaker of a yacht.

They were barely protected from the elements; almost as wet and as scared as if they were crouching out in the open. The raw power of the wind made any movement impossible outside where they huddled, wet to the skin, under the crude shelter.

Then, with an awful suddenness, everything stopped. The howling wind, the slashing rain—all ceased. No one was moving. Water dripping from the wall on the tarp became loud and insistent. There was shouting from the temple; replies from the lean-to. Everyone was fine so far.

Someone called out that this must be the eye of the hurricane. The still, quiet center. And it really was quiet. No birds were squawking and the jungle creatures were silent, as if the whole world were holding its collective breath. Mein Host said he could barely hear the waves after the roaring of the storm.

Eddie crawled out from the shelter and looked around him. The ground outside the monastery was littered with coconut husks; tree limbs; the long, curved branches of palm leaves; and hundreds of wooden shingles blasted from the roof of the living quarters, along with much of the living quarters itself.

When Eddie looked up at the wall high above him, I heard him calling my ward to see what was happening.

There was a long crack opening laterally like a jagged scar across the top of the end wall. Several tons of masonry teetered precariously sixty feet above them, directly over where Mein Host had advised they build the lean-to. Small pieces of rock and plaster were already coming down onto the wet tarp. In a matter of moments, everyone was out and running across the compound to the temple, to crowd into the pit. Compared to the lean-to, it was astonishingly dry.

The winds started again as the last of them scrambled down into the temple pit, now really crushing together, with the blue tarp stretched tight overhead. Unless the sea returned with a vengeance, I heard them reassuring each other, they might just have a chance of surviving.

The velocity of the wind was building up again, this time coming from the other direction. Everyone was pressed together in the pit, four of the men holding on to the corners of the tarp for all they were worth.

But everyone was not in the temple pit.

In the scrum and huddle, no one there had missed him yet. After refusing to go to the temple, Mein Host had crawled, unseen by the others, back into the lean-to shelter. The storm was now reaching its full fury again. Mein Host was sitting in a single lotus, his eyes closed in meditation. The top part of the wall could be seen swaying back and forth.

I had no way of understanding why the lad was doing this. He knew the wall was about to collapse. Was he becoming deranged by the danger?

Many years later, in trying to understand the event for himself, he wrote: "[I was] overcome, I suppose, with shame and a disbelief that I might have been that wrong. I insisted on staying and meeting whatever fate was my due."

It was at least ten minutes later when a worried-looking Eddie pulled the tarp back to find Mein Host sitting with a peaceful smile on his face. Eddie shook his shoulders. Like Eddie, he was wet through and through. Eddie was telling him to leave; he refused. Eddie was insisting; he still refused. Eddie then panicked, and still Mein Host refused to move.

Angrily snapping the tarp closed, Eddie disappeared. Mein Host sat on, placid-faced and resigned, apparently, to his fate. The whole top of the wall was now swaying several feet out of true. For some minutes I feared for his life before I realized it was not to be his time.

Eddie was back again with instructions from Mary Ann to drag the idiot—by force if necessary—back to the temple pit. Still the idiot refused to budge. He was now in a very strange state of mind. He writes of the death wish being powerful in him, and I watched impatiently as he tried to fight Eddie off.

Eddie was stronger by far and hauled his struggling friend out into the fury of the hurricane. Being ordered back by his Goddess reduced his resolve and he finally allowed himself to join Eddie in dodging flying debris, splashing through the water, and running to the temple, before jumping into a pit of resentment and recrimination.

He might have tried to justify his action, but his good sense told him he was just plain wrong. He'd made a terrifying mistake in recommending the placement of the lean-to, and he was a fool to believe that sacrificing himself would make up for it. I quote him again when he writes: "That [Eddie] had to risk his life for my stupidity, understandably, did not go down well with the rest of the group, but once again, they let me back in."

He goes on to tell what happened:

It was a terrible storm, coconut palms ripped up at the roots, and yet the surge of water I thought would swamp us never arrived in full force. The small cliff and the dunes had absorbed the worst of the waves. Whenever I peered out from under the tarp covering the hole in which we were huddling, I could see coconuts, large tree branches, pieces of masonry and roofing tiles flying through the air, embedding themselves in the trunks of other trees.

Many hours later, the wind and the rain subsided and we crawled out, surprised to have survived, intensely alive and surrounded by debris. The top fifteen feet of the end wall of the monastery had collapsed and crushed the lean-to in which I would have been stoically awaiting my fate.

For all Mein Host had put himself through up to this point, this was the first time he had ever been brought face-to-face with a current of shame and guilt that ran so deep that he would have vociferously denied it if accused of it on the previous day. If he had been sufficiently self-aware at the age of twenty-six, he would have understood this was one of the first clues as to his own angelic heritage.

❉ ❉ ❉

It was fortunate that Lemurian society was so basically stable when the neurological changes took place in the population. The transformation occurred over two or three generations and might well have created serious intergenerational conflicts, if the populace hadn't possessed a deep confidence, born of a history of thousands of years of continuous peace.

Their prevailing belief system, passed down through the centuries, was based on the principle that all that happened was meaningful and had a purpose. And that natural events—the rain, the storms, the seeping of the lava, the plants and animals, the Earth, the sun and stars—all occurred for reasons that could be interpreted and understood.

This was experientially reinforced on a daily basis by the Lemurian practice of Being Kind to one another under all circumstances. Although this might sound hollow or naive to the modern ear, for a culture that was aware of the profound meaning of life and all that life entails—whether or not that purpose was understood in the moment—practicing kindness was an inspired way of confirming their belief. Naturally, the presence of the immortals, Vanu and Amadon, when they visited the different islands also carried the implicit promise that life had a larger context and significance than what was immediately obvious.

Approaching their lives in this openhearted way, and with a long history to confirm its consistently beneficial effects on their culture, Lemurians, on the whole, accepted the withdrawal of midwayer guidance from their minds with admirable equanimity.

Yet, of course, there had to be the normal challenges that necessarily arise in a polarized material frequency domain. Left on their own, without the ready availability of midwayer guidance, mortals are more liable to error and misdeed. It is part of the mortal journey to learn from the consequences of your errors—just as it has become mine as a result of the rebellion—and to master the darker impulses of your animal heritage.

As I've already mentioned, it was in the priesthood that corruption first started appearing on Lemuria. Previously, when the midwayer presence was a constant, there had been no need for priests. The few people drawn to counsel others, though they might have been thought of as priests, made no claims of exclusive guidance; if anything, rather the opposite. Functioning as proxies for Amadon, they saw their purpose as helping people to reconnect with their own inner guidance.

When the midwayers withdrew from the minds of mortals, a new class of person started emerging who seemed to need to control other people and take advantage of their innocence and gullibility. And the Lemurians, many of whom were among the most spiritually advanced individuals the world had yet seen, were paradoxically all the more vulnerable to the lies and manipulations of this new priest class. Their very openheartedness led individuals to accept the priests' empty rhetoric.

This is no blanket indictment of the Lemurian priesthood; there were always some who maintained their honor. But the institution itself, with its strict hierarchy, its dogmatic statements, and its growing accumulation of wealth—all this signaled the sort of corruption I'd seen so often in Caligastia's territories in the West. Whereas the Prince would have pounced on the first signs of corruption and used it for his own ends, Amadon, on Vanu's advice, was wise enough to leave the priests alone.

One of the only actions I saw Amadon take was to speak personally to all the original counselors, urge them to continue their work with Vanu's support, and make sure they remained free of the priesthood. I believe it was to seal this agreement that Amadon introduced a mysterious and marvelous set of spiritual tools to a few special people—those more committed to helping and healing others than seeking control, power, and wealth for themselves.

The flowers of a climbing vine in the family Convolvulaceae had long decorated the exteriors of Lemurian houses on the islands in the cooler climates. The seeds of these flowers were among those brought from the mainland by the original settlers. That the flowers were so highly valued for their ethereal beauty was shown by the fact that the hardy little seeds had been carried all the way from the cooler climate of the Chinese mainland before even being brought over to the islands of Mu.

The name *Morning Glory* was first given to this flowering plant in Lemuria, although the Lemurians' hieroglyph for the plant more accurately reads "Dawn welcomes another glorious day." Colloquially, the flower was known as Glorious Dawn, and then later Morning Glory, as it entered the modern era.

Unlike the seeds from some other plants, which are nutritious and pleasant-tasting, the seeds of the Morning Glory plant lack both qualities. These seeds are small, hard, and indigestible, and I'm told they taste bad when ground into pulp. If there were a few occasions when a cook might have experimented with them as part of a meal, and had they been the seeds of either *Rivea corymbosa* or *Ipomoea tricolor,* I suspect the diners would have been unlikely to request a repeat of the meal any time soon.

In short, while Morning Glory flowers were ubiquitous on the northern isles as a decoration, the practice of using the seeds as a foodstuff was completely unknown when Amadon confided to the shaman the mysterious secret at the heart of a certain genus of this family of flowering plants. Since this is of particular interest to Mein Host, I'll try to relate the basic elements of the exchange Amadon had with one of these selected shamans, as they've come to be known in all cultures.

"You are one who has been chosen to enter the Mystery," Amadon was telling the man—Lemurian shamans were generally male—after he sat him down. It was dusk and they sat outside, close to the water that was lapping at the base of the basalt shelf. Between them a small fire was glowing.

"Guard the secret well and it will serve you in your work." Amadon's voice was stern and resonant. He poured out two handfuls of seeds in front of him on a stone slab.

"Look. See what I'm doing." He vigorously pounded hundreds of the tiny seeds, using stone against stone, until he had a double-cupped handful of fibrous material.

"Use between three and four hundred seeds for each journey." Amadon stopped grinding and showed the man a handful of ground-up seeds. I could see that the shaman was wrinkling his nose and laughing, unaccustomed to the smell and having no idea what Amadon had in mind. He clearly felt privileged at being chosen for whatever was going to happen and hid his nervousness with laughter.

Amadon mixed the crushed seeds with water and handed the shaman a stone mug full to the brim with a viscous milky fluid. "Here. Drink this," Amadon said. The shaman gagged a few times but managed to keep the thick concoction down.

Amadon was tapping quietly on the small drum he carried with him everywhere. The stretched lizard-skin head produced a taught, snapping sound that drew the shaman deeper into himself. The minutes passed and the drumming seemed to entwine itself with the rhythmic beating of the waves on the rocks beneath them.

The fire was burning brighter now. Amadon was periodically sprinkling on the flames a crushed mineral dust that sparkled as it reached the heat. He started talking in a singsong voice, and I realized that he was telling the story of the world as he remembered it. He sang of the wondrous arrival of the surgeons of Avalon almost 460,000 years earlier and of being among those chosen to contribute the biological gift that would become his beloved Vanu. He was singing of Dalamatia, the City of God, and of the noble Prince Caligastia and the promise of a new world.

The shaman's face assumed a beatific smile, and I watched as his spiritual body filled with light. The drumming changed rhythm slightly and Amadon's voice took on a more somber tone.

Now he sang of the rebellion among the angels, of the tragic and terrible conflicts that arose between members of the staff, of the great schism, and of Vanu's brave resistance. Amadon's voice echoed the sadness and poignancy of their exile and their long trek across half the world. I saw reflected on the shaman's face and in his emotional body that he was experiencing every nuance of Amadon's story. His face flushed with joy and his eyes were upturned in ecstasy when Lemuria entered the narrative—the long dangerous sea trip, the kindness of the dolphins, the early struggles, and their slow expansion into a great culture. Amadon sang of all these wonders and more.

The drumming suddenly stopped.

Amadon's voice adopted a new and authoritative tone. I wondered if someone else was speaking through him.

"This, this I wish you to know. I speak with the mandate of Vanu and of the Most Highs. As I have told you, at the time of the rebellion among the angels, your world was quarantined. You were isolated from the comings and goings of other planetary beings. You know little of the magnificent Multiverse."

The shaman was listening intently. He was clearly experiencing feelings unknown to him, and I sensed that Amadon's words were creating a visual accompaniment in the man's mind.

"Your world is being left to follow its own path, so hear this well. I spoke to you of Vanu's companions, Prince Caligastia's staff, and the demise of our city. I sang of their terrible deaths when the nutrient rays were cut off, how Vanu and I were spared this fate, so as to bring your forebears safely to our beloved Mu."

Here Amadon paused. The shaman was rocking silently to some rhythm only he could hear. I saw from his subtle energy bodies that he was fully conscious, fully aware of the significance of what he was being told.

I sensed that Amadon was coming to the point.

"What you do not yet know is what you are now feeling and experiencing. The plant will be your ally in your healing. You understand now? It is the spirit of this plant who will be your ally. She will be your teacher. She will guide your hands and your mind."

The shaman was silent throughout Amadon's recitation.

After a long silence, Amadon resumed speaking, once again in his singsong voice.

"In these desperate times, with our companions dead or recalled, Vanu discovered a terrible, yet wonderful truth. He beseeched me to remain mute until the time when ones such as you would emerge and be deserving of such knowledge.

"It is this. Displacement and redirection. Much of what was contained in those life-giving energies that poured down on us, on all of us—the nutrient rays that sustained the staff, warmed our spirits as the sun warms our bodies. What has been unrecognized by all is that these cosmic rays were long imprinting this world's second chakra, well before they were ever shut down."

Amadon paused again, watching the shaman's face, making sure that the man was following, making the connections for himself. But it was far too important to leave to guesswork, so Amadon continued: "You have no need to understand the details, know only that there are certain plants, sacred plants, power plants, that have been endowed with the spiritual capacity to empower human consciousness beyond its highest limits.

"You will discover power plants for yourselves as your species matures. There will be others. You'll find them on all continents and in all climates but the very coldest. There will be fungi and cacti; there'll be certain vines and flowering plants; there'll be roots and leaves and the bark of special trees. The spirits of all these will be your teachers.

"These, the seeds of our sacred Morning Glory, are your introduction to this realm of spirit. She will show you how to travel in your mind, how to speak to the dead, how to seek the aid of the Old Ones, how to retrieve lost souls, and see into past and future."

The shaman was showing signs of sensory overload, so once again Amadon held his tongue for what must have seemed to the shaman like an eternity.

"And, for some of you, she will bring you to the throne of the Most High."

The shaman's hands were dancing, forming mudras in the air before him. Amadon took this as the perfectly natural response of a sentient being seeking to balance and align his subtle energy bodies in the presence of massively accelerating energies.

"This is sacred knowledge. The journeys you will take are sacred journeys. Use these power plants with respect and wisdom. They are dangerous for the unprepared or the uninitiated. Others like yourself will value this knowledge; you will know them when you meet them. Like you, they will be the shamans of their people."

The man now had his eyes open and his full attention was focused on Amadon. He had returned from the Highest Heaven. He found that the fire was burned down to embers as dawn split the sky and birdsong filled the air.

Amadon offered the shaman water from a carved gourd bowl, which he drank with enthusiasm. They sat together in silence before turning to face the sun as the world dropped slowly beneath its warming rays.

"I leave you with two pieces of advice, my brother." Amadon's arm was around the shaman's shoulders, and the shaman appeared to be surprised at being addressed as such. His body relaxed.

"First. Never confuse the messenger with the message."

When the shaman looked confused, Amidon added, "The spirit of the plant is the messenger: she is not the message. Don't set her above yourself. Do not direct your devotion to her. She will show you the God of your heart. She is your ally—no more, no less. She requires respect, not worship."

"And the second?" It was the first time the shaman had spoken throughout the night. Amadon was smiling in appreciation: the man had been listening.

"Ah! The second thing. This is the most important. You would be wise not to talk openly about the sacred journey you have just taken. Absorb the knowledge you have gained, use it to deepen your healing work. Share it only with other shamans. I've told you that you will know these men and women when you meet them. Otherwise, you'd be wise to keep the Mystery to yourself. It's a sacred Mystery. It is not to be profaned."

Apart from a few random incidents of humans who mistakenly ate sacred mushrooms, the event I've recalled here is one of the earliest times in human history that an entheogenic plant was accorded the supreme respect such a plant spirit deserves. The plant devas have served the shamans of your species with loving devotion through generations of humankind and are entitled to your gratitude.

❂ ❂ ❂

So, what did happen at Xtul?

Why didn't they get wiped out by Hurricane Inez?

The storm was heading straight for the Yucatán coast, the worst and deadliest hurricane since 1928—it killed a thousand people in its long track through the Caribbean. In Veracruz alone, the coastal city on the other side of the Golfo de Campeche from Xtul, 293 people died in the hurricane's wake.

Yet if you carefully examine the track Inez took, as Mein Host has, you will find that it made a slight change in direction northward as it approached the Yucatán. It was just a small jog, but it meant that the hurricane merely brushed the coastline and Xtul.

However, as the people in the community pulled themselves, wet and bedraggled, out of the temple pit to survey the devastation around them, they agreed among themselves that it was another miracle.

They'd prayed to their gods and their gods had answered them.

They'd been saved from certain death and Mein Host, for one, was convinced that the miracle was a direct result of their meditations. If he had any remaining reservations about Mary Ann's divinity, her wisdom in choosing to stay and face the storm, her faith that she would prevail, and the power she wielded in harnessing the group mind to make this happen—all this appeared to leave him in no further doubt that he was serving the incarnate Goddess.

Every once in a while as I write this narrative I'm aware of Mein Host's embarrassment in retrospect that he ever made such foolish choices. I need to remind him that, foolish or not, beliefs of this sort are largely interchangeable. It isn't the authenticity of the belief that is important, but the manner in which the belief is held by the individual. Mein Host, by wholeheartedly throwing himself into accepting Mary Ann's divinity, will discover sooner rather than later the truth of his conviction.

At Xtul, however, in the fall of 1966, with Hurricane Inez still bearing down on the coast toward Veracruz, the community—like people granted a last-minute stay of execution—wandered the grounds checking the damage in a high state of ecstasy.

Everyone obviously felt it. How could they not?

In spite of the destruction of all they'd built or repaired over the months they had been there, they were filled with the pure joy of being alive. I could feel this joy more powerfully than I've ever known it and it was through my ward that I experienced it.

So this exquisite joy is another aspect of being mortal, I recall thinking at the time.

To Mary Ann's credit, she chose to use the general exhilaration to suggest that the community walk to the local village of Chuburna Puerto first, before anything was done at Xtul, and lend a hand in repairing the damage there.

I've previously written of the village solely as the source of the water with which the mosquito-covered water carriers twice daily stumbled back to Xtul, because that was the only contact they had with the villagers. There were the few Maya women who giggled and averted their eyes as the water carriers struggled with their loads, but apart from that the villagers had kept to themselves every bit as much as the community had shown scarce interest in the village.

The Maya have every reason to be an intensely private people. Despite some in the West's recent preoccupation with the Maya Long Count calendar and whether its completion on December 21, 2012, has signified the end of a world, or indeed the start of a new one, the Maya keep their deeper mysteries firmly to themselves.

Each morning after the storm, most of the community—I saw no sign of Mary Ann or Robert ever making the effort—could be found traipsing the four miles along the jungle path to the village. Some clambered up rickety ladders to replace the corrugated metal blown off the roofs, others worked with hammers and saws all over the small village, while still others cleared the mass of debris, only to walk back exhausted at the end of the day and face the desolation that was Xtul.

It turned out that the village had been hit harder than Xtul, largely because the villagers' shacks were flimsily built and there was simply more to destroy. Inez was just as violent in both places—after all, she'd blown the top fifteen feet off a three-foot-thick masonry wall.

"Now I understand why the villagers build such rickety makeshift shacks," Juliette told Mein Host as they were sharing a hand-rolled cigarette and taking a break from completing the roof on a nearby dwelling. The corrugated roofing sheets had been ripped off and hurled every which way all over the village.

"The whole place is up and running again in a few days." There was surprise in Mein Host's voice as he looked around at all they'd done. He handed the cigarette back to his friend.

"Yup! Build 'em shoddy. What's the worst that can happen?" Juliette smiled at the thought.

"People like us come along and make it all better for them?" Mein Host was laughing along with her.

"Hey!" she said sharply. She'd been rolling the cigarette between her fingers and staring distractedly at it. "There's printing on the paper. Is this what I think it is?" She took a long drag and passed it back.

"It's all I had. Never did much like the book of Revelation." He'd found the Bible, discarded and lying around in a corner of the broken down hut in Xtul; the tobacco he'd picked up in the village on one of his trips there.

"You heathen!" She said, half-meaning it. "Here. Gimme another drag! Then we'll get back to work."

He held the cigarette away a few times in mock revenge before handing it over. He wasn't quite sure whether Juliette was genuinely upset. She might have had a strict Christian upbringing. They'd made love, they'd slept in each other's arms, they thought of themselves as close friends, yet they knew almost nothing about each other's lives before joining the group.

"I wonder if Genesis would draw any smoother," she said thoughtfully. Her tanned, serene face was turned up toward the sun, blue eyes with their lightly epicanthic folds squinting with amusement, and a stream of smoke pouring from her long delicate nose.

Within a week the village of Chuburna Puerto was as good as new, or at least restored to its original ramshackle condition and ready for the next hurricane. They had all worked together, side by side, as brothers and sisters—short, strong, brown-eyed Maya and tall, lean, mainly blue-eyed Caucasians—with no language in common, apart from music and humor, to achieve something wonderful.

The villagers responded in the most gracious and unexpected way. They invited certain people in the community to join them in their group meditations.

Group meditations? The Maya? Hadn't the Spaniards stamped out all that spiritual stuff years ago? Yet, here they were, two alien cultures four miles apart, both faithfully practicing their own group meditations.

Mein Host was one of the few invited and found that the meditation quickly turned into a séance, with many of the women there falling into trances and speaking, he was told afterward, in the language of their ancestors.

"It was a very strange experience," he told Juliette after getting back to Xtul. "Nothing like our meditations. Often four or five tranced-out women were talking at once. God knows what they were saying. But the rest of 'em were right there, listening to every word. I could see how important it was for them. It was a big deal."

"What was it, though? What was going on?"

"They tried to explain it to me afterward, but I couldn't really get what they were saying. Looked more ancient to me. Didn't feel like their dead relatives. Wasn't like any séance I've ever read about."

"Is that it? That all you got? A lot of women jabbering in a strange language? They tell you anything more?"

"You'd have to have been there, Juliette. The room was full of spirits. I could feel them. Whatever was going on, it was real enough. I found myself crying. Others were, too."

"Really? You?" She said with a grin. "You don't believe in all that stuff, do you?"

"Nine months ago I would have said no—it's ridiculous, of course. Now, with the Beings, the gods, Mary Ann. With the miracles, the fish, the hurricane—it's like I don't know anything for certain any more.

"And you know what, Juliette? I love it. I love being in this state of knowing nothing. I feel entirely open, ready for anything." He was speaking with a conviction I hadn't heard in his voice before. I think Juliette heard it, too, because she wasn't arguing.

"If the Old Ones were speaking through tranced-out villagers," he said finally, "is that any weirder, when you think about it, than us asking the gods to spare us from the hurricane?"

"No weirder," she said, laughing. "No weirder at all."

⁂

I must have spent far too long in Lemuria because I received an unpleasant telepathic tongue-lashing from Daligastia, the Prince's aide-de-camp, when I finally made it back to the Western Territories.

There was a certain desperation in his outburst, which told me more about the general state of morale in Caligastia's camp than it hurt my feelings. Perhaps one of the few advantages in having an insubstantial emotional body is there aren't many feelings there to hurt. Besides, I'd been less and less aligned with Caligastia's cause after observing Vanu's work in Lemuria and getting a glimpse, from my trips to Zandana, of what might have developed on Earth. Yet I'd cast my lot with the Prince, and with Lucifer and Satan, and I had no choice but to make myself available to them for as long as this wretched affair continued. Realizing this called up a new feeling in me: a horrid, shrinking feeling of cowardice.

I'd never once told Prince Caligastia, or Daligastia for that matter, how I was really feeling, or what I believed was going wrong. Scarcely a justification, I know, but I was fairly certain they would consider any criticism from a Watcher the height of insolence.

Just as I was leaving Daligastia's presence, I heard him calling me back.

"So, Georgia," his voice dripped oil in my mind, "you have some, um, observations to share with us?"

I thought I'd masked those thoughts from him.

Again, the coolly sardonic voice: "It's come to our attention that you appear to actually prefer to spend your valuable time with that despicable Vanu; that is, when you're not on Zandana. Yes, we know all about your trips."

I was taken aback by his tone. Anger at my absence I could understand. But I'd seldom been addressed personally by him before and never in this sneering tone. Did he think I was spying for Vanu? Or that I might be a saboteur?

I'd barely formed the thoughts when Daligastia's contemptuous voice broke through again.

"There's nothing we need to learn from that traitor."

There was little point in replying: I was an open book to him. He was my direct superior.

"Vanu's Lemuria . . . ," the scorn in his tone was becoming painful. "Thinking he's doing so damn well. Proud of himself, isn't he? Towing the party line like that, like a good little boy. He always was: Yes, MA this . . . No, MA that . . . And he has no idea what it's really all about! That's the joke of it."

I must have seemed confused. It was no surprise that Daligastia was derisive of Vanu's progress, but a joke? This I'd never heard before. He continued, almost as if he were thinking aloud and he weren't directing his ridicule at me.

"And what do you think is going to happen to Vanu's wonderful Lemuria?" he asked rhetorically. "You think it's going to last? You think that's what this is all about? Life getting better and better? Wiser and wiser? A lovely peaceful world? Everybody being nice and kind to one another? You think that?"

Ignoring the slur cast on what I thought was an excellent ideal to live by, I felt bound to react somehow.

"But, Great One, isn't that why we're all here?"

Perhaps I surprised him, breaking into his train of thought, because I felt his attention turn once again to me.

"Is that what you Watchers think? You think that's what the rebellion was all about? We went through all that trouble just to build another happy little world for MA?"

"But, surely . . ."

"Thinking's never been you Watchers' strongest suit. Best leave it to those who can manage it. If you haven't connected the dots yet."

His tone softened and I realized that he was musing aloud again. Incapable of intelligent thought though I might have been in his mind, he appeared to need a (thoughtless) foil off which to bounce his thoughts. I knew better by this time not to respond to his questions.

"What do you think that 'voice' was all about? We all heard her. I know you did—you wouldn't be with us if you hadn't. She was supporting us all the way. And now where is she? Did she know we'd all be treated like traitors? That we'd be cut off? Isolated? Quarantined as though we had some terrible disease? You think she knew this was all going to happen?"

He had a point about that mysterious "voice." And it was a mystery. Soft, persuasive, humorous, enchanting in her tone and manner, she made us feel so special and loved. She was excited for us embarking on this great new adventure.

All the Watchers with whom I'd compared notes after the rebellion maintained that they'd heard her subtle encouragement to follow Lucifer. Yet no one knew who she might be. Some thought it might be a Supreme circuit opening up; others believed it was the voice of the Mother Spirit. And those who didn't hear the voice thought we were deluded if we spoke too openly about her.

She'd talked about the task ahead as a cosmic experiment, as something we would understand more fully as time passed. She spoke of needing us to complete a great cycle, that we'd been chosen for this special task and promised she'd be there at the end to welcome us home. She warned us that it wasn't going to be easy, that we'd be challenged to our very essences. But that only made us more determined. She hinted that we would be opening doors to entirely new territories.

We were enchanted. How could we resist this siren call?

Then, she disappeared.

Silence.

Nothing.

We were on our own.

"That is how Great Lucifer heard her voice." Daligastia broke the long silence. He'd read my mind again.

"He evidently believed it was the voice of the Supreme Deity—he had no doubt about that. He even told us he derived much of his courage from her. She had been with him all through the revolution. It was difficult for all of us when she withdrew."

Daligastia drew silent again. Not a telepathic peep out of him. It's how the telepathic circuits function. The greater encompasses and interpenetrates the lesser, as the greater can mask its thoughts from the lesser. The lesser is telepathically transparent to the greater, but not vice versa.

This is what finally convinced those of us who could hear her mysterious voice. She spoke to all of us, great and small. Whoever or whatever she was, she encompassed us all, from a System Sovereign down to the humblest cherubim. During the revolution she was a constant presence who could never be ignored. Frankly, sometimes it was as if it was her voice, and not Lucifer, who was leading the way. It was that strong.

What was Daligastia up to? I hadn't thought much more about this voice after she disappeared, and that was many millennia past. Actually it was something of an embarrassment since her sudden absence suggested she might have been some sort of mass delusion after all. It wasn't a happy memory, and I think I speak for most Watchers when I say we tucked away any memory of those cajoling tones behind us, and in the chaos and excitement of our revolution, I'd forgotten all about her.

Yet here was Daligastia bringing up the voice again—after all this time. I wasn't sure quite what to make of it, when his voice slid into my mind again. His tone was more gentle now, as I think he realized I really was a simple Watcher and unlikely to have considered myself an unwitting pawn in a larger conspiracy.

"You never concluded that we all might have been set up?" Daligastia asked abruptly. "This never occurred to you?"

I was unused to being this easily read. I can mask my mind from mortals, midwayers, and most of those of my order, but Prince Daligastia could pick thoughts out of my mind as simply as reading words out of book.

"Yes. Yes. I know she called it a great experiment," he sounded impatient. "That we were doing something that had never been done before. But did you know it had been tried three times before—just in this Local Universe?"

Well, yes, I did remember something about the previous three rebellions, and they were always called "rebellions" by the Melchizedek Brothers in their lectures, and not "revolutions"—thus automatically portraying them in the negative, as enemies of MA. However, I did notice that they were extremely reticent to talk about those three incidents, so prior to the uprising I hadn't given them any more thought.

I was wondering whether those who participated in the three earlier rebellions had also heard her voice, if they, too, had been persuaded by her tender promises.

"I blame the Melchizedek for that!" The anger was back again. "You know they told Lucifer almost nothing. You would think System administrators would have a need to know about any previous conflicts, wouldn't you?"

I knew better than to reply: this news was far above my pay grade. Yet it didn't altogether surprise me. MA never liked to admit failures. It was little wonder that they would have buried the information so deeply in the restricted archives.

"And none of us ever met, or even heard about, any of those who participated in those early revolutions."

Revolutions, I noticed, not *rebellions.* But what was he doing taking me into his confidence like this? I'd never heard Daligastia, or Caligastia for that matter, talking like this before. I hoped my own feelings of dissatisfaction weren't the cause of his unexpected intimacies.

"I have never seen the significance of that until now—one more clue that we were set up." He was thinking aloud again and evidently had forgotten to shield his thoughts.

This was going to be risky.

I shouldn't be here, listening to this.

Should I quietly take my leave?

I really don't want to be here when he realizes I've been listening.

And yet . . .

"And if it was some sort of setup, well, what then? Are we then the dupes? Have we fallen into MA's trap, damn it? Is that what happened? And we just blundered into it? Thinking it was all our own idea?"

I felt first his bewilderment and then a renewed anger building in his thoughts.

"Does MA take us for fools?! Is that it? They think we are dancing like marionettes to their tune? Who do they think they are playing with? They cut off the juice, damn it! They killed my staff without mercy."

He may well have gone on in this vein as his anger and

self-recrimination grew stronger, but this time I took it as my hint to quietly withdraw from the Great One's presence.

I wondered later, after I was well out of Daligastia's telepathic range, whether this would be a line of thought he planned to share with Prince Caligasta.

Somehow, I doubted it.

10

Return from the Wilderness

A Union of Opposites, *Homo Habilis*, Gabriel Stern Revealed, and Telepathic Probes

There was one unexpected bonus to the hurricane at Xtul. Food. Bags of corn and beans appeared at the gate, courtesy of the Mexican government. No gourmet fare by any means, but it appeared to be a welcome relief from the daily diet of fish, coconuts, and prickly pears. And there was enough of it to give the group several weeks of comparative luxury.

When all the houses in Chuburna Puerto were fixed up and the grateful villagers had given a feast for their new friends, the community had no choice but to confront the awful damage sustained by the buildings at Xtul. Not only was all the work they'd done to rebuild and repair the buildings destroyed by the storm, there was also extensive damage above and beyond this. The wooden structure that had been their sleeping quarters was now completely roofless and it was leaning to one side at a drunken angle. Roof shingles were scattered all over the landscape.

Yet I don't believe it was solely the ruined state of the place that made them question their continued life at Xtul. Certainly the hurricane was taken as a sign. And after one of their meditations it was evident from the answers they were receiving that their gods wished them to return to London, and to civilization.

Not everyone received this counsel—a handful of them were told to stay behind at Xtul to continue the building work. Although whether it was Mary Ann or the gods who were really behind the decision to leave or stay remained for each of them to work out for him- or herself.

As it is Mein Host's state of consciousness that interests me, I should add that he was among those instructed to return to England. Hurricane Inez, and the manner in which they were saved, had evidently made a deep impression on him. He confided in Juliette that he believed their salvation and the cool and inspired way Mary Ann had acted in the face of danger were profound confirmations of his revelation of her divinity.

The hurricane also had the effect of bonding the members of the community ever more closely. They had been through the wars together; they'd shared a wet and full-to-bursting foxhole. They had risked their lives for one another, and each of them knew how everyone else had responded in such a life-or-death crisis.

They had done their turn in the wilderness; it was now time for them to return to the culture that spawned them and share with others what they had learned.

In most cases, relieved parents were more than happy to send tickets to the children they believed they would never meet again. Mein Host's mother, Diana, for one, was delighted to see her son. In spite of my ward's youthful conviction that he would never return to London, she was sensible enough to have had her reservations.

Arriving back in England tanned, thin, and healthy, on a cold, wet, November day, in nothing but their torn and tattered summer clothes, the group must have appeared like rescued castaways to any who saw them deplane at Heathrow Airport.

Balfour Place, the mansion in London's upper-crust Mayfair district that the community had purchased before leaving, was much as they'd left it. They'd closed the place down for the duration. Strangely, Mein Host never once appeared to be aware that the financial demands of a sizable mortgage may have called them back, and not necessarily a sign from the gods.

After the excitement of Hurricane Inez, London was a gray and dull place. Under the surface, however, a new spirit was stirring in the arts and music, with the Beatles and the Rolling Stones leading the way into what soon would be labeled "swinging London" by the press.

Revolver, the Beatles' fifth album, had just been released. Mein Host, who'd recognized the genius of the group since their first recording, "Love Me Do," four years earlier, still remembers hearing *Revolver* for the first time. Having arrived back in London from the wilderness, music-starved for months and listening to the album's fourteen tracks on Jean, his former girlfriend, and her new husband's superb sound system, became a touchstone in his musical life. Each and every one of those songs moved him through a remarkable range of emotions, rendered all the more poignant by the recent dissolution of some of the barriers he'd erected subconsciously to protect himself from tender feelings. His hard-young-man front was starting to break down.

One of the features of the community's life, whether in Xtul or when they returned to England, was a surprising lack of individual self-reflection. This was all the more astonishing because the community had started three years earlier as a psychotherapy group. However, as you'll have no doubt learned from my narrative, from the time they arrived in Nassau, Mary Ann's personality became progressively more assertive. By the time the hurricane struck, everyone in the group recognized that they were in the presence of someone quite extraordinary—if not the incarnate Goddess.

Meanwhile, Robert had somewhat faded into the background at Xtul, busying himself with writing the books that would form the basis of the community's elaborate theology. Back in London, he started reemerging as the community settled into life in the city. However, he no longer made public appearances propounding the tenets of the community. His ribald rejection at the Oxford Union and at the London School of Economics before they left England doubtless convinced Mary Ann of the evident limitations of the man she was manicuring for the role of messiah. With no public appearances, Robert became, like Mary Ann, an unseen presence in the life of the community for all but the eight or ten people in their inner circle.

So Robert wrote and wrote—slim books, granted; self-published; and

printed by the community's press, with titles like *Humanity Is the Devil,
The Gods on War, The Seeds of Destruction,* and *And There Was Darkness.*
The words poured out of him in a heroic attempt to identify and explain
all the ills of humankind.

Although the books were written with a prophet's inflammatory
bluster and were unreadable in Mein Host's opinion, Robert had to be
credited with placing humanity within a larger Universe context in his
books—even if the context was not altogether correct. And he also should
be recognized for having the courage to write about Lucifer and Satan in
a thoughtful and compassionate manner.

Yet, even if his theology was faulty and confused, there was a core
to Robert's belief system—concerned with uniting opposites—that was
unlikely to have been inspired by Mary Ann but deeply resonated with
Mein Host. The experiences he'd been having at Xtul opened him up to
his dual nature and his subpersonalities in such a way that he was now far
more aware of his internal conflicts.

Mein Host had already come across the idea of the Union of
Opposites in his reading. The need to resolve opposing polarities within
the personality runs like a current through the perennial philosophy, as
well as being central to European mysticism and the practice of alchemy.
Robert's view of this was derived from Christ's admonition to "Love Your
Enemy." Robert had asked, quite reasonably, "Who but Satan was Christ's
enemy?"

This was a dangerous belief to introduce to a nation of people, many
of whom were purportedly Christian and steeped in the tradition of a
devil who was convenient to blame for their misdeeds. To these people,
the threat of reconciling with those they hated in the course of their
everyday lives was challenging enough—let alone the concept of a reconciliation with their Prince of Darkness. That was too much for most and
far too tempting a target for the press to ignore, so there'd be a periodic
eruption of hostility directed toward the Process—which was now being
branded by the media as a cult.

Even though they'd received some unpleasant attention from the
tabloid press before they left England, when the group returned from
Mexico they'd become zealots—with all the naiveté of true believers,

convinced of their truth and sure that the public would finally open their eyes to it.

The Process would flourish over the next decade, but the requirements of its demanding set of beliefs kept the number of adherents to a minimum. I believe, in retrospect, that this served Mary Ann's purposes well, in that it gave her a convenient whip to goad the group into ever-greater efforts to "bring in more people." Indeed, any effort to tone down the rhetoric in the publications being printed on the Heidelberg press, now installed in the basement of the Balfour Place mansion, would be met by Mary Ann with the instruction not to moderate but rather to amplify the extravagance of the rhetoric.

It quickly became obvious they were going to need a constant flow of money to support the mansion and the community together with the sizable slice passed along to Mary Ann and Robert.

And, thus, another new phase in Mein Host's life began.

⁘ ⁘ ⁘

Having spent that unpleasant interview listening to Daligastia ranting on about MA's betrayals, I'd retreated quietly out of his presence. I felt he was demonstrating a level of anxiety and self-doubt I'd never seen in him before.

I also wondered what would come of those angry thoughts of his about MA's having set him up. And not only him, but the lot of them—Lucifer, Satan, Caligastia, and all the other thirty-six Princes and their deputies—plus the large proportion of the mission staff on those thirty-seven planets and all of us Watchers, too. Could it be that we were all being manipulated by the very authorities we were rebelling against?

This wasn't good. What I'd seen of Caligastia's behavior in the past was bad enough. I feared what would happen if he were to take his deputy's thinking to heart. The Prince's pride—and he could be overbearingly proud—would be dealt a terrible blow if he believed he was just another of MA's puppets.

Whether or not Daligastia could handle it, I wasn't at all sure; perhaps he'd just tuck the whole dreadful thought away. Being of the same Order of Sonship as the Prince, he should be able to effectively screen his thoughts from Caligastia without making him suspicious. Surely he would know how his Prince would be certain to react? Who would know better?

Such was my thinking at the time, as I made my way across the still-desolated North African coastline. I assumed the radioactivity, which had poisoned the land for over ten millennia, had decayed sufficiently to permit life to return tentatively to the scorched landscape. Green patches were starting to appear, but there were almost no signs of the previous epoch. The great temples had disappeared into heaps of rubble, which were now being covered by the blown sand.

Yet as I moved farther south to the regions less affected by the war, I was able to observe that many of the larger animals had returned. I saw big herds of zebra and antelope, but far fewer lions than I'd expected, until I realized that the predators at the top of the food chain would have absorbed far more poison than their prey.

The saltwater marshes and the string of shallow lakes were brimming with waterfowl, and every once in a while I came across small clan groups of a human type I hadn't seen before. I've spoken earlier about Caligastia's threat to bomb the people back to the Stone Age and yet these humans bore little resemblance to their predecessors, if that is what happened—and if the effects of the Prince's war had reached this far down the continent.

They were larger, bulkier, with broad faces, large noses, and surprisingly thick, protruding brow ridges. They had nothing of the grace of the earlier humans. Yet they stood upright with muscular, well-built bodies that wouldn't look out of place in a modern gym. Their eyes were brown pools, deep-set under their heavy brows, and they seemed to me, as I peered into them from my invisible perch, to contain an odd mix of courage and sadness.

They were skillful hunters, when they could stir themselves, but they seemed mainly to prefer the safety of scavenged meat. They made use of the entire carcass after consuming everything edible—the skin for leather, the bones for weapons or simple flutes—and were just starting to throw organ meat onto the fire before eating it.

I watched individuals from different clans when they were threatened, for example, cooperating in trapping and bringing down a fierce water buffalo. But there were never that many of them and they lived simply, in caves, when they could find them; the rest of them appeared to spend most of their time looking for caves in which to dwell.

Apparently they had long since mastered fire, and the flints used to create the sparks were among each family's most treasured possessions; these were passed down through the generations for as long as they lasted. They'd become quite skilled at fashioning stone implements: I saw some beautifully made spears and arrowheads and an obsidian dagger polished to such a smooth sheen the children could see their reflections in the seven-inch blade.

They clearly valued one another. Although they were a simple people, they had spiritual lives. Everything around them possessed life— the Earth; the sky, with its clouds that formed pictures; the rocks, the plants, and the trees; all the animals. For them, everything was infused with spirit. In fact, I could tell from their amorphous and immature spiritual energy bodies just how deep was the sense of Oneness they felt with the world around them. When they killed an animal, they believed they were killing a part of themselves. And when they ate the meat, they felt they were restoring themselves with the spirit of the animal. When they scratched and painted animals on their cave walls, they believed they were possessing the animals' souls.

They appeared to care deeply for their elderly, frequently nursing them under extremely demanding conditions. They buried their dead in a squatting position with flowers and simple implements for use in the afterlife, following a respectful ceremony.

On the whole, they were a gentle people. They shared their food generously whenever they had it and it looked to me as though they were raising their children with loving care.

But, most of all, they made babies. More and more babies. With good reason, you might think, considering that only one in five children survived its first three years. But, from my observation, I'm inclined to believe the ever-increasing number of babies was more directly a result of those long hours amorously spent in their comfortable caves.

A contemporary anthropologist would place these people somewhere near the close of the Middle Paleolithic Age and most likely label them as

Homo habilis. A contemporary office worker, however, might well think of them as an indolent people. They spent, on average, no longer than two hours a day feeding themselves and almost all the rest of their time safe and happy in their caves.

And, of course, they were making babies!

So this was all that Caligastia was left with—a bunch of simple cavemen and their women and children.

The clock had been turned back almost half a million years. It was as though the Prince's mission had never been; nothing still existed of the civilizing ways the staff had so carefully introduced and nurtured before the uprising. As nature had once again reclaimed a ruined landscape, so too was a new line of human beings reappearing—a simple, primitive, and as-yet-uncorrupted people.

I was happy to see that there was no sign of any of Caligastia's midwayers. The people certainly didn't deserve that additional nuisance in their lives! Besides, I imagined these simple people would have been far less fun to meddle with in the cynical way the rebel midwayers manipulated the folk back before the terrible war.

Frankly, I didn't hold out much hope for the future. The people would probably be left alone for a few millennia, but I knew Prince Caligastia and his midwayers were just biding their time, and when they came back they'd be returning with a vengeance.

However, Caligastia was soon to have a far more serious problem on his hands, and one that promised to deprive him of his power once and for all.

❋ ❋ ❋

I have to admit: Mein Host is an odd creature.

I've heard him saying that he was capable of being totally committed to the Process—and to Mary Ann—while not buying into the theology being introduced by Robert. I think the lad must have been half-aware, even then, that he'd joined the Process for the experience—and not for a theological system so convoluted that it meant little to him.

This casual dismissal of the growing complexity of the theology appearing in Robert's books did not detract from Mein Host's adherence to the more fundamental challenge of loving his enemies. And, due to the emphasis placed on personal responsibility among the group, he was aware that this act of reconciliation needed to happen first within himself. He would need to balance and unite the disparate—and often conflicting—aspects of his personality before he could produce anything of real value. As his earlier entheogenic explorations had shown him, in no uncertain terms, the enemy who so desperately required the loving was inside himself.

Although he could never have framed it in this way at the time, his multiple personalities were going to have to play a part in this personal integration. As I write, he is astonished to hear me reporting that the previously mentioned Gabriel Stern, who had taken the helm during the Xtul experience, was subconsciously called forth by my ward on his return to London.

Perhaps some of you will recognize a counterphobic aspect to this, because it was only in situations in which my ward pushed himself to his limit, physically or psychologically, that Gabriel Stern would take over. To hear Mein Host trying to explain what happened when Stern stepped forward is to realize that he had no idea what was going on with this subpersonality.

"The nearest I can put it," he was telling Paul, his old friend from architecture school, "it's like climbing on top of myself. Then just throwing myself into whatever it is. Something else kind of takes over then, and it's pure magic. It's like I can't make a wrong move or say a wrong word. If I'm out in the city selling magazines, I feel as if I'm the king of the street. I know exactly who to ask, who'll stop and buy, who's not worth bothering with. It's spooky how it happens."

"But what's the trick? How do you get there?" Paul was never able to get over his natural reticence and tended to fall back on his Germanic stoicism when the going got tough.

"Beats me, Paul. Wish I could explain it better. Just feels like an act of will. I will myself into another plane of activity—that's what it feels like, closest I can get."

"What? Just like that? You just will it to happen?"

"Sometimes it happens just like that. Bang, and I'm there. Other times I just have to grit my teeth and plunge into whatever it is and, within a few minutes, I'll find myself in this other state of consciousness. Maybe that's where the will comes in, Paul—in making myself do it."

But it was only marginally about will—Paul had shown every bit as much willpower as Mein Host—and it had far more to do with Gabriel Stern's facility for taking over the primary personality.

Almost twenty years later, Mein Host, by then more aware of the impact of his childhood traumas, would call forth all seven of the subpersonalities, or alter egos, that he'd identified. He would have them sit on rocks and blankets around a fire burning in his imagination and ask them, each in turn, to tell their stories. Interestingly, this formal ceremony both led to the integration of his various subpersonalities and contributed directly to my eventual emergence. In fact, it was my ward's facility in handling the integration of his subpersonalities that has eased the way for my appearance in his life, as well as allowing him the confidence to permit our collaboration.

We'll learn more about the other subs as my narrative develops, but since Gabriel Stern was the one who emerged most often in the coming years, I will give a thumbnail sketch of him. In doing so, I hope I can also clear up some of the misconceptions about what psychiatrists have called multiple personality disorder (MPD) or, as it's now been renamed, dissociative identity disorder (DID).

DID is considered a controversial diagnosis by many in the psychiatric community. However, it has gained some support in recent years because advanced brain imagery has shown distinct neurological differences between a person's different subpersonalities, or alter egos.

I suggest that one of the reasons for the confusion and the rejection of DID by skeptics is that a certain degree of multiplicity is present in all human personalities. It may even be a quality inherent in personality itself—a reasonable coping mechanism whereby a primary personality delegates a situation to another aspect of itself, an alter ego better equipped to handle the matter.

At around this time, Mein Host encountered the work of the Italian psychologist Roberto Assagioli, MD, a younger contemporary of Freud and Jung and the developer of psychosynthesis. My ward had been reading widely in psychology since he was a teenager, but he'd never come across talk of using subpersonalities for therapy and personal growth. He learned that psychosynthesis believed, as John Rowen later tried to summarize in his 1993 book *Discover Your Subpersonalities,* that "subpersonalities exist at various levels of organization, complexity, and refinement throughout the mind." And that the integration of these "leads to the discovery of the Transpersonal Self, and the realization that it is the [Transformational Self] that is the final truth of the person, not the subpersonalities."

Psychosynthesis was to supply a crucial clue to finally unraveling Mein Host's understanding of his multiplicity. Most important was his recognition that, while he appeared to have a mild case of DID, that didn't mean anything was "wrong" with him. He wasn't sick or crazy—not that he ever believed he was—but he discovered that other, "normal" people didn't have any distinct subpersonalities and had no idea what he was talking about.

There were one or two exceptions, of course, the most significant of which would be facilitated by companion angels. When he was eventually to make contact with his companion angels in the early 1980s, he was able to appreciate the advantage of being familiar with his subpersonalities. He said at the time that he never felt any danger of being "taken over by a negative entity" because his experience with his subs had taught him he could always return to the primary personality. He knew, come what may, that he was in charge.

He was introduced to psychotherapist Armand DiMele by a mutual friend, another psychotherapist who intuitively recognized that Armand and Mein Host would share a sense of kinship. He was correct. Despite the two men having had entirely different life experiences, or perhaps because of that, they were fascinated with each other. They were both thirty-eight when they first met in New York City, with a mere three-month age difference between them. Armand was at the top of his profession and was known as a forceful and provocative speaker who used words and music to induce in his audiences profoundly transformative experiences. He ran his own successful clinic in Manhattan, as he still does, employing a number of other psychotherapists in a wide variety of healing arts.

Armand was a worldly man of Sicilian/French ancestry, who'd grown up on Manhattan's Lower East Side and become a wealthy Wall Street trader before turning to psychotherapy. As much a magician as a therapist, he was known to be as brilliant as he was effective, and, as such, he was also an extremely controversial figure. Mein Host, who as public relations officer for the Process had to handle many of the controversies generated by the community's radical public statements, found that he had much in common with this unusual man.

We'll encounter Armand later in this narrative, since he played an important role in helping my ward finally decode the puzzle of his multiplicity. Suffice it to say here that, as a psychotherapist, Armand was treating a number of patients with DID when Mein Host first met him in the late 1970s. The two became immediate friends, long before either knew of the other's interest and involvement with the multiple personality issue—Armand professionally and Mein Host experientially. When they started opening up to each other, each learned a great deal from the other's stock of knowledge. Armand had never encountered anyone aware of the disorder and healing it within himself by his own means, and Mein Host had never come across a therapist with any understanding of the condition.

He learned the essential clue from Armand. It was to enable him to finally unlock the whole pattern. His friend told him that, over the course of hypnotic treatment, one subpersonality was invariably aware of all the others. This was the one who desired the healing and ultimate wholeness and with whom he, the therapist, could work. This was the one that Armand called the "angel," as that was how this particular subpersonality would frequently refer to herself.

It should come as no surprise that, in Mein Host's case, that "angel" turned out to be me—although he wouldn't realize that until somewhat later. I should emphasize here that I am not merely one of my ward's subpersonalities. He didn't create me as a coping mechanism as he did Gabriel Stern and the other subs. As a Watcher I am a fully independent being who, because of my particular long-standing relationship with Mein Host, chose to first make myself known to him consciously under the guise of a beneficial sub. And since Armand had told him about the "angel" subpersonality he'd encountered in his psychotherapy practice,

I felt it an appropriate situation to introduce myself. Yet for all that, it would take another twenty years for us to become sufficiently at ease with one another to embark on this most intimate of collaborations.

Most of Armand's patients suffering from DID had complete amnesia—a barrier of forgetfulness—between the various subpersonalities. These were the people who might well wake up in a strange bed with no idea of how they got there or walk the streets of an unfamiliar town with no memory of having traveled there.

Yet these patients are at the extreme end of a spectrum that spans the entire human personality. Everyone, I'm sure, will have had the experience of presenting different aspects of the personality in different situations, or seeing how the personality changes under the influence of alcohol or drugs. Only in extremely traumatic circumstances will there be a dissociation, in which the different personalities will have little or no knowledge of the others. These cases merit a diagnosis of DID, because such people can suffer terribly from the ensuing chaos in their private lives and will frequently attempt suicide.

So Gabriel Stern can be considered an aspect of Mein Host's personality who moved into the fore as Mein Host's primary personality dissociated when he was a terrified child under the rain of Hitler's bombs during the London Blitz of World War II. Gabriel reappeared intermittently during the lad's childhood, including once when, as a ten-year-old, he was staying with his mother's sister's family in County Limerick in Ireland. At that point, he was set upon by a couple of young ruffians a few years older than he was. Mein Host has since said he was surprised to find that he seemed to know the various pressure points on the boys' bodies that created the maximum amount of pain and that sent them limping off in puzzled disgrace. But, of course, it was Gabriel Stern who knew those moves.

Then, again, as an adolescent at the English boarding school Mein Host attended, Gabriel Stern stepped forward to endure the many formal beatings administered to Mein Host. And Stern was the one who ultimately defied the brutality of the school authorities.

Mein Host's personality was not actually dissociating—he had no radical lapses in memory, no waking up in unexplained locations. In addition, he retained his memory of the events in which Gabriel Stern emerged.

So is it as simple as that? Gabriel Stern is an aspect of Mein Host's ego? An alter? A subpersonality?

Well, yes and no. And this is where, from my point of view, it gets so intriguing. At two or three years old, Mein Host's ego could barely be considered substantial enough to have created an alter ego as mature as Gabriel Stern. Yet here was Gabriel, stepping in and bravely taking whatever punishment was being doled out, from bombs to beatings to flagellation.

So what was going on?

Only now, as I write, am I being shown something I find remarkable. As a Watcher, I'm familiar with other Watchers—angels who aligned with Lucifer—being assigned to the thirty-seven dissenting worlds, and I suspect that we are being prepared for mortal incarnation. What I didn't know was that some of the angels who remained loyal to MA have taken it as their mission to overlight certain mortals under particular circumstances. Overlighting is best understood as when an angel chooses to resonate with, or overlight, a mortal's spiritual body, much to the benefit of that mortal. These loyalist angels say their purpose is compassionate; their overlightings are brief, and they claim to have no desire for mortal incarnation.

Putting all this together, I believe I can complete this digression with a measured assertion that the Gabriel Stern we've met was originally created by an angelic overlighting, at a time when the primary, unformed personality was dissociated. This unusual personality continued to manifest intermittently, until Mein Host's midtwenties, whenever he was under extreme stress. Subsequently, Gabriel Stern has only made rare appearances and never, I'm told, accompanied by an angel.

However, when I return to the chronology of my story of the community settling back into life in London in the winter of 1966, we will find Gabriel Stern, by now a well-developed subpersonality, gradually morphing into yet another personality. This sub was drawn forth by necessity and, in this case, named Micah Ludovic by Mary Ann. Mary Ann, I hasten to say, did not create the Micah subpersonality. She would have said when she saw this aspect of Mein Host manifesting that she'd chosen to nurture it, and how better to foster that aspect than by naming it.

❉ ❉ ❉

You will recall Caligastia's abortive invasion of Vanu's Asian territories and how, after crossing the desert of the Arabian Peninsula, the Prince's vastly depleted army became bogged down south of the Caspian Sea.

As the centuries passed, the survivors settled in the area, expanding south and west into Persia and Mesopotamia, finding the fertile region between the Tigris and Euphrates rivers particularly to their liking. Others mated with the rare nomadic tribes that passed through the area and reverted back to a more migratory life.

These people were sufficiently far from the war zone that they had not been affected by it or the dreadful radioactive fallout; as a consequence, they were living out relatively normal lives for those times.

The two kings whom Prince Caligastia had ordered to carry out his revenge against Vanu and who led the failed invasion across the desert were now almost mythical figures. They had subsequently settled by the Caspian, leaving a bloodline that had swollen over the centuries into a large aristocratic class. The kings themselves were among those who were the direct descendants of the Prince's staff.

I knew that the sixty members of Caligastia's staff who had followed their Prince had been instructed to mate with mortals and have as many children as possible before they died. It had been hard not to notice the enthusiasm with which the staff carried out their orders.

No doubt, this was one of Caligastia's reproductive strategies to ensure that his influence continued long after the death of his staff. Existing in a parallel frequency domain and unable to enter the minds of mortals unless consciously invited, both Caligastia and his deputy sorely needed physical beings through whom they could continue their work. The singularly robust genetic complement delivered by the Avalon surgeons, when they created bodies for the staff, had remarkable staying power—just as long as the bloodline remained uncontaminated.

The hereditary gifts of the bloodlines descending from the Prince's staff were profound and continue to have their distant echoes today in some of the royal lineages of Europe. Intermarriage with "commoners" over the last few hundred years has guaranteed that these bloodlines have been thoroughly adulterated; but some forty-two thousand years ago, when there was still a memory alive of a time when superhumans walked the Earth, these ancestral genetic lines were demonstrably powerful.

Well-developed individuals in these royal bloodlines were physically larger and stronger than their commoner counterparts, with gracefully formed bodies and finely chiseled features. They were extremely long-lived—many hundreds of years, in some cases—with bodies so healthy they rarely succumbed to disease. When injured, their wounds healed with astonishing speed. Many of them were viewed as magical beings, since they possessed some limited telepathic ability, as well as a facility in what has recently become known as remote viewing.

Caligastia had made it his business to follow and nurture these blood-lines within his territories, using his midwayers to help pave the way for the vast fortunes and the power bases designed to serve his ultimate purposes. However, he'd been so disgusted with the performance of his expeditionary forces and was still smarting from the failed invasion so many thousands of years earlier, that he'd chosen to entirely ignore what the survivors were doing in their campaign against the settlements. Since the passing of time meant little to Caligastia, he still thought of those in his invasion force who survived as traitors and cowards. I believe that by holding this grudge, and forbidding any of his midwayers to even spy on them, Caligastia seriously misjudged the survivors' expanding numbers—that is, until they finally arrived in Mesopotamia to build one of the most lasting and powerful of the great antediluvian civilizations. Then he was forced to take notice.

Some of skills developed by artisans under Caligastia's regime—before they left for the invasion—were passed down through the generations, and now large sandstone buildings were starting to be built, clustered together where the two great rivers drew closest. The boats that plied those waters also broadly followed a design once perfected ten millennia earlier by West African shipwrights.

Yet by expanding west into Mesopotamia the people were also stray-ing unknowingly into a region traditionally dominated by Caligastia's increasingly baleful presence.

Since the war, which the Prince had directly instigated and then just as promptly lost, Caligastia had been rendered relatively power-less. Another being might have felt crippled with shame at the terrible crime he'd committed, but if Caligastia felt any shame, he was far too proud to ever admit it. His machinations had resulted in laying waste to a vast swath of territory, from deep into the African continent to encir-cle the Mediterranean, including much of southern Europe and stretch-ing as far east as the current Turkish/Persian border, and he'd remained unrepentant.

Yet it was obvious to us Watchers that Prince Caligastia had effec-tively destroyed the very beings he'd taken such pleasure in manipulating.

I received some insight into Caligastia's thinking when I was required to report to him soon after I arrived in Mesopotamia. Previously, I'd had more dealings with Prince Daligastia, since Watchers fell under his command, but Prince Caligastia was still my titular superior so I had no choice but to meet with him in his grandiose palace close to the eastern coast of the Mediterranean, in present-day Israel.

He'd created this fanciful structure, with its translucent walls, impos-sible cantilevers, and topless towers, with his powerful mind. The pal-ace floated free of gravity in a subspace frequency domain available to celestials. The arched halls reached as high as the nave of a Gothic cathe-dral, yet there were no columns supporting the ornately sculpted ceiling. Like an M. C. Escher drawing, free-form staircases angled up and down without logic in the vast internal space. Light filtered dimly through gaps between the heavy crimson drapes, the tops of which reached up into the arched roof.

Yet, for all Caligastia's efforts to impress the rare visiting celes-tial, the palace was a tawdry affair. The attempt at magnificence was ostentatious and unseemly, given the appalling effects of Caligastia's governance.

The atmosphere inside was tinged with a gloomy red. Since the Prince had kept me waiting, I had a chance to drift up to look more closely at the bone-white, molded ceiling panels I'd admired earlier from a distance; what I saw confused me at first. They weren't at all the abstract, sculpted forms that I'd first believed, but a living bas-relief of a mass of slowly writhing, naked human beings locked in endless sexual congress.

Then I heard the Prince's voice in my mind, calling me down to his reception chamber. This turned out to be a more intimate room, clinging to the side of the main hall, its glazed floor revealing a void falling away into darkness beneath me. It engendered a most unsettling feeling in me. It didn't help me to know that this was a deliberate effort to throw visitors off balance.

I hadn't seen Prince Caligastia for many thousands of years by this time, preferring Vanu's company on the other side of the world, and the planet Zandana, when I was able to get away from this world altogether. Yet there was no avoiding it: when my master called, I had no choice but to respond.

And I had to admit, I was shocked at his appearance.

I remembered the Prince as a shining presence; even as he was self-importantly proclaiming his divinity, he was beautiful to behold. But, as human beings are said to have the face they deserve by the age of forty, so also had Caligastia's appearance changed in ways that reflected his increasingly criminal behavior. His face, which I'd recalled as finely formed and ascetic, now looked bloated. His long golden hair had thinned out, lost its sheen, and hung limp around his shoulders. The piercing blue eyes had a terrible darkness in them and had sunk deep under a brow once admired for its nobility.

He was slumped in an elaborately carved throne when I entered, that huge head lolling to one side, but I caught the gleam of his eyes watching me as I approached the throne and made my salutations.

If it seems curious that my description of Prince Caligastia is not dissimilar to that of a human being, there is a very good reason for it. MA has always regarded it as essential for those celestials most intimately connected with mortal beings to have bodies recognizably similar to theirs. This is for the celestials' benefit, in that it allows them closer identification with those they care for, as well as for the benefit of the mortals, who feel far more secure when they see that celestials have familiar humanoid forms.

It should also be evident by now that while each frequency domain may have its own "physical" laws, within each frequency domain those laws function interdependently with the senses of the creatures existing within that domain.

So while the Prince's floating palace was a manifestation created purely by Caligastia's mind, as I stood there facing him on the throne, it all felt as solid and real to me as the world Mein Host inhabits feels to him. Yet, for all that, I knew my thoughts would be transparent to the Prince's telepathic scrutiny, so I maintained my silence until I heard him again in my mind.

Telepathic probing has its limitations: the thoughts of a conflicted mind reveal nothing but conflicted information. When thoughts are spoken and put into words, a certain resolution is reached. A telepathic probe has to deal with raw, unfiltered data, so unless a subject's thoughts are extremely focused and any conflict surrounding the examined issue is resolved, such telepathic scrutiny is best considered a broad sweep, merely lighting up general areas of mental interest.

I was aware I was still emotionally invested in our revolution working out successfully—so that everyone wins. Despite the disorder caused by Lucifer's act, the Multiverse, as I'd experienced it, has always seemed to me an essentially benign affair. It wouldn't function as smoothly as it does if there wasn't an overall movement toward goodness, truth, and beauty. So I still held out hope—even at this late stage—that we could somehow reverse the decline; that Caligastia might shine again; that somehow it would all turn out for the best.

Running counter to this increasingly hollow hope was my disgust at all the terror and mindless brutality I'd witnessed at the hand of Caligastia's leadership, or the crimes committed in the Prince's name. The truth is that I had no idea which of these two different streams of thought in my mind would be the one that dominated, which he would use to berate me. For I was quite certain that was why I was there.

I'd been aware for some time that Caligastia never much liked me— Watchers tend to be considered spies by those with as much to hide as the Prince—and, besides, I was sure he would have taken note of my prolonged absences.

I tried to distract my mind by thinking that the Prince would be wanting news of what I'd observed of the new blossoming culture in Mesopotamia. But, within moments, I could tell from his telepathic tendrils that his interests lay somewhere else entirely. He seemed to care nothing for my optimistic observations: it was that session I'd had with with his deputy Daligastia that had piqued his interest.

No. It was more than mere interest.

The Prince was obsessed.

And he was angry.

11

A Terrible Secret

The Prince's Paradox, Divided Loyalties, High-Class Call Girl, and the Devas' Dream

London in the cold, wet winter of 1966 must have seemed all the more drab to Mein Host and the others having returned from the tropical heat of the Yucatán. After their initial exhilaration at being back "home" wore off, the lackluster tones of the city began reflecting their mood. The glorious freedom of the group's time in Xtul had all too soon been replaced by the demands of a large house in an expensive city.

Mary Ann and Robert, however, were by now comfortably ensconced in their elegant apartment at the top of the mansion, busy with their inner circle in trying to come up with ideas to support the place. No one wanted to go back to the offices and the day jobs they'd left behind, so the solutions needed to be something peculiar to the Process that would also draw attention to them.

Over the course of their discussions, they were not talking about simply supporting the mansion. Mary Ann's ambitions for the Process were far broader—she wanted it to become famous, rich, and powerful.

Although Mein Host wasn't present for some of the key decisions made by the Omega—this was now the collective term used for Mary Ann and Robert—this period became a time of intense activity for everyone in the inner circle. Yet no one knew what direction they were going to take. Were they still a psychotherapy group? Were they becoming a religion? Were they something between a psychotherapy group and a religion? What was the central theme that drew them all together? What was it they had to offer a cynical public?

They were sure they were special. Hadn't they been saved by their gods from a devastating hurricane?

Perhaps they'd been precipitous in leaving London so hastily last time—yet I never once overheard anyone making this assertion. At this point, no one would doubt Mary Ann's wisdom. Besides, hadn't they become fused into a coherent whole in Xtul? Like a squad of soldiers on a battlefield, the group were bonded by the hardships and danger they'd faced together.

The Process was just starting to be branded as a "cult," with all the insulting connotations associated with that label. But, of course, that is exactly what the Process was, a cult in the original sense of the word, denoting homage paid to a divinity.

While the reputation of cults in general hadn't yet been dishonored by the crimes of Charles Manson, Heaven's Gate, or Jonestown, it was not a term any group—however cultish—would apply to itself. Yet every religion has started with a small group of dedicated devotees gathered around a charismatic leader or leaders. Whether it is Buddhism, Christianity, Islam, or Mormonism, all were considered cults during their early, formative periods. And because no religion ever welcomes a new one horning in on its territory, the term *cult* became a derogatory way of dismissing competitors.

Cults, however, whether or not they develop into full-fledged religions, all have certain cautionary similarities that are far better understood now than fifty years ago. Most obvious: for members of a cult, the only truth that is authentic is theirs—none other. However carefully masked this hubris is by an appearance of tolerating other beliefs, at the heart of every religion lies the conviction in the absolute rightness, and in some cases the divinity, of its leadership. This belief is also the essence of a cult—it holds the members entranced, it can lead to the betrayal of friends and family and to some terrible abuses by cult leaders, and it can also prompt acts of unexpected courage and self-sacrifice.

I admit that it amuses Watchers to note that the improbability of a belief appears to make little difference to the conviction with which that belief is held. Researchers into mind control over the past half-century have probed this phenomenon in depth and now better understand it. They've determined that, frequently, the irrationality of a cult's central belief in the absolute authority of its leader makes that cult hard to identify with from the outside, yet powerfully persuasive for cult members on the inside.

Even if the Process had no clear idea yet of its central message, there was a sense among members of the community that some years later was summarized in a key line from the baseball movie starring Kevin Costner, *Field of Dreams:* "If you build it, they will come."

It was the mid-1960s and coffeehouses had been springing up over the previous decade as a generation of urban young people enjoyed the freedom and variety of expression possible in their easygoing atmospheres. Mein Host, with his aversion to alcohol, and growing up in Chelsea throughout the 1950s, had long preferred coffeehouses to pubs.

So it seemed like a perfectly natural suggestion, when the subject inevitably came up for discussion, to find somewhere in the mansion that could function as a coffeehouse. This had never been considered when Mein Host had originally designed and completed the mansion's conversion before they left London, but since the basement had a separate entrance, a high ceiling, and stretched the full length of the building, this gave them some good options.

Plans were quickly drawn up to convert the largest of the five rooms in the basement into a coffeehouse and a small adjoining room—already complete with appropriate plumbing—into a simple kitchen. The sixteen-foot-high ceiling allowed the community's carpenters to build a gallery around four sides of the main room. This was reached by an extremely narrow circular staircase with open risers, which would later become the bane of the pretty young waitresses teetering up and down, trays stacked high with healthy sandwiches and a nutritious drink with the unlikely name of an Ogmar.

Mary Ann's direction for the decor placed heavy emphasis on the colors red and black, with strong and provocative artwork on the walls. There were prints of some of Gustave Doré's darker etchings from *Paradise Lost,* and on the wall in one corner was Mein Host's unsettling painting *I for Eye,* a piece with a score of dolls' eyes. The eyes were embedded in the painting and designed to tremble at the lightest footstep, so that twenty pairs of improbably bright blue eyes gazing out from a swirl of colors would quiver and wink at the diners—a somewhat disconcerting experience for the fainthearted. Yet they might have considered themselves warned. *Satan's Cavern,* the name Mary Ann chose for the coffeehouse—more for its dark humor than its inviting allure—generally succeeded well enough in keeping the fainthearted away.

News of this weird new coffeehouse spread among London's cool and hip. As people talked up the delectable, healthy food and drinks concocted from ambrosia—the very food of the gods—and the beautiful, clear-eyed girls who'd wait on you and sit and talk to you about all your problems, Satan's Cavern soon became the most select of hangouts. Any day of the week you would find artists, writers, and musicians making the scene there. Among those there were people whose names have now become synonymous with the era: Marianne Faithful, Brian Epstein, William Burroughs, Mick Jagger, Stefanie Powers, Chögyam Trungpa Rinpoche, Jane Asher, Pete Townshend, and Hunter S. Thompson—he even included a knowing reference to Satan's Cavern in his book *Fear and Loathing in Las Vegas.* And, as Mein Host comments, it would be hard to get hipper than that!

In a room lit only by candles, with tables tucked intimately under the balcony and a couple of alcoves with red velvet–cushioned bench seats, Satan's Cavern had an ambience that was at once sacred and profane. The name *Satan's Cavern* was such a bold statement, so transparently provocative, that it terrified some people and confused others. A number of patrons felt completely at home there. Some believed it was a joke, while others arrived with their dismissive arguments at the ready. Consequently, it was always a spirited place, full of loud conversation and fine music. Members of the community who became the waiters and waitresses were good-looking, charming, and well-practiced in the art of listening. Years later, when the Process had aroused the suspicion and anger of the wrong people, the standing joke among the pretty young waitresses in Satan's

Cavern was how, at any given time, there were more undercover police and spies eating in the place than there were regular patrons. Nothing, I should add, ever came of their official investigations because the Process, in spite of the dubious and controversial reputation it gained over time, was careful not to break the law.

However, there were other reasons an intelligence agency might have wanted to keep the Process under observation that only Mary Ann would be aware of, and it was a secret she'd never even told her husband, Robert, let alone anyone else in the community. It was, perhaps, the one secret that, if revealed, would have instantly prompted the disintegration of the community. She'd come to regret this secret many times over the course of her life. It was shameful enough that she would die with it many years later, her secret still unrevealed.

It must have seemed so innocent to her when she was first approached, simply being asked to keep her eyes and ears open and report back to her contact in British Intelligence. She was working as a "high-class" call girl at the time of the Profumo affair in 1963, when the British Secretary of State for War was mixed up in an espionage scandal, so the request would likely have appealed to her patriotism, along with tacit permission to continue her proscribed profession. What she could never have known was the Intelligence agencies would continue to play a part in her life as the Process grew in size and influence. This was the secret she most dreaded coming out.

As a Watcher, I could observe from the state of Mary Ann's emotional body that this secret came to form the core of one of her deepest inner conflicts. On the one hand, her relentless ambition was driving the Process toward becoming wealthy and influential; on the other was her fear of being exposed should the community ever become too visible and vulnerable to official investigation. This conflict would manifest time and again over the years when she would cancel a number of potentially successful projects just as they were breaking through, for no good reason that those involved could divine.

❉ ❉ ❉

I hadn't noticed it before, but then I hadn't been in Caligastia's presence for many millennia: the Prince was starting to smell horrible. The odor seemed to permeate the reception chamber—not an odor of the material world; hard to describe, but redolent of burned or decomposing flesh. And, yes, Watchers do have a sense of smell. We are especially sensitive to what you might call "psychic odors," the smell emitted by a being as a result of her or his thoughts and actions.

Mein Host discovered that he possessed this faculty quite by accident in his early twenties. However, I don't believe he attributed it to the community's psychic work, since I never heard him talk about it to anyone in the Process.

It happened inadvertently on a #137 bus while it roared down London's Baker Street. As the conductor moved steadily up the aisle, taking money and punching tickets, my ward tells me he became aware of a truly horrible smell that seemed to be emanating from the man. Looking around, he noticed that no one else in the crowded bus appeared to be aware of the stink. He saw no wrinkling of noses, no suddenly averted eyes, no hankies held to delicate nostrils.

The smell became worse the closer the conductor came. Yet, mysteriously for Mein Host, it seemed to disappear entirely when the man was actually standing beside him, punching his ticket. It grew stronger again as the conductor moved farther up the aisle. This suggested that it wasn't a physical smell—it wasn't something the conductor had eaten. As my ward came to understand this, as well as the fact that other people hadn't noticed the smell on the bus, he first became aware of psychic odors. This, he tells me, has been confirmed in a number of similar experiences he has had over the years, and has been extremely useful in discerning something of the inner nature of the people he has met.

The Prince's eyes were watching me intently while he gestured for me to stand before him. I knew he was telepathically "scoping me out." I did my best to keep any thought out of my mind of my distaste at the stink that hit me on entering.

"Well?" I heard the derision in his tone. "Well? I know you were there with Daligastia. So what are your thoughts, Watcher?" His deputy had obviously been in contact with him about his doubts.

"You think I did not know this, Watcher?" The tone was demanding, turning boastful. "I, who am God of this World!? Do you believe that your God would not know the true wickedness of the administration? Do you understand now the real depth of our revolution?"

He picked up on my confusion immediately.

"It was as Prince Lucifer told us. MA will say anything to discredit us. They have cursed us as traitors. They have accused us of insanity. And now you believe that the MA leaders were setting us up? Am I correct, Watcher?"

I was no less confused. I still remembered that sweet, encouraging voice that whispered in our minds of the freedom to come. Surely . . .

Caligastia's voice broke through again, softer this time and with an edge of sardonic humor.

"And if she did? What then? You take no pleasure in paradox, Watcher, do you? You are still young."

This was getting too complicated for me. Watchers, as you may have discovered for yourself, are not complicated creatures. My previous encounter with Daligastia's bitter resentment had been painful and obviously must have colored my thinking. Yet here was the Prince taking the whole affair as a joke.

"Not a joke, Watcher!" he said rather sternly. "But can you not see the paradox?"

Clearly, I couldn't.

"Think deeper, little sister."

Was that something like affection creeping into his tone? Affection from Caligastia? Now *that* was a paradox. That was a real oxymoron.

He still sat slumped on his throne, his face an expressionless mask. But those eyes continued to bore into me, informing me more than anything he might have said that I was clearly a disappointment to him.

Wait a moment, I thought. Had he really expected me to understand all the intricacies of System politics? Me, a simple Watcher?

It wasn't for me to fathom whether or not our revolution was one of MA's false-flag operations and we'd all been deceived. Or if the administration itself had been duped by its senior officials, who had grander plans in mind. Or whether, as MA would have it, we were all just a bunch of rebellious villains who needed no supernatural encouragement from a mysterious "voice" to rise up against the authorities. These covert motives mattered little to me at the time! All I knew was that our great revolution wasn't working out as I'd hoped it would.

Was I really expected to know what was happening on the higher levels?

Was that my blindness? My stupidity?

As I said before, all these behind-the-scenes machinations were way above my pay grade.

Prince Caligastia stood up for the first time. He seemed to regain a little of his old nobility as he loomed over me.

"It is true, Watcher. This matter is more complicated than you can know. A paradox, I called it before. I trust there will come a day when you will more fully appreciate the essence of my dilemma."

This was a vulnerable side of the Prince I'd never seen before. It hadn't occurred to me that he might have a dilemma or indeed have any reservations, for example, about his claims of divine authority. His voice continued before I had the chance to realize that he was likely trying to manipulate my sympathies.

"I have reviewed your papers on Zandana's progress with interest, but I would have you remember that my destiny here on Earth is very different from my Lord Zanda's. You will find no deeper understanding by comparing our two worlds."

He paused, giving me a chance to absorb the implications of what he was saying. Was he claiming that Earth was being primed to be a special world? Or did he believe that he was the one with the special destiny? Or was it simply his own grandiosity speaking?

His face softened for the first time during the meeting and I remembered how seductive he could be when he was in his prime. In those moments I wondered if I'd misjudged Prince Caligastia. He must have been aware of what I was thinking, yet he wasn't responding with his customary anger. I felt his kindness warming me as he spoke again in my mind.

"I called you here, Watcher, because I need your witness."

My astonishment must have leaked through. Caligastia needing me? I didn't think he even knew I existed among all the Watchers who served him.

"It is as I suspected. MA is trying to interfere with our plans again. It is more serious this time and my midwayers cannot penetrate their shield. I have no wish to make myself known. Which is why you are required as a witness. You will, of course, report directly back to me. I will make my appearance when the situation demands it."

I recalled from the training lectures back at System Headquarters that there would come a time when MA would send the second of its missions to the planet. This held true on all third-density worlds when their inhabitants reached a certain level of development. We were told this would be a biological mission designed to uplift the mortal genome by the addition of what is colloquially called "violet blood." This would be initiated by the arrival of an uncommonly fertile pair of off-world beings of the Order of Material Sons and Daughters, whose thousands of offspring and their descendants would interbreed with mortals over the millennia, ultimately upgrading the genetics of the entire human race. This is the pair whose names will descend to you as Adam and Eve, although I never once heard Prince Caligastia honor them by name. He always called them "those violators," or "those wretched usurpers," or when he was feeling more ingratiating, it would be simply "the visitors."

This must be what the Prince was concerned about.

"I was informed that you would understand." Those cold, azurite eyes held me in their gaze. Understand? Understand what?

He appeared to overlook my querulous questions. My self-doubts were of no concern to him. He knew I would have to do his bidding.

"This mission is a direct interference with my world. I was not informed of its arrival. It is one of MA's power plays and it is an insult to us all. I have been in contact with Prince Lucifer. He instructs us to get rid of the two usurpers as soon as possible. I have decreed that they will be taught a lesson that MA will not quickly forget."

The edge was back in his tone. His statements shocked me. My head ached with the impact. Did I really understand? Whoever would have informed him that I did?

"Do not be concerned." His voice softened again. "You will find what I am looking for. Search carefully along the coastlines of both great seas. That is where reports of unusual activity have been observed."

I felt the meeting drawing to a close.

"I will expect you to report back to me, and only me."

I must have seemed puzzled, since I'd always presented my evaluations to his deputy. The responsibility for Watchers and midwayers had long been delegated to Daligastia, so the instruction to sideline my immediate superior took me by surprise.

"To me, only." He emphasized. "I do not wish Daligastia to be involved in any way, nor do I desire him to know my plans. And, should you be approached for information by any but me, I expect you to stay well-shielded. And silent."

Prince Caligastia took a step back and sat down heavily again on his baroque throne. His eyes were no longer on me and seemed blank and unfocused, as though he were reflecting within on how he was plotting to outwit MA and rid himself of this troublesome intrusion.

I bowed my head and started backing away.

"Go, little sister. Be on your way with my blessings."

And with that, said in a remarkably gentle tone, the Prince slipped back into himself.

In a thought I was out of his phantasmagoric palace and was soon relishing the freedom of my own limitless realm. As a Watcher assigned to the original mission, and one who had chosen to follow Caligastia into the uprising, I had no choice but to obey my Prince. I would scout out the mischief and report back as instructed.

I had no idea how much trouble I was about to get into and how confused and further divided my loyalties were going to become.

❉ ❉ ❉

Who was Mary Ann to wield such absolute power over her followers? And what was this secret, so egregious that it was never spoken about?

I've resisted revealing what I've come to understand about Mary Ann's background because Mein Host knew almost nothing about the woman's past until much later, and I needed to avoid getting too far ahead of myself. However, even when he came to learn more about her past, he still held her in awe. He appeared to be caught in the web she'd spun around him.

Mary Ann was born in the Glasgow slums in 1931, as the Great

Depression was hammering an economy that had always been depressed. The Gorbals had long been considered among the worst slums in the British Isles and they weren't about to get any better throughout the thirties.

She was the illegitimate daughter of a man who was said to have disappeared at her birth and was never mentioned again and a woman for whom she appeared to have nothing but contempt. She was an only child raised by a woman who didn't deserve Mary Ann's scorn, since she must have struggled mightily with a variety of menial jobs to support her increasingly strong-willed daughter.

When she alluded to this time in her life in speaking to her inner circle, Mary Ann would talk proudly of her independence and throw out mental images of this tiny tattered girl of five or six, dancing and singing for pennies on the frozen streets of the city. She would frequently conjure up images like this of her poverty-stricken background as a way of proudly proclaiming her remarkable rise in fortune and prestige from the gutters of Glasgow. She enjoyed contrasting it with those in her inner circle of a more affluent background, whom, in class-conscious England, she could then make feel guilty for those silver spoons in their mouths.

Since I did not accompany Mary Ann through the early years of her life, I can only repeat what I've heard her say when my ward has been in her presence. Nor can I confirm the truth of her more outrageous stories, but with what I have come to know about her over time, I believe she took pleasure in creating that ambivalence.

Among the most unusual and telling of the stories she would relate was how, as a young girl, she would leave her body at night and find herself in an out-of-the-body state projected into Hitler's bunker during planning sessions with his generals, gathered around a large table covered with maps. She spoke with amusement at how she would walk around behind the generals whispering into their ears, and of the Führer's terrible temper tantrums.

True or not, it seems an unlikely fabrication with which to regale her inner circle, unless she merely concocted the story to shock the others. That was very much part of her style. She seemed especially prone to trying to unsettle Hugh, the only Jewish member of her circle.

She never talked about her adolescence, or the limited schooling she must have received, but she gave the impression that she couldn't wait to get away from Scotland and down to the Big City.

London, in the years immediately following the war—she would have arrived as a sixteen-year-old in 1947—presented few options for a young, poorly educated girl from the Glasgow slums. Having endured the worst of Hitler's bombs and all the deprivations of a long war, the dazed citizens of England's capital city were still struggling to reestablish a semblance of normal life. The exhilaration felt by Londoners at the end of the war had long since worn off when people had the chance to take stock of their appalling situation. The country was financially broken, the people were exhausted, the city half-destroyed, and many of the best and bravest of a generation of young men and women were dead or crippled.

Having made such a sacrifice, many English people regarded the constant presence of American troops still based in England with mixed emotions. "Of course," they'd tell one another over a beer, "the war wouldn't have been won without the Yanks. But just look at 'em poncing around thinking they beat the Nazis by themselves." Another might point out that they'll be paying off the Yanks for the rest of their lives. Then someone else would chime in with how the Yanks have all the money and get all the girls.

Under these depressing conditions, a young girl from out of town might be forgiven for falling into life on the street. However, Mary Ann was far too intelligent and ambitious to settle for that unsavory profession and would contrast it proudly with her own decision to work as a high-class call girl.

She soon found her niche.

By the time Mein Host first encountered Mary Ann in 1963, she was in her early thirties and had married Robert—my ward's friend from architectural college. She'd styled herself as a wealthy, jet-setting, professional career woman, not mentioning anything too specific. Apparently Robert had met her in Scientology, in which Mary Ann, by her account, had risen to a position of some importance, briefly becoming a favorite of its leader, L. Ron Hubbard.

However, neither she nor Robert were convinced by Scientology, and both left after a couple of years. She would often describe it as "Hubbard's ego trip," or she'd say, "Hubbard's just trying to make a lot of little Hubbards." And she'd speak contemptuously of the shocking condition of Hubbard's teeth because he was too cowardly to go to the dentist. Although both Mary Ann and Robert had left Scientology, and before they'd become targets of Hubbard's "fair game policy," they'd invited Mein Host to a Scientology lecture to support one of Robert's younger brothers who was still involved. My ward told them afterward that he wasn't surprised they'd left because he was "utterly unimpressed by Scientology."

Mary Ann maintained a special loathing for L. Ron Hubbard. It doesn't take a psychologist to suspect that her hatred of Hubbard stemmed from their being so similar in character. Both were convinced of their own rightness, both imposed their interpretation of reality on others, both cultivated an aura of secrecy and mystery around themselves, and both felt justified in living well at others' expense.

Although Mein Host had been close to Robert during the first three years of their architectural training, Robert had dropped out of college, and they hadn't seen each other for two years before Robert made contact with his friend again. At that point, Mein Host first met Mary Ann.

I've already written in *Confessions of a Rebel Angel* about his instant dislike of the woman and how this visceral distaste so radically transformed into reverence three years later when he believed she'd revealed herself to him as the Goddess.

So this amounts to the little information Mary Ann had allowed to leak out about her life before the Process. Mein Host didn't learn much about this until a number of years after the community had returned to London from Xtul. By this time Mary Ann was the fully ensconced Oracle of the Process, and starting to groom her husband as a messiah, with herself as the power behind the throne.

Yet these were still early days, and Mein Host knew as little about Mary Ann's ambitions as he did about her background. He believed that she'd revealed herself to him as the Goddess, and that was enough for the lad. In his devotion to her, he had left his old life entirely behind him—

his career, his friends, his family, his sweetheart, his books and guitar, and his independence.

If I were to "read" him at that point in his life, I would have to say he appeared to be completely committed in his devotion to Mary Ann and would no doubt remain so for the rest of his life. He certainly showed every sign of that being the case.

And the dark and terrible secret that Mary Ann carried to her grave?

Let me approach this elliptically, since I've only just revealed this secret to Mein Host and he's not at all happy about it.

Here's the key that my ward might have used to unlock this secret had he known it at the time to form the question: How does a woman with half a dozen prosecutions in England for prostitution come and go so easily from America, a country that doesn't readily grant permission for entry to people with criminal convictions? My ward was also far too young and naive to suspect that an intelligence agency would ever approach a call girl for pillow-talk information on her clients. It would have been the last thing to think. It would have been an unimaginable betrayal.

But, of course, Mein Host knew nothing of this.

✣ ✣ ✣

I was mightily relieved to be out of Prince Caligastia's presence.

The stink took some time to wear off, so I took the opportunity to relax, not wanting to take its remnants with me on my investigations. I knew I had to carry out the Prince's instructions, but as time has passed and I've seen something of the disaster Caligastia has wrought on the planet, I no longer felt compelled to respond immediately to his every whim.

The Mediterranean Sea, especially along the North African coastline, had changed radically since I'd last seen it, evidently as a result of the war. Natural events would change the shape of the sea many times before it finally arrived at its present form.

I watched pods of dolphins numbering in the thousands moving as a single being, leaping together in rhythmic arcs that looked from the air like a great loom, weaving the ocean into a turquoise sheen. Islands appeared under me like shark's teeth piercing the surface, surf frothing around the base of sheer cliffs like chiffon skirts. I found myself more drawn to the islands.

I chose Crete for some brief rest and recreation. I liked its wildness. It hadn't yet been settled by mortals and I felt a natural resonance with its magnificent White Mountains on the western side of the island. I soon found a harmonious place on Mt. Volakias, a perfectly circular, grassy plateau, surrounded by high rock walls, broken only where the Gorge of Samaria starts cutting down through the mountains to the sea.

I took my time. I lay down for some twenty of your years, cushioned by the thought of the friendly grass beneath me. I had the curious sense that the mountain was trying to tell me something, yet as I dreamt on I could never quite grasp what it was. It kept slipping through my fingers as I moved in and out of dream states.

And, yes, angels need to sleep and dream in much the same way as you do. It's an arena in which many different species can interact in what you might call a "virtual reality." Companion angels, in particular, use Dreamtime to train, or minister to, their mortal wards.

As I lay there, half-aware of your world, no animals disturbed my peace. Small, brightly colored birds bobbed and fluttered in the long grass. Clouds of midges flew all around, their millions of tiny wings refracting sunlight into scintillating rainbows. Only the eagles soared and circled on the updrafts, wafting up the gorge as the land cooled at night.

What was the mountain trying to tell me?

The images were so strange—ancient things, incomprehensibly old, even by standards of eternity. I dreamt of ancient and enormous sea creatures that moved languorously through the abysmal depths. I saw their extraordinary transformation as millions of years passed, and noted their endless patience and the cosmic message they'd waited so long to convey to the beings they hoped would emerge. I dreamt of their small clan and of the love connecting them as they fell down through the inexhaustible wastes of time. I saw them living and dying many millions of years later, their great bodies fossilizing into the massive undersea mountain ranges that became their burial sites. I watched them easing their great bulks onto the land, moving so imperceptibly slowly that they could be mistaken for the landscape itself.

What it meant, I had no idea. Or, indeed, why the White Mountains were singing to me of that particular song.

Then another long song started in Dreamtime. I recognized in it the dreaming of the Rock Devas. I felt their long, slow, telluric rhythms, the sudden explosions of volcanic lava, the mountains thrust up and buckled by colliding tectonic plates, the glaciers that gouged deep into their flesh.

Then I started catching glimpses of the profoundest ennui, a weariness born of the ages, a sense of ancient restlessness, as though eons of stability desired more from life. And so it was that the Rock Devas dreamed the plants and trees—they carpeted themselves with meadows and forests, they dreamed of many colors and flowers blossomed, and with the trees and flora came the Nature Spirits to care and minister to the natural world.

I was drifting in and out of Dreamtime, trying to make sense of what I was being shown. Next, it was the Plant Devas dreaming, and theirs was a yearning for mobility, for a release from their rooted capture by rock and earth. In their dreaming, their desire to serve a higher purpose was recognized by the insects, the birds, the fish, and all the animals that live off the plants and grasses.

And now it was the animals dreaming of their gods. Their pack leaders morphed before their eyes into jackel-headed immortals striding through Dreamtime: the fish dreamed of their Oannes; the lizards dreamed of their reptilian gods living in underground cities; snakes dreamed of dragons; birds dreamed of the great beyond.

Dreaming, dreaming, dreaming—everything around me was dreaming of life, glorious, radiant life.

As I lay there entranced by Mt. Volakias's epic creation dream, I slowly became aware of some unusual activity emanating out of the gorge. After trying to ignore the odd sounds, my curiosity got the better of me and I moved closer to the edge, where I could see the cliff on the other side of the gorge rising precipitously from the valley floor.

Yet what seemed to be appearing on the rock face riveted my attention. I was still drowsy, but it looked as if the faults and fissures in the wall of rock were almost imperceptibly reconfiguring themselves amid a violet mist of midwayer activity. I could see that they'd already molded massive petroglyphs in a hieroglyphic language known only to them.

I lay quite still and silent on the rim of the canyon, staring up at this enormous bas-relief, enjoying the thought of the long grass tickling my nose, and not quite believing what I was seeing.

Who could these midwayers be?

I had rarely seen any of Vanu's small contingent on this side of the world. Being outnumbered four to one by Caligastia's forty thousand–plus active midwayers had apparently made penetration of Caligastia's territories nearly impossible. So it must have been part of the Prince's group. And yet that didn't make sense—Daligastia was known to keep a brutally sharp eye on his midwayers, continually fearing their defection. Although midwayers cannot leave the planet unless they're taken off by MA, Vanu had always made it clear that he and Amadon would welcome any rebel midwayer prepared to forsake the rebellion, change sides, and join them in Lemuria. However, until all 40,119 rebel midwayers would be removed some thirty-eight thousand years later, only a scant few were known to have actually taken up this offer and defected to Vanu and Amadon's side.

One of the ways I've observed that Daligastia was able to keep such strict control over his unruly midwayers lay in keeping them constantly busy. They were given no time no reevaluate their cause and were tacitly encouraged to believe they were separate, godlike beings who lived to control the human experiment. I knew this was how they thought about humanity—as the human experiment. I believe it affirmed their sense of detachment and upset the fragile balance all beings experience between service to others and service to self.

Midwayers are introduced on all inhabited worlds in their early stages of protocivilization—their primary function being to serve the Prince's staff in their long-lasting task of supporting generations of planetary mortals in their climb from their animal natures to the higher spiritual values of empathy and mutual respect.

Following the uprising, Daligastia's midwayers had become increasingly self-serving, until the atomic war had rendered them harmless, the human genocide having deprived them of their playthings. All that happened over ten millennia earlier, and now the rapidly growing new human settlements centered around Lake Van, spreading into the Balkans and central Europe, were starting to repopulate North Africa. Into this mix came the migration south of natives, unaffected by the radiation and retreating from the cold in the frozen northern regions. All this movement among the descendants of those who survived the war also led to frequent clashes between the neanderthal tribes moving north from Central Africa, much to the latter's disadvantage. Regardless, a small number of neanderthals managed to make their way into Europe and slowly evolved a primitive cave-dwelling culture.

I knew Daligastia had put his midwayers back to hard work, requiring them to attach themselves to the leading individuals, families, and clans who were emerging in the newly founded cities as the ruling classes, the priests, and the military, as well as the rich traders. The midwayers slipped all too willingly into their roles as household gods, with their promises of wealth and protection for men and women who were sadly unaware that they were falling into Prince Caligastia's web.

Perhaps this digression will cast light on the degree of my astonishment in observing what was being incised on the rock face in the Gorge of Samaria. They clearly had to be Daligastia's creatures, and yet somehow they had managed to break loose long enough to create this magnificently precise petroglyphic summary of what I took to be their historical memory.

As I observed all this activity from my perch in a frequency domain imperceptible to the midwayers, it came to me that I was seeing something new. I could sense that they were operating outside Daligastia's command structure and were exercising their individuality in a far more creative manner than I'd ever previously believed possible in that species. I'd seen the way some midwayers derived pleasure from playing with the clouds, forming and dissolving them into immense vaporous biomorphs and constantly shifting simulacra, but molding their designs into solid rock was of a far higher order of difficulty.

In those moments I first formed a strange and new understanding about the nature of life in this world—life on all sentient levels working here. I felt there was something fundamentally paradoxical about this planet—perhaps the same paradox that Prince Caligastia had teased me about.

Yet, oddly, it felt more like a blessing to me. I saw that however severe the inevitability of the planet's downward spiral was, there would always be individuals and small groups drawn from every race and sentient species who would find artful ways of challenging the destructive forces of their eras.

The rebel element in me was now starting to revolt against the rebels. Of course, this was the very paradox that was bothering the Prince. He must have understood by now that any of his efforts to produce an advanced civilization were bound to end in disaster. And for reasons he was still too proud to admit, he would likely have been carefully chosen from thousands of contenders to be the primary agent of this world's downward spiral into isolation and technological savagery.

I saw the unfortunate dilemma into which both Princes Caligastia and Daligastia had unwittingly fallen—if MA had indeed set them up. Whenever they placed their energies and the considerable power of their midwayers into proving MA wrong by attempting to create a viable human culture, that culture would invariably descend—sooner rather than later—into chaos and bloodshed. On the other hand, if the Princes were to be as expressive as they really wanted to be—and both maintained an unrelenting fury at MA's dismissive and condescending attitudes—and if they then focused their influence on making life on the planet as progressively intolerable as possible, wouldn't they merely be serving MA's more base purposes?

After a while I drew away from the gorge's rim to sink once again into the long grass of the sunlit plateau. I felt almost overwhelmed with all this new information. I was relieved to find that the mountain was silent—I wasn't sure I could handle any more Dreamtime sagas right now.

This was probably the first time I actually relished being a Watcher. I am merely an observer. I'm unable to make anything concrete occur in your material reality.

I watch and I report.

That's all.

While I can be held responsible for my choices and decisions, surely I cannot be blamed for any of the multiple disasters brought on by the active meddling of Caligastia's proxies in the affairs of mortals.

As I was congratulating myself on apparently avoiding any moral responsibility for the appalling state that I saw as the inevitable destiny of the world to come, I recalled with a jolt Caligastia's instructions. I could feel him getting anxious about me. I tried to keep his anxiety at bay. I recall thinking: I'm only going to observe. Watch and report. Even if I have no choice but to share the feelings of those I observe, I create no effect on them. The sole exception to this fundamental injunction has been the rare occasions when I've been required to intercede—mainly by simple misdirection—in some of Mein Host's incarnations at which I was present.

Now I could feel the psychic pressure from Caligastia for me to not only report on what I'd observed, but if I saw an opening I was to try any small act of sabotage against the two off-world visitors that the Prince had convinced himself were already somewhere in the world. Thus, it was in this uncomfortably ambivalent frame of mind, which persisted through-out my search of North African coastline, that I finally stumbled onto what the Prince had instructed me to find. It was on a slim peninsula extending out from the eastern coastline of the Mediterranean.

What I found surprised even the seasoned Watcher I felt I was becoming. That's how little I knew about how much more seasoned I would have to become before winning a mortal incarnation.

In the Prince's words, I was still a "very young Watcher."

12

The Birth of a Cult

The Visitors' Arrival, Exalted Bloodlines, Extraterrestrial Secrets, and the Mindbenders of Mayfair

You, my tenacious reader, now know a great deal more about Mary Ann, the self-proclaimed Oracle of the Process, her background, something about her singular abilities, and what might be motivating her than Mein Host or anyone else in the community knew for many more years.

The 1960s was a far more innocent and trusting time, and it wouldn't have occurred to anyone who had fallen under Mary Ann's spell to question her authenticity. They would have laughed scornfully, had you raised that issue, and told you that Mary Ann was the most authentic person they'd ever met. Skilled as they'd become in the art of turning tables, they might well have said that it was her very authenticity that had drawn them to her.

There was some truth to this. Mary Ann was certainly authentically herself. And she was evidently fully convinced of the cosmology she was to evolve that would become the belief system of the Process: Church of the Final Judgment. So to dismiss her as a con artist and her followers as mere dupes—as some of Mary Ann's more vociferous critics have contended—is overly simplistic and would do her, or her followers, little justice.

I have no doubt that Mary Ann was convinced that she was the incarnate Goddess. I no longer observed her after Mein Host left the community in 1977, but from the brief correspondence he had with her before she died, she was still showing no signs of self-doubt.

I can't be sure how strongly others in the community believed Mary Ann was divine, as Mein Host did, but from what I've observed of their actions, everyone there must have believed it to some extent. When she took the name Hecate some time later (Hecate was a Greco-Roman goddess best-known for her hounds and her dark magic), it seemed to confirm for them they were the guardians of this deeply hidden secret; a secret that became so sacred it was never openly discussed. They believed they were the Elect. They thought of themselves as the privileged few, the only ones to whom an incarnate Goddess had revealed herself.

Or, in Mary Ann's case, the one and only Incarnate Goddess Herself. For one thing was certain: Goddess or not, she was a woman who openly accepted no equal.

Robert was still being groomed by Mary Ann to be what I've heard her call her "front man." This had to lie in the future since Robert, as stated earlier, no longer made any public appearances and was now operating exclusively behind the scenes.

Much has been written by others about *PROCESS* magazine, and Mein Host has previously published stories about some of his experiences as the magazine's art director, so I have no wish to duplicate what is already generally known. Yet, there were occasions when he served as art director that I believe became deeply formative in the development of my ward's character.

As should be clear by now, this is no apologia for Mein Host's choices or actions. We Watchers tend to emphasize the best in people, especially when we observe that our wards' intentions are broadly aligned with their destinies. Hard though it was for me to appreciate the reasons Mein Host gave himself for his devotion to Mary Ann, his companion angels had made it clear at the time of his Goddess revelation that this was his freely chosen path.

Designing *PROCESS* magazine drew out an aspect of Mein Host I hadn't observed before. His long architectural training allowed him the precision to create handmade four-color separations, and his innate design sense carried over fluidly from architecture to graphic design. Although he clearly loved architecture, magazine design came naturally to him and he especially enjoyed how he was able to apply his intuition to it. The design process was very different from the long, slow, rational decision-making that the field of architecture required.

Recently, the eight issues of *PROCESS* magazine that the community produced between 1967 and 1975 have been gaining some underground notice as a major influence on the psychedelic graphic design seen now in many contemporary magazines. Mein Host was astonished when he learned, some thirty years later, that his design work was being recognized in such glowing psychedelic terms. He had stopped any exploration of psychedelics when he joined the group, and he hadn't taken entheogens for at least three years prior to designing the magazines.

Although he would not have been aware of it at the time, he had been intuitively creating a methodology for himself that has enabled him to work wisely with entheogens over the course of this lifetime. Rather than using entheogens to escape from or avoid everyday reality, from his earliest experiences with LSD and DMT in the late 1950s, he appeared to be intuitively aware that entheogens were a gift of great value, a lens through which he could confront and master his demons. The art of it, so he believed, was to bring back the information received in the higher realms of entheogenic consciousness and allow what he learned to slowly transform his character.

His so-called psychedelic magazine design was a good example of this. He was unaware of the psychedelic artwork coming out of San Francisco in the same period and knew of no others working in this style. Indeed, he would hardly have considered it a distinct style—it was simply a manifestation of his individual design sense. He had evidently sufficiently integrated his prior entheogenic experiences so as to be able to express what he had learned in his unique graphic style, which was only later identified by others as psychedelically inspired.

To Mary Ann and Robert's credit, they quickly recognized Mein Host's unusual design sense and gave him a remarkably free hand with all the graphics. In their weekly editorial meetings, they'd made it clear that neither time nor money (within reason) was to be spared to produce the very finest, the most beautiful, the most provocative and successful magazine of its kind and its era.

Yet for all the subsequent accolades, the magazine also became the unwitting vehicle of Mein Host's next fall from grace in Mary Ann's eyes. It was a hard and humbling fall, and his eventual emergence from the dark cloud of his Goddess's disapproval was as ironic as the original cause of his fall from grace.

The Process art department occupied the room in the basement of Balfour Place closest to the street that the public passed on their way to Satan's Cavern. It was a long room, about fifteen feet wide, with drawing boards and light boxes down both long sides. Angle-poise lamps bowed low over work surfaces; strips of red masking material and pages of Letraset—a dry transferable lettering unknown today—with missing letters covered all available surfaces. The one window at the end wall was blocked off, so that day or night meant little to those working continuously for days on end without sleep, pushing themselves to their limit whenever the deadline was looming to get it to the printers.

There were seldom more than two or three people working in the art department on the early magazines, although over time the number grew to half a dozen as more skilled illustrators joined the community.

As art director, Mein Host very much ruled over the art department, and I could tell that he felt himself fortunate to be working with two of his closest friends in the group. Peter, his friend from pre-Process days and the big Irishman who caught fish for the community at Xtul, soon became the editor, while Andrew, Robert's younger brother, willingly took on the job of production manager. These three regularly met with Mary Ann and Robert to discuss and plan the magazine. From what I observed of their interactions, they worked surprisingly well together.

The final and most important part of the operation was the darkroom. This was impossibly tiny and wedged under the staircase some fifteen feet along the corridor from the art department and opposite the door to Satan's Cavern. In the era before computers and programs like

Photoshop, the darkroom was where all the visual magic occurred—and for that a magician was needed. In what was to happen with remarkable frequency, exactly the right person became a member of the community at exactly the right time. Within a few months of returning from Mexico, and when the first magazine was on the drawing boards, a young German with a background in photography walked into Satan's Cavern and within weeks had joined the community.

Ewald was a brilliantly inventive young man who invariably rose to the technical and aesthetic challenges posed in the darkroom by Mein Host's innovative designs. While Ewald was never included in the editorial discussions and didn't get to meet the Oracle or Teacher for many years, *PROCESS* magazine could never have flourished as it did without his technical flair.

Balfour Place hummed with activity throughout 1967 as the Process felt driven to make its way as an uncharacteristic voice in swinging London.

The community's highly disciplined life—free of drugs, sex, and alcohol; with no personal money, possessions, or freedom; and a twenty-four-hour-a-day dedication to a higher cause—made an unlikely contrast to their increasingly liberated, and licentious, peers in the outside world. In a way, members of the Process didn't fully acknowledge—or, even notice—they were becoming curiosities, living anachronisms. Devotees of the Goddess in a godless city, living like monks in a world they believed was corrupted beyond redemption.

Strange contradictions faced anyone curious and bold enough to penetrate the challenge the Process presented. Having dared themselves to enter Satan's Cavern to eat, they might be heard to remark on their astonishment at the delicious food—for Satan! And if one of the beautiful young female waitresses had sat down with them and listened with such apparently genuine interest to their woes, then wherever did Lucifer and Satan come into the mix?

All the members of the group had been allowing their hair to grow out for the past three years. By now many of the men had neat beards and wild manes reaching halfway down their backs. They looked like hippies; yet they were neat, clean, and they all dressed alike—at that stage it was simply black pants and tops, justified by the simplicity it brought to the community laundry. To many people, Processeans presented an incongruous sight when they started wearing uniforms and selling their magazines on the streets of the city.

They were the first of many groups to have discovered how much money can be made, and how many magazines can be sold, by directly approaching people on the streets of a city. Processeans—as they were now calling themselves—were charismatic, flamboyant, and terrifyingly self-confident to the timid pedestrian, as a pair of them would prowl either side of Kings Road, catching the eyes of prospective buyers. Yet, when people stopped to talk, they found these odd creatures invariably courteous and charming, and frequently extremely funny.

They could talk with an unselfconscious ease about archaic myths as if they were real—Jehovah, Lucifer, and Satan, and what Christ meant to them. And yet their magazine was cool and modern. They were living highly regimented lives of poverty, celibacy, and obedience, but they appeared, both men and women, to grow progressively more beautiful as the months and years passed. More than a few times I heard visitors to Satan's Cavern ask some version of the same question: "What did you do with the plain ones? Throw 'em back?"

It was something of a mystery, even to the members of the community themselves. Yet being English and brought up to be modest and self-effacing, this increasing pulchritude was seldom mentioned—although it didn't go unnoticed by Mary Ann. It should be no surprise to hear that she ascribed the phenomenon to the potency and value of her brilliant insights and to the effectiveness of Robert's teachings.

A less egotistical viewpoint would hold that members of any small group of dedicated young people, all devoted to what they believe is a higher purpose, will exude a certain kind of beauty. Their skin will glow with inner health, their enthusiasm will be infectious, their hair will be glossy, and the pupils of their eyes will be so dilated it will be hard not to fall a little bit in love with them.

Of course, there were misjudgments and misadventures, one of which sent some of the more fainthearted among the audience scuttling for the doors. At one of their weekly "Processcenes" held in the main assembly room—they might have been called "happenings" in San Francisco, although the Process developed the concept independently—it became evident how far the community had moved from generally accepted values.

The evenings, for which an audience had made a small donation, were designed to be provocative as well as instructive. They also provided a platform for individual members to express, in an artful and engaging manner, what most interested them. The emphasis was always placed on improvisation, on intuition, and on allowing the words and ideas to flow freely.

One evening, for example, featured an animated and unscripted discussion between a member dressed as the pope and the other as Aleister Crowley. Promoted without irony as "Great Priest Meets Great Beast," the performance was thought to be a huge success in that it offended almost everyone in the audience.

When it came his turn, Mein Host pulled off an oddly prescient little theatrical event. Surrounding himself with bits and pieces of recording equipment, old TVs, and a couple of oscillators, and with a microphone in his hand—all connected to audio speakers—he conducted an elaborate three-way conversation between individuals from three different extraterrestrial races, discussing the state of this planet from their point of view. Some of the comments made by the three (purported) extraterrestrials—having somehow bypassed my ward's rational mind—turned out to be rather more truthful about the deteriorating state of the biosphere, and our treatment of our fellow humans, than the audience might have expected.

However, it was Paul who managed to send the timorous scurrying from the room. Paul, the tall, elegant, somewhat austere man—one of those with whom Mein Host studied architecture—had taken up flagellation with considerable enthusiasm at Xtul. Once the community returned to London, this practice was quietly stopped. According to Mein Host, it just hadn't seemed to matter anymore. No one had told them to stop. It just faded out.

Apparently not for Paul. He strode up the aisle between a packed house as the room darkened. With his back to the audience and a sole spotlight focused on him, he slowly stripped off his shirt and folded it carefully before placing it on a high chair next to him.

The room fell utterly silent.

I felt that people weren't quite sure what they were watching.

Then I saw a shudder ripple through the room as the audience grasped what Paul had in his right hand. A five-foot-long piece of rope with a thick knot every five inches, one end coiled around his hand, hung down to the floor beside his bare right foot.

He allowed for a long theatrical pause, during which I doubted anyone in the room dared to breathe, before whipping the rope over his left shoulder in a terrific thwack.

I saw every person in that room physically recoil, mirror neurons squealing, as though they had just scourged themselves. There was a scuffing of feet and the legs of chairs squealed against the hardwood floor as people pushed nervously back in their chairs.

Another thwack echoed through the room. More recoils, and this time some gasps and moans. Red welts were starting to appear on Paul's back, as the brutal self-punishment continued. By the fifth thwack a few people were starting to edge out the door. By the ninth, the room was all but empty.

Paul, still with his back to the almost-empty room, was in a world of his own. He continued to flagellate himself mercilessly. I could see from his subtle energy bodies that he was in a state of painful contrition.

And, I recalled thinking, what a contrast this was from watching Mein Host reaching his heights of ecstasy whenever he flagellated himself. And then: what a strange thing this Process community is, that two such completely different people had been drawn into Mary Ann's orbit and had become so closely aligned in their aspirations.

⁂

The two off-world visitors—the pair that Caligastia sneeringly referred to as "usurpers"—appeared to have settled into their small outpost when I first stumbled on them on the fertile peninsula at the eastern end of the Mediterranean. After leaving Crete, I'd worked my way all around the coastline and might well have missed the strange visitors if it wasn't for the flurry of midwayers operating in the subspace regions around their settlement.

I could see why Caligastia had sent me on this mission. It didn't require that many of Vanu's midwayers to throw up enough confusion in subspace to prevent the Prince's midwayers from piercing the veil. They wouldn't have had the chance to see what was going on.

So this is what some of Vanu's midwayers had been up to! I'd seen those midwayers at work on their petroglyphic history on the rock face in the Gorge of Samaria. Of course, it couldn't have been any of Daligastia's crew—I should have known better. He kept them far too strictly under his thumb to permit such trivial pursuits as "decorating rocks," to quote Daligastia's mocking words when he heard about it.

Observing the two off-world visitors for the first time brought back to mind much of what I'd been taught in the training sessions back at System Headquarters. Unlike the few brief extraterrestrial visitations I've observed while I've been here, I knew these two visitors were posted from the Inner Worlds, from Jerusalem, the System headquarters planet, on this the second of MA's formal missions to the planet.

We were told these "Material Sons and Daughters," as MA calls them, were "biologic uplifters," deposited—much as we were for the Prince's mission—on the face of a primitive planet, with the intention of building on what the Prince's mission should have accomplished. While I'm sure their teachers had briefed the visitors on the condition of Prince Caligastia's world before they arrived, I doubt if anything could have prepared the pair for the chaos and opposition they'd find when they got here.

I was aware, as I'm sure Caligastia was too, that one of the primary functions of this magnificent couple—and even in my eyes they were magnificent—was progenerative. They were bringing a genetic boost I recall the tutors called "violet blood," designed to contribute an important added refinement to the human genetic pool.

I have called this pair magnificent and that was no understatement. They were humanoid, of course, but both male and female stood well over nine feet tall and were beautifully formed—strong muscular bodies with long legs and broad across the shoulders. Their skin was fairer than any I'd yet seen, almost translucent, and as they moved around the compound, I could discern that their auras were tinged with a tone of light violet. Their fine-boned faces were dominated by a pair of the brightest of cornflower-blue eyes, and their long blond hair blew wildly in the offshore sea breeze. They were the first such strikingly blue eyes I'd yet seen on the planet.

The pair were clearly closely bonded and, from what I could observe, they appeared to dislike spending any time separated from each other. Frankly, they couldn't keep their hands off one another. They were obviously reveling in the beautiful new bodies the Avalon surgeons had created for them. I recall thinking how fortunate that was for them when I remembered that they were here to make children—hundreds of thousands of children.

The tutors had explained that these children, the products of interbreeding with the indigenous mortals, would be delivering violet blood into the genetic stream of all planetary mortals. They impressed on us that this approach to injecting a genetic uplift, while slow and somewhat tedious, was regarded as the most natural way of accomplishing the task. They had tried cloning and other reproductive techniques in earlier experimental worlds. However, nothing had been as successful over the long term as what they called this "more natural technique," since it allowed a reasonable period of enculturation for the violet blood to spread throughout the world.

Good luck! I thought as I watched the beautiful pair going about their day. They had no idea of what they were up against. Caligastia wasn't going to let MA's two proxies slip out of his control, however pretty they were.

I found myself fearing for the future of their mission.

I decided I wouldn't report back to Prince Caligastia immediately—I was fairly certain he'd have heard about the visitors' arrival from another of his Watchers. I hadn't seen any of my kind near the settlement, but I'd been around the Prince long enough to know he would never have entrusted a task like mine to a single Watcher. He was far too suspicious. Besides, I was aware by this time that Caligastia didn't fully trust me. I was bound to serve him—I had no choice about that. Yet he must have been telepathically aware of how I was starting to feel about his uprising—even if he showed nothing of it in our meeting.

I had an uncomfortable mix of emotions when I realized this. I'd been learning to deal with powerful emotions in their pure form, but these emotions were fluctuating, sometimes aligned and sometimes opposed, and I felt they were tearing my emotional body apart. I had to stay cool and think this through.

First of all, I had to assume that I would have been transparent to him. It was a shock when I let this sink in. It had unpleasant implications.

Then it registered that Prince Caligastia cared absolutely nothing for me. I was merely something he'd used to accomplish his ends, a useful idiot. I had stood behind him throughout the uprising. I truly believed he was our brilliant leader, our guiding light. Yet I meant nothing to him!

The resentment I now felt toward him for so profoundly deceiving us—deceiving me!—was colored, and, yes, slightly mitigated, by a sense of relief that MA's new mission was here to restore some balance to this difficult and corrupted world. I didn't hold out much hope for their chances, but at least they were here. So, I stayed on, observing for the next few decades.

Many years' preparation had evidently been invested in readying the garden/park for the two off-planet visitors. Now that they had arrived and started their work, word of their presence was spreading to the mainland. In response, more and more of the local tribes were drawn to the peninsula, making for a remarkable sight. MA's beautiful pair greeted all newcomers with open arms and put them to work finishing the high wall to close off the peninsula from the mainland.

I'd observed that they'd been having problems for some time with wild animals straying onto their land; evidently there were instructions not to kill those creatures. Neither of the two visitors appeared to be afraid when a pride of lions moved into the settlement before the wall's completion, but the humans, now living and working alongside the visitors and their growing number of children, were utterly terrified.

Thus I imagined that the wall became an unfortunate necessity in the visitors' eyes. It was the first sign I saw that they were making compromises that I'm sure they weren't happy about. They were here to teach and uplift the mortals; they wouldn't have wanted to demonstrate fear. So they had justified building the wall by maintaining that it was to protect the livestock that they intended to domesticate from the intrusion of predators.

Interestingly, the visitors appeared to have a gently subduing effect on the most vicious of animals. I assumed this was a telepathic effect, although the signal was outside the range of frequencies to which I'm sensitive, so I couldn't tell how they were doing it.

One morning I observed Vanu and Amadon entering one of the simple, yet strikingly elegant, houses I'd seen the visitors sharing.

Now that was a surprise!

What were Vanu and Amadon doing there?

Then, of course, it all came together in my mind.

Under normal conditions, it should have been the Planetary Prince who would have made all the arrangements for the visitors. It should have been Prince Caligastia who'd have gathered the tribes together with the good news of the coming of these special visitors; who would have had the people busy by the thousands, preparing the peninsula for their arrival; who would have proudly passed the baton of a thriving global population over to the visitors; and who would have pledged to support the new mission in all ways possible.

But this was clearly an exception. So Vanu had taken over, had he? Evidently, Caligastia was being sidelined and Vanu had been called in to do his best to prepare for the illustrious visitors' arrival.

Now this was certainly intriguing. I knew it would only infuriate Caligastia more. He would see it as a direct insult to his self-proclaimed divinity. That MA's bureaucracy hadn't asked his permission for the intervention; that the Melchizedek Receivers who'd sanctioned it had done it without his knowledge—all that was humiliating enough. But then to discover that his sworn enemy, Vanu, was fulfilling *his* role—the Prince's role! That was going to push the Prince over the edge.

With this understanding, I realized I'd been deluding myself if I believed for a moment that Caligastia would not find a way of outwitting this unworldly pair. Beautiful and brilliant though the visitors may have been, compared to Caligastia they were innocents.

Besides, I'd have thought that Vanu and Amadon would be preoccupied with their Lemurian experiment. I hadn't been over to the islands since well before I was last on Zandana. So much had been happening, both here and on Zandana, that I realized I'd given no further thought to Lemuria's fine culture.

When I was last on the islands, the civilization that the people of Mu were building—with Vanu and Amadon's guidance—seemed to be entering its mature phase. They had become a seagoing culture and, over the previous three thousand years, they'd spread widely all over the Pacific. Lemurian artisans and missionaries traveled as far as northern India, as well as setting up numerous settlements in the Americas that would later develop into great cities.

Over the millennia, their basic philosophy of kindness had taken root and produced a remarkably peaceful people. Their worship of Father Sun and Mother Earth was so simple and direct that their religious devotion had become a personal matter and required no priests to officiate or intercede on their behalf.

The three oracular centers discussed earlier had thrived and waned over the centuries, largely due to the people's fears of natural disasters. Since so many of the islands straddled volcanic areas, earthquakes and eruptions were not infrequent. In those times the oracles were thronged with islanders anxious for a vision of their future.

Both Vanu and Amadon had mated with numerous native women and had produced hundreds of children over the centuries. These were the source of the bloodlines that ultimately became the dominant families of the many islands of Lemuria—the famed Kings (and sometimes Queens) of Mu—as the millennia passed, and human nature gradually asserted itself in its need for leadership and ceremony. As Vanu had to surrender his teaching and worship of the One True—but invisible—God, to the peoples' need for visible representations in the form of Father Sun and Mother Earth, so also had he to accept that human beings at the current stage of development still required their kings and queens. Yet for all Vanu's reluctance to allow this gradual change to occur, the royal families that came to dominate in Lemuria's later period proved, in general, to be remarkably adept rulers.

246 The Birth of a Cult

Sharing the same exalted bloodline, it seemed that the kings had found ways to live at peace with one another. Through a complex network of clan ties and an emphasis on preserving the bloodlines, they gained the respect of the people by maintaining the peace. With rare exceptions, the kings truly believed themselves to be the servants of their people. And in their ancestral assemblies, held with an almost ritual observance four times a year, all the kings gathered to settle their issues with mutual respect and kindness as their guiding light, and as an example to their people.

Apart from some minor inter-island skirmishes, there hadn't been an actual war since they'd arrived on the islands twenty thousand years earlier: a period of continuing peace many thousands of years longer than any later civilization has managed to achieve.

※ ※ ※

Mein Host was riding high. He thrived in the intensity of the community all functioning together with the single-minded intention of making a success of the Process. If there is some truth to the anthropologist Margaret Mead's suggestion that a handful of totally dedicated people working together can transform the world, then the Process was well on its way.

All the members were encouraged to do what they loved to do and what they did best. If an idea was practical enough to be done, and it brought in the much-needed money, it was adopted. Mein Host's interest in extraterrestrial matters, for example, led to lectures by the likes of Brinsley Le Poer Trench, author of *The Sky People,* and Desmond Leslie, whose 1953 book *Flying Saucers Have Landed* was cowritten with George Adamski.

In a maneuver that Caligastia would have appreciated, all three of these men—along with many others—were viciously pilloried, deceived and lied to, and dismissed as irrelevant, as the U.S. and British governments became increasingly dominated by a need for secrecy.

It is now known that an arm of U.S. intelligence had been well aware of extraterrestrials since the late 1940s. And that, by using the press and academia, this highly secretive cabal created, and has sustained, a deliberate fog of derision and disinformation in order to deny the existence of UFOs and the reality of extraterrestrial life.

While denial was initially understandable in terms of the Cold War, so much has happened since then that no one in the military or government wishes to admit to a sixty-year deception of the public and all that implies. This includes the extensive exchange of ET technology, the various secret treaties and agreements, the careers ruined by official ridicule, and the large number of abductions. All that transpired after the fateful decision to keep extraterrestrials a secret from the world's public has now become exceedingly embarrassing.

What will the public think, for example, when they hear what Dr. Steven Greer discovered in talking to military whistle-blowers? Those in the know, he was told, were able to justify their talk of UFOs as truthful because UFOs were not "unidentified"; they were all too "identified." These people maintained this absurd deceit over the years by privately calling the craft ETVs (extraterrestrial vehicles).

But, as I write in early 2011, this massive sixty-year conspiracy of silence and denial must end soon, or the extraterrestrials will step in and declare themselves more openly on their terms. There are many signs that this is already occurring with individual contactees and contactee groups cropping up all over the world.

Meanwhile, courageous, independent investigators, like George Adamski, Desmond Leslie, and Brinsley Le Poer Trench, were derided or patronized by the scientific and military community, who themselves were being deceived by a cabal about which they knew nothing. More serious, perhaps, than the public humiliation of those early believers in ET life is that the general public has been deprived of some of the advanced, clean-energy, ET technologies that the military has kept to itself.

Since much of what is known now about extraterrestrials and their presence on the planet was the most closely guarded secret on the planet in 1968, I'm using this digression to illustrate a quality I've observed in Mein Host, and which I've also admired about the Process. For better or worse, they were prepared to follow their own drummers.

Mein Host claims that the reality of extraterrestrial life always seemed completely natural to him. A brief encounter he'd had five years earlier with a young man he intuitively knew was an ET had merely confirmed for him what he already felt was true. It's to his credit that my ward trusted his intuition in the face of the scornful dismissal of many of his friends and colleagues and will be seen to have been correct all along. And it's to the community's credit that the Process would give voice to those speaking a forbidden truth.

The Process was starting to become more widely known by 1967. Satan's Cavern, now wisely renamed simply *The Cavern,* was drawing in more and more adventurous souls. Attendance at the community's weekly lectures, films, and happenings was growing, as puzzled Londoners tried to figure out what the Process was all about.

And the Process wasn't making it easy for them. Even then, in the early days before Robert's elaborate theology confused almost everybody, they seemed to many to be a mass of contradictions.

The central issue that most people missed was that the Process was about experience—most of all, about extreme experience. Whatever the group took on, they would push themselves to the extreme. They prided themselves on this. They were just as interested in other people's extreme views or experiences. I've heard Mein Host saying that only by going through these extreme experiences can people find out who they truly are.

However, showing a film like Luis Buñuel and Salvador Dalí's *Un Chien Andalou* one week and Leni Riefenstahl's *Triumph of the Will* the next might be guaranteed to confuse and antagonize the public.

And, indeed, trouble was brewing once again in the background.

The second issue of *PROCESS* magazine was a radical improvement on the first. Yet, paradoxically, every single copy of that first issue was sold.

On a whim of Mary Ann's, the first issue was devoted to opposing Britain's joining the Common Market. It was an odd choice. No one in the community had any particular political interests and, although Mein Host wouldn't have noticed it at the time, it was one of the first of Mary Ann's miscalculations. She believed that because the issue of whether or not to join the Common Market—now the Eurozone—had been dominating the news, people would want to buy the magazine.

They didn't. At least, not for that reason.

And the Common Market wasn't a subject likely to draw anyone's attention on a newsstand.

The magazine sold out simply because of the charisma and persistence of the Process members who went out on the streets of London to sell it.

The indifference of Londoners to the subject matter became a challenge that Mein Host, for example, discovered he could overcome with self-deprecating humor and courteous persistence. Others came up with their own successful approaches.

In those days, before panhandling became a common practice in Western cities and the public had grown ever more cautious at being unexpectedly approached by strangers, selling magazines on the street was an exhilarating exercise for those Processeans capable of throwing themselves wholeheartedly into it. Yet, to be fair, successful selling was clearly due as much to personal charisma as it was to hard work. And not everyone possesses charisma.

When some members returned to Balfour Place having consistently sold less than a dozen magazines a day, and a few others had just as consistently sold between fifty and seventy-five daily, there was bound to be some envy and resentment directed at those who were successful. And who was among the most successful but my ward?

I say this not to praise him unduly but merely to establish when the germ of the envy directed toward him first started coalescing among some of those closest to Mary Ann. This envy would resurface periodically during Mein Host's thirteen years with the group.

I've previously mentioned Mary Ann's technique of juggling her favorites, raising up one while humiliating another. Mein Host's success at selling the magazines quickly became one more weapon she could use against the half a dozen members of her inner circle who proved reliably inept at "bringing in the money," as she liked to put it. And she was merciless in her ridicule.

Much of this occurred behind Mein Host's back, in meetings at which he wasn't present, so he continued to sell hundreds of magazines and bask in Mary Ann's acclaim, completely unaware of the ill will and envy gathering in the wings.

The second issue of *PROCESS* magazine, financed from the sales of the first, was larger in format, had more pages, and was printed on semigloss magazine paper. However, it followed the principle established by Mary Ann in the first issue and focused on a single subject—this time it was to be Freedom of Expression.

The green cover features a solemn-faced Marianne Faithfull, standing in profile and gazing out over the Thames, yet she is separated from the river by a fence of viciously pointed iron railings. Her left hand grips the top of one of these points, her right hangs down by her side. She is dressed in a two-piece velvet suit, buttoned up the front, with a high, turned-up collar and a white ruffled shirt, over which her blond hair is blowing in the breeze.

It was a modest photo of the singer, almost demure, and its symbolic intention was clearly to create a sense of thirsting for a freedom the river was promising. Yet, as in so much of the graphic imagery that was to emerge from the Process, the visual clarity of the image—of a beautiful young woman yearning for the freedom to express herself—was complicated by an unintended dissonance. A foggy, bereft London in the distance and a view of the Thames at low tide, its wide banks muddy and desolate and littered with household debris, suggested that the yearned-for freedom might carry with it some unfortunate consequences.

The decision to concentrate on a single subject was both unconventional and ingenious, in that it allowed for contributions from a variety of extreme viewpoints. While this was wholly consistent with Robert's metaphysical teaching of the Union of Opposites, for many readers it was baffling and, in some cases, even offensive.

Readers might open the magazine and find on one page the graphic of a large swastika, together with text discussing the Nazis' suppression of any freedom of expression, all tucked neatly into the symbol's negative spaces. Then, on the opposite page, was an equally large graphic hammer-and-sickle, with text examining the Soviets' repressive approach to free speech. This was clearly designed to shock readers. The text in both cases—however rationally argued and by no means an endorsement of either ideology—was unlikely to have ever been read, so viscerally overwhelming were the symbols.

Only those who have some understanding of graphic design would have appreciated the endlessly laborious hours spent cutting lines of text and pasting them—with what I observed as mind-numbing precision—around the contours of the symbols. These kinds of graphic effects, Mein Host assures me, are now nearly effortlessly generated on a computer. Two generations of graphic designers since then will have forgotten how it used to be done—when *cut-and-paste* really meant cutting and pasting.

Mein Host then art-directed a photo session in a local graveyard with Marianne Faithfull. I watched him with some amusement as he positioned her flat on her back, lying on a grave, with a rose between her folded hands. Richard, a fellow Processean and another of my ward's longtime friends from architecture college, took the black-and-white photos.

Although Mein Host was still shy on first encountering famous and beautiful young women, the session with the relaxed and compliant singer largely cured him of any embarrassment. Unaware of quite what she was lending her name and image to, yet charmed by Richard and Mein Host, she willingly struck any pose suggested and was so kind and natural that my ward learned one of the prime lessons of the media age. Celebrities—however beautiful and haughty, however detached or narcissistic, however arrogant or dismissive—are all people, too. And frequently, as he was to discover over time, they are rather ordinary people at that, many of whom actually appreciated being treated as ordinary people.

This insight allowed him to form a surprisingly easy friendship with the young actress Stefanie Powers, who was prized for her intelligence, her beauty, and her self-effacing humor in the short-lived TV series *The Girl from U.N.C.L.E.* She was known as one of the few "real people" on television.

As soon as Mein Host met the actress to interview her for the magazine, there seemed to be an immediate buzz of mutual recognition between them. They were like the closest of friends who'd known each other their whole lives. It was not primarily a sexual attraction, although it might well have been interpreted as such given the sense of intense intimacy both of them experienced in that first, and their few subsequent, meetings. Mein Host called it "a joining of hearts."

With Stefanie Powers he felt the same sense of spiritual closeness—

although he wouldn't have known to describe it as spiritual—that he'd felt with Jean, the ex-girlfriend he'd parted with four years earlier to join the community. And there were a few others, too, with whom he'd felt this unexplainable affinity and an almost telepathic intimacy. Since this work is in part concerned with the impact incarnated angels have had, and are having, on the planet, I don't think I'm overstepping in revealing that I believe Ms. Powers is a mortal of angelic spiritual heritage.

Mein Host's natural empathy and his ability to strike up a rapport with others, as well as his newfound ease with the rich and famous, later led to his being appointed the public relations officer of the Process, with instructions from Mary Ann to get friendly with celebrities wherever and whenever possible.

The third issue of *PROCESS* magazine heralded Mein Host's next fall from favor—the one I intimated was coming a few pages ago.

Through no fault of the singer, the third magazine will always be known as "the Mick bloody Jagger" issue.

Mein Host had crossed paths with Mick Jagger a few years earlier in London at Michael Hollingshead's* Pont Street apartment, so it seemed like a natural step to ask Marianne Faithfull, Jagger's girlfriend at the time, whether he'd care to be interviewed for the third issue. He was more than willing. So a short interview, conducted by Richard, with Ewald taking the photos, was featured along with some other remarkable photographs of the singer. At the time, the Rolling Stones were at the height of their fame, and having an interview with Mick Jagger, with his picture on the cover, was a big coup for a relatively unknown magazine.

You would have thought that, wouldn't you?

Yet, far from that, the Mick bloody Jagger issue turned out to be the first indication of a rift in the Process that would open and close over the years. The focus might change dependent on exigency, but it invariably boiled down to those best described as Process fundamentalists and those who thought of themselves as pragmatists. It was a rift that would ultimately break the community apart in the late 1970s.

---

*Michael Hollingshead, known on two continents for his mayonaise jar full of acid, has been popularly credited with turning Timothy Leary on to LSD 25.

❖ ❖ ❖

When I surveyed the peninsula, I was able to see how much time and work had gone into preparing the place for the visitors. From three thousand feet, it looked more like a vast, beautifully laid-out park. The meadows and forests were watered by an interlocking network of rivers and canals, from which sprang the narrow threads of irrigation ditches coiling through the landscape like silver snakes. I saw no wild animals whatsoever until I'd moved farther eastward toward the mainland.

Before fully completing the great wall across the neck of the peninsula, I could see that they were now finishing a smaller wall that ran outside and parallel to it. This smaller wall was being built some ten miles away so as to enclose a long rectangular piece of land spanning the width of the peninsula. They were leaving this enclosure as a natural zoological preserve.

It was certainly beautiful and peaceful but as I had a chance to observe more closely I noticed that there was something unfinished about the place. Many of the small brick houses used by Vanu's volunteers were still roofless shells, and the irrigation ditches, which looked so spectacular from far above, often turned out just to be roughed-out trenches.

I had no doubt that Vanu had done the best he could. I'm sure it hadn't been easy. Caligastia clearly knew something was stirring the people up and would have done everything he could to stamp out any disturbance.

I'd also discovered that Vanu had to cope with a massive wave of desertions among his workers when it had come out that he hadn't known exactly when the promised visitors would be arriving. He'd begun work on the park over seventy years before the visitors eventually made their appearance, and with each passing generation it had become increasingly hard to raise the necessarily volunteers. What I was looking at must have been the result. Hardly what MA and their agents would have hoped for, or ever expected.

Happily, there were only a few volunteers around as I closed in on the main compound, not that they would have been able to perceive me. At that time I preferred to avoid getting too close to mortals. The weight of their emotions all too easily flowed into my energy field, dragging me down into their fears, their hatreds, and all their painful emotional conflicts.

Moving cautiously, I slipped unnoticed in my dimension toward one of the central compounds, around which were gathered seven of the neat brick buildings I'd seen earlier from the air. I had to pause as I entered the sweeping meadow that acted as the forecourt to this particular little settlement. It was breathtakingly beautiful.

I'll risk a brief digression here because it occurs to me that the attentive reader might wonder how I can perceive the beauty of the material world from a fifth-dimensional reality, which must be as solid and real to me as your three dimensions are to you. You'd be justified in asking how this might occur.

I can only pass along what I've come to understand of the physics of the Multiverse and, of necessity, what I know is limited by words to metaphor. For a fuller appreciation, I recommend personal experience, because techniques for exploring the dimensions are more accessible to mortals these days.

Modern physics, for example, teaches of the vast empty spaces that appear to exist at the atomic and subatomic levels of matter. Just because instruments capable of detecting and measuring this apparent "emptiness" don't currently exist doesn't mean it is empty space. Within this empty space the other dimensions, and the many frequency domains within those dimensions, are found.

Watchers understand this "empty space" as a living, multidimensional membrane. This is a membrane of potential that can resolve itself to manifest as particles in a variety of different dimensional frequency domains.

Through the carefully laid-down processes of evolution—as happened in this world, first with the devic realms, then with the ever-widening explosion of organic life-forms—all will be equipped with bodies and senses tuned to their survival in their particular frequency domain. As life gains sentience, so also do the creatures' senses reach out to experience, and then to understand, the frequency domain in which they exist.

In this way the Local Universe—itself a subset of the Multiverse—can be thought of as manifesting within a range of frequency domains we all share, angel and mortal. My fifth-dimensional existence interpenetrates the three dimensions a human being perceives as the mineral, the vegetal, and the animal realms. I can move fluidly through each of these dimensions if I wish, so it could be said that I exist within your reality.

I trust you will appreciate that the above description is a merely a metaphor. This is particularly important to understand since each dimension has its own laws, which may be rather different from each other. Mein Host has to catch a plane to fly to New York City, for example, whereas I merely "find myself" there, as needed. This holds true for all planetary travel, although I can move as slowly or as fast as I wish when I'm functioning as an observer.

Thus, the landscape I was admiring as I looked around the broad meadow and over to the houses beyond, tucked neatly into the forest, was much the same landscape that you would see if you were standing where I was.

No trees had been cut down and the only wood used in the houses was carved from fallen lumber. Under Amadon's direction, the volunteers had obviously become masters of the creative use of brickwork. All the houses had barrel-vault roofs and domes made entirely of bricks. Towers reached up above the rooflines, drawing in fresh air to the houses' inner chambers. Rainwater was channeled down from the roofs into bulbous brick reservoirs that seemed to grow out of the ground. Through the gaps between the buildings, I could see a river that had been ingeniously damned and rechanneled to create a pair of small streams running behind the houses—one carrying away the waste and the other bringing in fresh water.

Two of these simple houses were considerably larger, though still modest in appearance, and I found myself drawn toward the one I'd seen Vanu and his deputy enter sometime earlier. As I drew closer, I could appreciate just how large it was—large but not monumental or ostentatious. It was large simply because its occupants were large.

I passed through elegantly proportioned, domed rooms with elaborately patterned, tiled floors, interspersed with colorful plantings and palm trees that reached up to the high sloping ceilings, through arched doorways into what I can only call a botanical wonderland. Flowers of every type and color bloomed in profusion throughout the space. Orange and lemon trees grew in big ceramic pots. Fruit I was unfamiliar with hung on bushes that bordered the enclosure. As I made my way through the greenery, I saw different species of grasses being grown in boxes on long benches under what were clearly controlled conditions. I recall thinking, as I paused before leaving the greenhouse/laboratory, that the visitors must have advanced botanical and biological knowledge to have put all this together.

Then the combined scent of all the plants and flowers almost overwhelmed me.

My head was still swimming when I found myself in the garden at the center of the building. Open at one end to a park that stretched into rolling hills, the garden was dominated by a grove of old-growth trees, around which the house must have been built. The twelve trees, with their massive trunks, stood in a rough circle. Four fountains, carved out of single granite blocks, burbled at the cardinal points of the grove. In the middle of this sacred grove was the reason I was here. I was finally in the presence of the two off-world visitors who, with Vanu and Amadon, were seated around a massive stone table, the top slab polished to an obsidian sheen.

So is this what Caligastia had in mind?

He had slipped me into the very center of those he thought of as his enemy. This is what I mean by a Watcher's relative choicelessness. Yes, I had a certain degree of freedom when I was looking for the visitors. But now that I'd found them, I had no choice but to stay and serve my master.

I was relieved to see that my presence seemed to have gone unnoticed. The visitors were leaning forward, intently listening to Vanu. Beyond the table and playing among the fruit trees growing in the courtyard were children—lots of fair-haired little children.

Clustered beneath the covered arcade, bordering the central court on three sides and shielded from the harsh sunlight, were the leaders from among those volunteers who'd stayed on after the visitors arrived. Grouped behind them I could see some of Vanu's midwayers, when I scanned through their frequency domain.

"You need to know what you are facing here," Vanu said to them. "It is vital that you do not underestimate Prince Caligastia."

I didn't manage to overhear the visitors' reply, but I sensed that Vanu must have been as shocked as I was to see the pair so nonchalantly dismissing his urgent warning.

They must have been thoroughly briefed back on System HQ.

Did they know something we didn't?

Or were they merely overconfident?

AFTERWORD

Threads and Metathreads

No Apologia for Lucifer, *Homo Angelicus*, Hints of What's to Come, and a Supreme Surprise

I, Timothy, am always intrigued to see where Georgia chooses to break her narrative—we still don't know anything of the promised fall from Mary Ann's favor, for example, and that one is a doozie! I've joked with her about how she seems to enjoy a good cliffhanger. Here, I find that Georgia has left us just as the two main threads of her story are moving into their next critical phases in which the primary players will be challenged and tested by both success and failure. How brief or how grandiose those ambitions will turn out to be—and how ignominious the failures—remains to be seen.

When I took on this project with Georgia it soon became obvious her story wasn't going to fit into a single volume. *Confessions of a Rebel Angel,* her first book, clocked in at 449 pages, which must have made it an exceptionally long read for some in this age of Tweets and Instant Messages. I believe she has shortened this volume out of a courteous consideration for our shorter attention spans. Yet this inevitably means there will be more volumes to come, perhaps many more, and I am simply going to have to follow wherever her narrative takes us.

It was never my conscious intention—although it may well have been Georgia's plan—to draw parallels between the events surrounding the rebel angels and what I go through as my life unfolds in Georgia's narrative. As she shows me the less obvious undercurrents running through my life *while* I am writing, this process has been changing me. In a sense, my knowledge pool has deepened during this act of mutual discovery. This, in itself, is creating what I'm starting to think of as a metathread in which both streams retrospectively inform one another. This then creates yet another current of understanding: the macroscopic is reflected in the microscopic, and the latter serves to demonstrate in a very personal manner the effects and influences of the macroscopic on contemporary life, as it is lived out by the narrative's protagonists.

Inevitably, this metathread affects both Georgia and me as we proceed further and further with this narrative. Although I regard myself as very much the junior partner in our collaboration, and, as I have previously remarked, I retain almost nothing of what is written during the day, I am aware that my own viewpoint and feelings are being refined and transformed over the course of writing.

This could translate, for some readers, into thinking of me as an unreliable witness or, at the very least, an inconsistent one. However, I make no claims to authorial consistency. I am not writing a novel in which I know the end before the beginning. I am discovering as I write. I generally don't even know what the next sentence is going to be unless I'm doing some research that Georgia requires!

I believe that if Georgia's point of view and her analysis of my life are to have any real value, it will be because we have both been honest and open about all our feelings—positive and negative. There is little point at this crucial juncture in purposely distorting, exaggerating, or making up our experiences and what we have learned from them.

Georgia's books are clearly not about polishing her own image, or that of Lucifer and the rebel angels, or about me trying to impress the reader with the curious facts of my life. They aren't an apologia for Lucifer and the rebel angels, but an honest attempt to unearth and understand the true dynamics of the angelic revolution and how it has played out through history on both this planet and the other worlds affected by the uprising.

Although some might consider writing so closely with a fallen angel as dangerous business, I trust after reading her words it will be clear she is openly and honestly seeking her redemption in writing her *Confessions*. As the time-frame of a half-million years covers the long and frequently tumultuous history of this world and the civilizations that have risen and fallen during that time, her *Confessions* will, of necessity, need a number of volumes to fulfill the task she has set for herself. *Revolt of the Rebel Angels* is the second volume of Georgia's *Confessions*.

In the next volume, *Rebel Angels in Exile,* we will find the Process blossoming into the bold and provocative cult that caused such a stir in the late 1960s and early '70s in both England and America. The members are unlikely to be aware that, like a number of contemporary spiritual groups that flourished briefly during that period, the Process was acting as a training arena designed mainly for incarnate rebel angels.

As Georgia likes to point out, almost all incarnate angels are unaware of their angelic heritage. She emphasizes that this is as it should be, because awareness of this deeply buried self-knowledge needs to be earned by each individual to be truly meaningful. Yet as world events move toward the inevitable global crisis and transformation, Georgia believes it is now crucial for the angel incarnates among us—those whom she has named *Homo angelicus,* implying a new spiritual mutation of our species—to awaken to their true natures.

She also reassures us that this spiritual mutation is a perfectly natural process and her writings are merely a small part of the much larger global transformation taking place, a transmutation still mostly occurring behind the scenes and in the hearts of human beings. She urges us to understand the real dynamics of this transformation—that while the events on the world stage as viewed through the nightly TV news, or read in reports from the more hysterical fringe of the press, may appear to suggest that the end of times are upon us, this is simply not true.

If I am to put this in more physically mundane terms, what we see occurring on the planet is much akin to boils breaking out on the body of the world. This is, in reality, the long-overlooked or suppressed corruption that has seeped into almost all human power structures since the time of the revolution among the angels, now breaking through to the surface. Knowing this can give us a deeper understanding of, and more compassion for, the people who are still struggling to free themselves from the oppression of others.

Rebel angel incarnates, says Georgia, are not only here for their own redemptive purposes but also to bring the wisdom garnered from lifetimes of previous experience to the massive transformation the human species is soon to undergo.

Yet, I have to admit, I have not found it easy to accept that I am a rebel angel incarnate. Although I'd had clues enough prior to Georgia coming forth in my life, I was reluctant to admit it to myself and pushed it away for at least fifteen years. Like most people, I'd been indoctrinated with the popular belief that the rebel angels were up to no good. It was only when I dug deeper into the subject of the Lucifer rebellion that I started to understand some of the dynamics behind the angelic uprising and found compassion and forgiveness in my heart for Lucifer and the rebels. Only then was I able to more fully accept the truth of who I felt myself to be. Then, as I traveled around the world, I realized that I was being guided to encounter other women and men who identified with the rebel angels. I was careful not to impose my preconceptions on them and used what I like to think of as skillful questioning to draw out their personal feelings. I became progressively more confident from these encounters, yet because I had no wish to bias the discussions I justified remaining silent about the possibility of being a rebel angel myself.

My character tends to be somewhat timorous by nature so any claim to be an angel, albeit a rebel one, was certainly not something I was eager to make. In fact, as a reader of my 2011 book *The Return of the Rebel Angels* pointed out, I hadn't broached the issue of struggling with my identity as an incarnate rebel angel until the very end of a more than four-hundred-page book. I was that sheepish about it! But life has progressed since Georgia and I started working on her *Confessions,* and I have to thank her for this narrative as well as the considerate way she is making my angelic heritage more available to me. And from the letters I've received since the publication of Georgia's *Confessions of a Rebel Angel* in 2012, I feel I've reaffirmed for myself that I am not alone in this understanding of self.

I don't believe being an incarnate rebel angel is all I am. It's more like assuming an identity or playing a role that feels powerfully resonant with deep memory and reflects in the choices I've made and the challenges faced over the course of my various lifetimes, culminating in the events and encounters of this present life of seventy-three summers to date.

The future volumes of Georgia's narrative will confirm that we are no longer subject to Prince Caligastia's behind-the-scenes devilry or the self-centered machinations of all those tens of thousands of troublesome rebel midwayers. And although life on this planet remains, for the moment, dark and difficult for all but a few, if Georgia is correct we will soon be participating in an event of such Multiversal significance that the world and those of us living here will never be the same.

But how soon? Isn't that what we would all like to know?

Georgia says this isn't to be known by any being—angel or human—only that what unfolds promises to be a Supreme Surprise.

APPENDIX

The Angelic Cosmology

Different versions of the so-called War in Heaven appear so frequently in indigenous legends and mythologies from all over the world, as well as in the sacred books and traditions of major religions, that the war is more than likely based on a real event. I believe the most authoritative account can be found in *The Urantia Book,* where it is referred to as *The Lucifer Rebellion.*

Thirty years after first reading *The Urantia Book,* I still regard it as the most reliable source of information about both extraterrestrial and celestial activities. It is broken down into four parts devoted to the following subjects: the Nature of God and the Central and Superuniverses; the Local Universe; the History of Urantia (their name for this planet); and the Life and Teachings of Jesus Christ. (For a definition of terms common to both *The Urantia Book* and this book, please refer to the glossary.)

According to the Urantia model, there are seven Superuniverses, which together compose the material Multiverse. These seven Superuniverses form the substance of the finite Multiverse and circle the Central Universe, which can be visualized as the hole in the center of the toroidal form of the Multiverse.

Each Superuniverse contains one hundred thousand Local Universes, each of which has its own Creator Son (ours is Christ Michael or Jesus Christ) and its own Divine Mother—these are the creator beings of their domain. This pair of high beings modulate the energy downstepped from the Central Universe to create and form the beings and the planetary biospheres in their Local Universes. Each Local Universe sustains ten million inhabited planets divided into ten thousand Local Systems.

Each Local System, in turn, contains one thousand inhabited, or to be inhabited, planets, and each has its own System Sovereign (ours was Lucifer) appointed to govern the System. Each planet, in turn, has a Planetary Prince (ours was Prince Caligastia), who oversees their particular worlds.

According to *The Urantia Book,* Lucifer and Satan (Lucifer's main assistant) came to believe that an elaborate conspiracy had been concocted by the Creator Sons of the Local Universes to promote the existence of a fictitious Unseen Divinity, which the Creator Sons then used as a control device to manipulate the orders of celestials and angels within their creations. Having announced the existence of this conspiracy, Lucifer demanded more autonomy for all beings and for System Sovereigns and Planetary Princes to follow their own approaches for accelerating the spiritual development of their mortal charges.

The revolutionaries quickly gained followers, and the rebellion spread rapidly to affect thirty-seven planets in our System, with Urantia, our planet Earth, being one of them. Choice was given to the many angels involved with supervising System activities as to whether to join the rebel faction.

Lucifer's charge—that too much attention was being given to ascending mortals—appeared to ring true to a large number of angels, as well as the thirty-seven pairs of administrative angels: the Planetary Princes and their assistants who were responsible for the orderly progression of mortal (human) beings on their worlds. The revolution was effectively suppressed by the administration authorities and recast as a heinous rebellion, its immediate consequence being the removal of Lucifer and Satan from their posts in the System.

At the time of the Lucifer Rebellion, the vast majority of the fifty thousand midway angels on Earth—40,119—aligned themselves with Lucifer and Satan. They were destined to remain on our planet until the time of Christ when, according to *The Urantia Book,* it was one of Christ's occulted functions to remove them. It is a brief reference and no further details are given in the book as to where the rebel midwayers were taken. However, with the removal of these rebel midwayers, a mere 9,981 loyalist midwayers remained here to fulfill the tasks of five times their number.

As a result of all of this, in contrast to a normal planet (one not quarantined) on which angelic companions and the presence of helpful midwayers and extraterrestrials must be commonplace knowledge, we Earthlings have slumbered in our corner of a populated Multiverse, unaware of who we are and how we got this way. Having been quarantined and isolated from normal extraterrestrial activity for the long 203,000 years since the rebellion, we first lost touch with, and then forgot entirely, our rightful place in the populated Multiverse. Given this, we were bound to evolve as a troubled species. Our world is one of the few planets that, due to the Lucifer Rebellion, have been thrown off their normal patterns of development.

This disquieting situation, this planetary quarantine, has persisted for more than two hundred thousand years, only to have finally been adjudicated, in my understanding, in the early 1980s.

Given that the planetary quarantine has finally been lifted, the rest of the Multiverse is now able to make legitimate contact with us. More recently what we are witnessing is both the return of the rebel midwayers (the Beings of the Violet Flame), who are now coming back to assist us in the coming transformation of our world; and perhaps of more personal interest to my readers, the many angels who aligned with Lucifer at the time of the rebellion are incarnating as mortals. It appears these rebel angels and Watchers are being offered human incarnation as a path to personal redemption and as the world is emerging from an interminably long Dark Age to shake off the shadows and fulfill its remarkable destiny.

Glossary

Many valuable insights in books have contributed to the themes and fundamental questions that *Revolt of the Rebel Angels* seeks to explore, but the most reliable and comprehensive exposition of God, the Multiverse, and Everything that I have come across remains, after thirty years, *The Urantia Book*. A number of the concepts, individuals, and words below are drawn from it and marked (UB), but the definitions are the author's.

Amadon (UB): originally a human being, it was Amadon's bioplasm that was used to create Vanu's material vehicle. Amadon also became Vanu's staunch companion and closest aide. He remained on-world with Vanu to maintain the Multiverse Administration's developmental plans for the planet, until both were returned to Jerusem some 37,000 years ago.

Angel: a general term for any order of being who administers within a Local Universe.

Astral Energy/Astral Realm: a slightly shifted frequency domain, accessible in dreams and out-of-body experiences, in which humans have an astral counterpart—an Astral Body.

Atman, Indwelling Spirit, Thought Adjuster (UB): an essence of the Creator that indwells all mortal beings, human and extraterrestrial.

Avonal Sons (UB): a Descending Order of High Sons who accompany a Magisterial Son (UB) on his mission. While the Magisterial Son appears in a material body, the seventy accompanying Avonals remain in a contiguous frequency domain.

Caligastia (UB): a Secondary Lanonandek Son who served as Planetary

Prince of this world and who aligned himself with Lucifer.

Celestial Being (UB): a generic name for a high angel.

Central Universe (UB): the original formative Universe whose energy is down-stepped to create the Master Universe that includes the seven superuniverses.

Creator Sons (UB): co-creators—each having a female complement, the Mother Spirit (UB)—of each of the seven hundred thousand Local Universes (UB).

Dalamatia (UB): constructed on the Persian Gulf by members of the Prince Caligastia's staff, this city became the center of the Prince's activities.

Daligastia (UB): a Secondary Lanonandek Son who served as Caligastia's right-hand aide.

Demons: negative thoughtforms.

Decimal Planets (UB): on every tenth inhabited planet, the Life Carriers (UB) are permitted to experiment with the initial seeding of biological life by applying what they have learned from the previous nine implantations. Earth is a decimal planet.

Devas: the coordinating spirits of the natural world. All living organisms are cared for by devas (or nature spirits). In the human being, the deva coordinates and synchronizes the immense amount of physical and biochemical information that keeps our bodies alive.

Enactments: a form of spontaneous and unscripted psychodrama practiced by the Process and intended to reveal the unconscious and compulsive patterns of behavior in both the individual members and the historic events under examination.

Etheric Realms/Etheric Body: collective terms for the higher frequency domains and the beings that exist within those realms. Many observed UFOs are etheric craft. The human subtle energy systems are also referred to as etheric bodies.

Extraterrestrial: mortal beings, such as ourselves, who hail from more developed worlds with access to our frequency domain.

Frequency Domain: the spectrum of frequencies that support the lifeforms whose senses are tuned to that specific spectrum.

Entheogen: the great ethnomycologist R. Gordon Wasson's name for visionary and hallucinogenic plants that places the etymological emphasis back onto sacred.

God: in my personal experience, God is both the Creator and the totality of Creation, manifest and unmanifest, immanent and transcendent.

Guardian (Companion) Angels (UB): angels who function in pairs to ensure that their mortal wards grow in spirit over the course of their lifetimes.

Indwelling Spirit, Atman, Thought Adjuster (UB): *See* Atman, Indwelling Spirit, Thought Adjuster.

Intraterrestrial or **Ultraterrestrial Beings:** the beings who inhabit our neighboring frequency domain, and whom *The Urantia Book* calls the midwayers or midway creatures.

Gibram Island: an isolated and uninhabited island off Zandana's great southern continent prepared for the exiled barbarian invaders who were not able to be assimilated into Zandan's more advanced society.

Janda-Chi, Prince: the secondary Planetary Prince of Zandana.

Jerusem (UB): an architectural sphere (created by the celestials) and the planet headquarters of this Local System of one thousand three-dimensional worlds, existing at a higher-frequency fifth dimension.[AQ1]

Jesus Christ: the Michaelson (UB) of our Local Universe (UB) who incarnated as Jesus Christ in the physical body of Joshua ben Joseph; he is also known as Michael of Nebadon—the name of his Local Universe (UB).

Life Carriers (UB): the celestial order responsible for the development and seeding of organic life on all inhabited planets.

Local System (UB): Jerusem, our Local System, named Satania (UB) is believed to currently possess between 600 and 650 inhabited planets. Earth is numbered 606 in this sequence (UB).

Local System HQ Planet (UB): the political and social center of the Satania System.

Local Universe (UB): a grouping of planets that comprises ten million inhabited planets.

Lucifer (UB): deposed System Sovereign and primary protagonist in the rebellion among the angels.

Magisterial Son (UB): a celestial being of the Avonal Order who appears as a material being of the realm to adjudicate a dispensation prior to entering a new one.

Master Universe (UB): the Multiverse that contains the seven Superuniverses (UB).

Material Sons and Daughters (UB): an Order of celestials that carry out the second of the Multiverse Administration's missions to planet Earth: known as the "Adam and Eves," each male and female pair is a biological uplifter who, with their progeny, adds "violet blood" to the human gene pool.

Melchizedek Sons (UB): a high order of Local Universe Sons devoted primarily to education; they function as planetary administrators in emergencies.

Michaelsons (UB): a generic term for the spiritual ruler of any given Local Universe. Our Michaelson is Jesus Christ, who incarnated in the physical body of Joshua ben Joseph.

Midwayers or **Midway Creatures** (UB): intelligent beings who exist in a contiguous frequency domain and serve as permanent planetary citizens.

Mortal Ascension Scheme (UB): the process by which all mortal beings who live and die on the material worlds of the Local Systems pass up through the seven subsequent levels to the System's capital planet as they embark on their Multiverse career.

Mortals (UB): intelligent beings with immortal souls whose bodies emerge as a result of biological evolutionary processes on a planet. Mortals' physical bodies live and die before they are given the choice to continue their Multiverse career, following their life review.

Multiverse: the entire range of frequency domains on every level of the Master Universe (UB).

Nebadon (UB): the name of our Local Universe.

Prince's Mission (UB): the first of Multiverse Administration's missions to the planet that arrived 500,000 years ago and settled on the Persian Gulf in the city Dalamatia until the angelic rebellion about 203,000 years ago when, shortly after, the city disappeared under the waters of the Gulf.

Satan (UB): Lucifer's right-hand aide who coinstigated the angelic rebellion 203,000 years ago.

Sephira: the senior female member on Zandana's Administrative Council.

Superuniverse (UB): a Universe that contains one hundred thousand Local Universes (UB).

Supreme Deity (UB): a God in the making; an experiential Divinity derived from the spiritual experience of all sentient beings, material or celestial.

System of Planets (UB): a grouping of planets consisting of one thousand inhabited, or to-be-inhabited, planets.

System Sovereign (UB): the administrative angel, together with an assistant of the same rank, who has overall authority over a Local System. Lucifer and Satan were the pair in charge of this System of third-density planets.

Thought Adjuster, Atman, Indwelling Spirit: *See* Atman, Indwelling Spirit, Thought Adjuster.

Thought Forms: quasi-life-forms existing in the astral regions, drawing their limited power from strong emotional thoughts projected from humans, both consciously and unconsciously. Thought forms can be negative or positive. Localized negative thoughtforms are referred to as fear-impacted thoughtforms.

Ultraterrestrial or **Intraterrestrial Beings:** the beings who inhabit our neighboring frequency domain and whom *The Urantia Book* calls midwayers or midway creatures.

Unava: the Chief of Staff to the two Planetary Princes of Zandana, Prince Zanda and Prince Janda-Chi.

Universe Career (UB): a mortal's destiny, unless chosen otherwise, to rise through the many hundreds of levels of the Multiverse to finally encounter the Creator.

Universe(s) of Time and Space (UB): a synonym for the Master Universe to describe the manifest Multiverse.

Vanu (UB): the leader of the forty members of the Prince's staff who stayed loyal to the Multiverse Administration after the revolt among the angels and the only one of the original staff who remained on the planet, together with Amadon, after his colleagues were lifted off and taken back to Jerusem.

Vimana: a small, circular 20- to 30-meter antigravity scout craft used in the early millennia of the Prince's mission and originally a gift from a benevolent space-faring race. Vimanas were "mothballed" for long periods of planetary history only to reappear in such encounters as found in the Vedas. Although Vimanas can manifest in three-dimensional reality, they are essentially etheric vehicles operating at a frequency outside the small section of the electromagnetic spectrum visible to human perception.

Violet Blood (UB): the potential of an infusion of a slightly higher-frequency genetic endowment, which results in more acute senses and a deeper spiritual awareness and responsivity.

Walk-In: an extraterrestrial being who, by prior arrangement with a specific human, takes over the physical vehicle often at, or just before, the moment of the premature death of the original occupant.

Xtul (pronounced "shtool"): the Maya estate on the Yucatan coastline occupied by the Process community in 1966 and '67 and contributing to the community's dangerous and mythic past.

Zanda, Prince: the primary Planetary Prince of the planet Zandana.

Zandan: the capital city of the great southern continent of the planet Zandana.

Zandana: regarded as a "neighboring planet" at approximately the same level of development as Earth, also subject to the Lucifer rebellion and subsequently quarantined. A frequent destination of Georgia's when she needs some recreation.

Index

About the Author

Timothy Wyllie chose to be born in London in 1940 at the height of the Battle of Britain. Surviving an English Public School education unbroken, he studied architecture, qualifying in 1964 and practicing in London and the Bahamas. During this time he also worked with two others to create a Mystery School, which came to be known as the Process Church, and subsequently traveled with the community throughout Europe and America. He became art director of *PROCESS* magazine, designing a series of magazines in the 1960s and '70s that have recently become recognized as among the prime progenitors of psychedelic magazine design. In 1975 he became the director of the New York headquarters, organized a series of conferences and seminars on such unorthodox issues as out-of-body travel, extraterrestrial encounters, alternative cancer therapies, and Tibetan Buddhism. After some fractious and fundamental disagreements with his colleagues in the community, he left to start a new life in 1977. The record of Wyllie's fifteen years in the Mystery School of the Process Church and the true account of this eccentric spiritual community appears in his book *Love, Sex, Fear, Death: The Inside Story of The Process Church of the Final Judgment*, which was published by Feral House in 2009. It is slowly becoming a cult classic.

A profound near-death experience in 1973 confirmed for Wyllie the reality of other levels of existence and instigated what has become a lifetime exploration of nonhuman intelligences. Having created his intention, the Multiverse opened in a trail of synchronicities that led to his swimming with a coastal pod of wild dolphins, two extraterrestrial encounters—during one of which he was able to question the ET mouthpiece as to some of the ways of the inhabited Multiverse—and finally to an extended dialogue with a group of angels speaking through a light-trance medium in Toronto, Canada.

Wyllie's first phase of spiritual exploration was published as *The DETA Factor: Dolphins, Extraterrestrials & Angels* by Coleman Press in 1984 and republished by Bear & Company as *Dolphins, ETs & Angels* in 1993.

His second book, *Dolphins, Telepathy & Underwater Birthing,* published by Bear & Company in 1993, was republished by Wisdom Editions in 2001 under the title *Adventures Among Spiritual Intelligences: Angels, Aliens, Dolphins & Shamans.* In this book Wyllie continues his travels exploring Balinese shamanic healing, Australian Aboriginal cosmology, human underwater birthing, dolphin death and sexuality, entheogenic spirituality, the gathering alien presence on the planet, and his travels with a Walk-In, along with much else.

Wyllie's work with the angels through the 1980s resulted in the book *Ask Your Angels: A Practical Guide to Working with Your Messengers of Heaven to Empower and Enrich Your Life,* written with Alma Daniel and Andrew Ramer and published by Ballantine Books in 1992. After spending time at the top of the *New York Times* religious bestsellers, *Ask Your Angels* went on to become an international success in eleven translations.

The Return of the Rebel Angels and *Confessions of a Rebel Angel* continues the series he began with *Dolphins, ETs & Angels* and *Adventures Among Spiritual Intelligences,* presenting further in-depth intuitive explorations of nonhuman intelligences. It draws together the many meaningful strands of Wyllie's thirty-year voyage of discovery into unknown and long-taboo territories into a coherent and remarkably optimistic picture for the immediate future of the human species, with the inconspicuous help of a benign and richly inhabited living Multiverse.

The Helianx Proposition or The Return of the Rainbow Serpent, also thirty years in the making, is Wyllie's illustrated mythic exploration of an ancient extraterrestrial personality and its occult influence on life in this world. Published by Daynal Institute Press in 2010, it includes two DVDs and two CDs of associated material. The CDs contain 19 tracks of the author's visionary observations augmented by Emmy-winning musician the late Jim Wilson, master of digital sonic manipulation.

Wyllie is currently continuing to work with Georgia on her *Confessions,* a multivolume personal exploration of the angelic realms over the past half a million years of their presence on the planet. The third volume, *Rebel Angels in Exile,* will be published by Inner Traditions • Bear and Company in 2014.

Wyllie lives in a house of his own design at the foot of a mesa somewhere in the wilds of the New Mexico high desert, where he can hear the subtle whispers of the unseen realms.

BOOKS BY TIMOTHY WYLLIE

The DETA Factor: Dolphins, Extraterrestrials & Angels, 1984 (currently in print as *Dolphins, ETs & Angels,* 1993).

Ask Your Angels: A Practical Guide to Working with the Messengers of Heaven to Empower and Enrich Your Life, 1992 (cowritten with Alma Daniel and Andrew Ramer).

Dolphins, Telepathy, & Underwater Birthing, 1993 (currently in print as *Adventures Among Spiritual Intelligences: Angels, Aliens, Dolphins & Shamans,* 2001).

Contacting Your Angels Through Movement, Meditation & Music, 1995 (with Elli Bambridge).

Love, Sex, Fear, Death: The Inside Story of the Process Church of the Final Judgment, 2009 (editor, with Adam Parfrey).

The Helianx Proposition or the Return of the Rainbow Serpent, 2010.

The Return of the Rebel Angels, 2011.

Confessions of a Rebel Angel, 2012.